Y0-BRF-557

Teacher Unions in Public Education

Teacher Unions in Public Education

Politics, History, and the Future

Edited by Nina Bascia

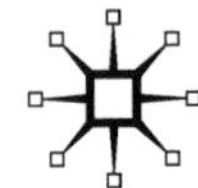

First published in 2015 by PALGRAVE MACMILLAN® in the United States—a division of St. Martin's Press LLC, 175 Fifth Avenue, New York, NY 10010.

Where this book is distributed in the UK, Europe and the rest of the world, this is by Palgrave Macmillan, a division of Macmillan Publishers Limited, registered in England, company number 785998, of Houndmills, Basingstoke, Hampshire RG21 6XS.

Palgrave Macmillan is the global academic imprint of the above companies and has companies and representatives throughout the world.

ISBN: 978-1-137-43618-4

Library of Congress Cataloging-in-Publication Data

Teacher unions in public education : politics, history, and the future / edited by Nina Bascia.
pages cm
Includes index.
ISBN 978-1-137-43618-4 (hardback)
1. Teachers' unions—Cross-cultural studies. 2. Public schools—Cross-cultural studies. I. Bascia, Nina.
LB2844.52.T43 2015
331.88'113711—dc23

2014050082

A catalogue record of the book is available from the British Library.

Design by Amnet.

First edition: July 2015

10 9 8 7 6 5 4 3 2 1

Contents

Part III: Renewal

List of Tables and Figures

Tables

Figures

CHAPTER 1

Perspectives on Teacher Unions: History, Discourse, and Renewal

Nina Bascia

This book locates teacher unions at the crux of teachers' efforts to navigate the enduring tensions between their own low status in the educational system and the necessary autonomy and working conditions to teach effectively and well. These tensions link papers that are otherwise varied in their conceptual and empirical underpinnings. The chapters, which are essentially a series of case studies, reveal the complex, dynamic nature of teacher unions engaging in a wide variety of activities and pursuing multiple strategies.

The chapters have been written at a time when teaching, public schooling, and teacher unions themselves face unprecedented threats in the face of neoliberal educational reforms. Choice, competition, incentives, and accountability have become central principles in the global policy agenda and in the restructuring of educational systems. Jurisdictions around the world have seen increases in governmental support for educational privatization (Ball and Youdell 2008). Many countries are experiencing a chronic underresourcing of education, especially for children living in areas of social and economic deprivation. The convergence of these tendencies has resulted in greater standardization in programming, reporting systems that emphasize surveillance, and an infrastructure that is lacking on support for teaching and learning (Bascia and Osmond 2013).

Teachers are at the center of many current educational reform efforts. New policies place tight controls on what is taught and how teaching is carried out and require that more of teachers' time and energy be spent on administrative tasks (Carter, Stevenson, and Passy 2010). New inspection practices affect teachers in terms of "workload, bureaucratization, stress, demotivation, alienation and insecurity" (Verger, Altinyelken, and De Koning 2013, 149). The crisis in teaching and teachers' work has led to significant proportions of the teacher population exiting the profession. Teachers' needs for organized representation thus are more pronounced than ever.

Teacher unions have become key defenders of public education at exactly the same time that they face significant challenges: their marginalization is in fact a goal of many reform efforts, and this marginalization, in turn, may lead to teachers' inability to recognize the importance of organized action (Bascia and Osmond 2012).

The authors whose chapters are contained in this book are both academics and unionists and include many of the leading teacher union researchers working today. While much of the mainstream educational research maintains that teacher unions should be outlawed or their powers greatly reduced, the authors in this book challenge this position; instead, they recognize the important role teacher unions must play in defending public education and in minimizing the damage caused by ill-thought-out educational policies. The authors do not idealize these organizations but instead recognize their limitations and the necessity for union renewal.

Arcs of History

The papers in this book reveal continuity and change in relationships between teacher unions and teachers, the public, and government. The early chapters most explicitly chart the history of teacher unionism, emphasizing the emergence of teacher unions, recent governmental relations, and the career histories of teachers who have carried out their social activism within the organizational frameworks of their unions. Particularly in their juxtaposition, these historical views allow us to see where teacher unions have come from and the persistence of tensions that were present at their origin.

In the United States, Canada, England, and Australia, teacher unions found their organizational footing around the turn of the twentieth century, in relation to emerging systems of mass education. When reformers of the late nineteenth and early twentieth century created the bureaucratic organizations that are the basis for today's school systems, they drew upon then-popular scientific management techniques and bureaucratic organizational models to centralize decision making, specialize offices and staff roles, and develop rules governing production. They looked to contemporary German and Prussian schools, which offered centralized, highly structured procedures and a sequenced curriculum compatible with an assembly-line view of the educational process (Darling-Hammond 1997). Within these school systems, educational administrators asserted their authority over teachers by claiming special "scientific" expertise (Carlson 1993; Gitlin 1996; Kean 1989; Manzer 1970; Tyack 1974; Urban 1982). Teacher bargaining rights initially grew out of demands for protection from arbitrary or sexist treatment by administrators (Strunk and Grissom 2010).

During the twentieth century, as public education systems became larger and more standardized, teacher labor movements arose to advocate and establish collective bargaining legislation. In gaining the right to bargain within the parameters of contemporary labor law, teachers found their purview restricted to issues of salary, material benefits, and working conditions; unions could not fundamentally challenge the status hierarchy that excluded teachers from participating in educational decision making (Carlson 1993). Between the 1970s and the end of the twentieth century, the scope of teacher rights, protections, and benefits contained in collective agreements expanded to include, for example, class size limits, evaluation procedures, a voice for teachers at the school level, how staffing decisions were made, and the parameters of teachers' professional learning (McDonnell and Pascal 1988). But because of legal restrictions regarding decisions on such fundamental concerns as curriculum content and funding policy, unions' influence could only be exerted through informal persuasion.

In more recent decades, in many jurisdictions, governments that have constitutional authority over educational policy have tended to centralize and standardize many of the decisions affecting teachers' work, and unions' abilities to negotiate have been restricted to an ever-shrinking range of issues. Governmental and public media criticism of public education, teachers, and teacher unions has increased, and so have legislative efforts to reduce the influence of unions on education. Many of the chapters in this volume illuminate how unions have sought to counter this turn of events by taking action in the courts (the British Columbia Teachers' Federation), in the public media and in the streets (the Wisconsin Education Association), and within their own organizations. In some historical accounts, union-governmental relations have been consistently contentious; in others, changes in government are accompanied by changes in relationships with unions, though often for the worse (as in Alberta, Canada, and England). At the root of these dynamics is the constitutional authority that governments hold over education and the fact that teacher unions' involvement in educational decision making can always be changed by governmental fiat.

Much can be learned by looking within teacher unions and by tracing their organizational histories and the career histories of the people that inhabit them (Bascia 2008, 2009; Murphy 1990; Rousmaniere 2004; Urban 2000). Challenging the image of teacher unions as monolithic, faceless organizations, these studies provide a fine-grained picture of how subgroups and individuals identify and pursue different strategic directions, often simultaneously. While union leaders obviously wield a great deal of influence, involved teachers and other staff also assert their effects on the micropolitical climate and impel the organization in a variety of possible directions, often simultaneously (the British Columbia Teachers' Federation). Teacher unions are complex organizations, undertaking collective bargaining, public communications, governmental relations, and activities that engage teachers with one another and with community members, thus blurring traditional organizational distinctions between what is "inside" and "outside" union purview.

Discourses

Language plays a significant role in framing the basic terms of social engagement. "What can be said and thought, but also . . . who can speak, when, and with what authority" is defined and maintained through discourse (Ball 1990, cited in Foley 1999, 15). Access to or control over discourse and communication is an important "symbolic" resource that defines the power base of a group or institution (van Dijk 1996). Discourse constitutes, establishes, reinforces, and challenges relations of power. Changes in discursive patterns are related to changes in power relationships. The chapters in this book reveal how teacher unions and governments employ discourse to set the terms of engagement; the degree and type of engagement between unions and their teacher members (Yonkers, New York); and norms among teachers regarding the costs and benefits of participation in unions (several states in the US Midwest).

Many teachers' organizations have been slow to recognize their power to contribute to public discourse about teachers, schools, and unions themselves. They inform the discourse about teachers by negotiating many conditions of teaching through collective bargaining, attempting to influence educational policy, and through the press. They may reinforce or assert images of teachers as victims or heroes, technicians, intellectual workers, political activists, and/or professionals (Bascia 2000; Mitchell and Kerchner 1983). Governments and teacher unions engage in the definition and redefinition of their relative power positions in the public domain through discourses about teaching and schooling, through policy positions, and through statements made in the press. "Professional communities" of teachers use discourse as the means by which they establish the legitimacy and value of union participation among themselves (Bascia 1994).

In recent years, however, as the dominant discourse has become increasingly antieducation, many teachers' organizations have become convinced (or, if you like, have adopted the prevailing discourse of national and international meetings of teacher union staff) that they are uniquely situated to persuade the public toward greater respect and support for education. Organization staff members are increasingly self-conscious about their direct communication with teachers and administrators and statements they make in the press. Public relations is a common organizational function in teachers' organizations of any size.

Renewal

Much of the mainstream educational research is sharply critical of teacher unions, viewing them from a distant vantage point. It is preoccupied with unions' diminished influence in collective bargaining and role in shaping policy, and with their loss of credibility with the public. The chapters in this book, on the other hand, allow us to observe unions close up as they engage in a range of alternative activities, some long-standing projects that have not been well publicized and some representing wholly new organizational directions.

In this period of neoliberal educational reform, teacher unions' priorities have shifted away from attempts to increase their credibility with official decision makers; in this neoliberal climate, this strategy has proved to be ineffective. Instead, unions focus more exclusively on supporting teachers themselves, forging new relationships with parents and community members, and shoring up public education.

Teacher unions are, more than ever before, turning their attention to developing strategies that address teachers' occupational needs directly. While unions have been providing a wealth of informal and nonformal professional learning programs for teachers for decades (Bascia 2000), the new types of union-supported projects are less focused on supporting teachers' adaptations of officially sanctioned reforms and more focused on building and extending support for teachers' autonomous professional learning (the British Columbia Teachers' Federation).

Some chapters report on teacher unions' adoption of new strategies for organizing teachers. In England, where teacher organization has taken place at the local (district) level, the transfer of decision-making authority to schools has prompted at least one teacher union to focus its attention on building union capacity at the school level. Across the United States and in England, teacher unions (and caucuses within unions) have begun shifting toward a culture that draws on organizing practices that hark back to earlier eras. At the same time, unions in these contexts are developing a form of social movement unionism in which unions seek to connect their industrial and political campaigns to a broader base of parental and community support.

Finally, in places where teacher unions were previously intent on maintaining working relationships with decision makers, some unions are taking their own direction. In Alberta, for example, where the teachers' association had been concerned with persuading the provincial government to join them in moving toward a more progressive vision of education, in the face of governmental hostility the Alberta Teachers' Association currently is moving ahead in developing its own vision for new educational directions. This autonomy is likely to serve the organization well through times of tumultuous working relationships with decision makers.

Adding It All Up

Taken together, the chapters in this book reveal many of the organizational faces of teacher unions, characterizing them as partners with governments in setting educational policy and as opponents to governmental policy; as shapers of public discourse about teachers and education more broadly; as strategic actors shaping future educational directions; as flexible organizations, transforming themselves in relation to changing environments; as standing for solidarity and democracy; as affiliated with broad social movements; as settings for teacher activism; as reflections of teachers' sense of collective affiliation; as organizations that support teacher professionalism; and as contested spaces where teachers and other educators compete for primacy. Despite the variety of their activities, the unions depicted in this book all face challenges from antagonistic decision makers and the public media. What is noteworthy is the resilience demonstrated by these organizations in the face of tremendous hostility.

It is not the intent of this book to provide teacher unions with a checklist of strategies to improve their comparative advantage. While teacher unionists are generally interested in learning from one another's experiences and curious about the approaches taken by others, there is no one-size-fits-all blueprint for change that would work well across the wide variety of contexts in which unions operate. Instead, the main contributions of this book are taking teacher unions seriously as organizations *for teachers* and charting the challenges inherent in representing the concerns of this occupational group.

These chapters arise from papers presented and conversations begun a number of years ago among teacher union activists and researchers in the Teachers' Work/Teachers' Unions special interest group of the American Educational Research Association. It is hoped that this book will deepen and extend these conversations.

References

Ball, Stephen, and Deborah Youdell. 2008. *Hidden privatization in public education.* Brussels, Belgium: Education International.

Bascia, Nina. 1994. *Unions in teachers' professional lives.* New York: Teachers College Press.

Bascia, Nina. 2000. "The other side of the equation: Teachers' professional development and the organizational capacity of teacher unions." *Educational Policy* 14 (3): 385–404.

Bascia, Nina. 2008. "Learning through struggle: How the Alberta Teachers' Association maintains an even keel." In *Learning in community*, edited by Kathryn Church, Nina Bascia, and Eric Shragge, 169–86. Dordrecht, Netherlands: Springer.

Bascia, Nina. 2009. "Pushing on the paradigm: Research on teachers' organizations as policy actors." In *Handbook on educational policy research*, edited by Gary Sykes, Barbara Schneider, and David Plank, 785–92. New York: Routledge.

Bascia, Nina, and Pamela Osmond. 2012. *Teacher unions and educational reform.* Washington, DC: National Education Association.

Bascia, Nina, and Pamela Osmond. 2013. *Teacher union–governmental relations in the context of educational reform.* Brussels, Belgium: Education International.

Carlson, Dennis. 1993. *Teachers and crisis: Urban school reform and teachers' work culture.* New York: Routledge Chapman and Hall.

Carter, Bob, Howard Stevenson, and Rowena Passy. 2009. *Industrial relations in education.* London: Routledge.

Darling-Hammond, Linda. 1997. *The right to learn: A blueprint for creating schools that work.* San Francisco, CA: Jossey-Bass.

Foley, Griff. 1999. *Learning and social action: A contribution of understanding informal education.* London: Zed Books.

Gitlin, Andrew. 1996. "Gender and professionalization: An institutional analysis of teacher education and unionism at the turn of the twentieth century." *Teachers College Record* 97 (4): 588–624.

Kean, Hilda. 1989. "Teachers and the state 1900–30." *British Journal of Sociology of Education* 10 (2): 141–54.

Manzer, Ronald. 1970. *Teachers and politics: The role of the National Union of Teachers in the making of national educational policy in England and Wales since 1944.* Manchester, UK: Manchester University Press.

McDonnell, Lorraine, and Anthony Pascal. 1988. *Teacher unions and educational reform.* Washington, DC: RAND Corporation.

Mitchell, Douglas, and Charles Taylor Kerchner. 1983. "Labor relations and teacher policy." In *Handbook of teaching and policy*, edited by Lee Shulman and Gary Sykes, 214–38. New York: Longman.

Murphy, Majorie. 1990. *Blackboard unions: The AFT and the NEA, 1900–1980.* Ithaca, NY: Cornell University Press.

Rousmaniere, Kate. 2005. *Citizen teacher: The life and leadership of Margaret Haley.* Albany: State University of New York Press.

Strunk, Katherine, and Jason Grissom. 2010. "Do strong unions shape district policies? Collective bargaining, teacher contract restrictiveness, and the political power of teachers' unions." *Educational Evaluation and Policy Analysis* 32 (3): 389–406.

Tyack, David. 1974. *The one best system: A history of American urban education.* Cambridge, MA: Harvard University Press.

Urban, Wayne. 1982. *Why teachers organized.* Detroit, MI: Wayne State University Press.

Urban, Wayne. 2000. *Gender, race and the National Educational Association: Professionalism and its limits.* New York: Routledge Falmer.

Van Dijk, Teun. 1996. *Discourse, racism and ideology. La Laguna*: RCEI Ediciones.

Verger, Antoni, Hulya Kosar Altinyelken, and Mireille De Koning (eds.). 2013. *Global managerial education reforms and teachers.* Brussels, Belgium: Education International.

PART I

Histories

CHAPTER 2

Gender and Status: Ontario Teachers' Associations in the Nineteenth Century

Harry Smaller

Rise of Local Teachers' Associations

In March of 1843, Robert Murray, the first superintendent of education for Upper Canada (now Ontario), received a letter from Tomas Graffe, "one of the five of the committee of the School Teachers' Society, Established in Brockville in 1843." Writing on behalf of the "101 Teachers in the Johnstown District," Graffe explained that, in spite of previous efforts made by Murray on their behalf, they had still been unable to get access to the grant monies. As a result, many teachers had "not the necessary means of procuring Board for the present year."[1] Similarly, in the same month, another letter to Murray reminded him of an answer he had given at a meeting of "the schoolteachers of the District at Woodstock" when he was asked "what amount a teacher of a Common School should receive from the School Fund." The teacher explained, "some of the most efficient teachers have abandoned their schools."[2]

There is no question that these letters, and a multitude of others to the Education Office in Toronto beginning in the early 1840s, were written because of a dramatic change that had recently taken place in the colonial government's intervention in the education of the colony's children. Up until that time, there was very little state involvement in these matters, and schooling mainly took place through the initiative and support of local parents, teachers, and churches and other local organizations.[3] With the political and social upheavals of the late 1830s, however, the colonial government soon began the process of enacting and administering legislation for the purpose of centralizing, standardizing, bureaucratizing, and controlling schooling practices, all aimed at the "proper" socialization of the colony's youth.[4] This included new controls on teachers, and over the ensuing years, regulations were established on many aspects of their work—salaries, curricula and textbooks, training and certification, conditions of work, and hiring and tenure conditions. No longer were teachers responsible for, and accountable to, only parents and their local communities. Thus began the development of a bureaucratic system through which power (both administrative and ideological) was vested in the hands of these education officials, local and provincial. As teachers were soon to learn (and this continues to this day), bureaucratization resulted mainly in the diminishing, or negating, of their input in the overall decision-making processes—both within the hierarchies of school staffing structures themselves and within the ever-expanding schooling jurisdictions.

In addition, this burgeoning system did little to challenge existing traditional patriarchal relations within the community. Murray himself seemed quick to interpret the new legislation from a masculine perspective. As he noted in one letter, early in his term,

> It does not appear the School Act of 1841 even contemplated the employment of Female Teachers in the Common Schools. The masculine pronoun is invariably used in the Act, when speaking of Teachers. This is clear for the third clause of the eighth Section. Besides, if they are to receive any of the public money they must be examined before the Township School Commissioners as to learning and ability.[5]

Unfortunately, given the precarious employment situation for teachers through much of the early history of state schooling, and the common practice of local school boards in hiring "women at half the price,"[6] male teachers themselves were often party to these patriarchal sentiments, ones which considerably clouded relations within and around teachers' associations, then and since. Ahira Blake, for example, in an 1843 letter to Murray on behalf of the "Prince Edward District Teachers' Association," complained bitterly about female teachers taking away jobs from the male members of his organization.[7] Henry Livesley of Simcoe wrote a similar note the same month, citing also another common complaint, nepotism: "Females, in some cases the wifes [*sic*] and daughters of school commissioners," were, he claimed, being favored in the hiring process.[8]

With the replacement of Murray by Egerton Ryerson as provincial superintendent in 1844, relations of control, gender, and status only worsened for teachers. Given his subsequent promotion of even more constraining legislation and regulations and increasingly hierarchical governance structures, it is not surprising that these local teachers' associations also grew in number and strength. Regardless of the distances between rural schools, teachers increasingly found ways to come together; as a result, their letters to the Education Office intensified, as they reported on the results of these local association meetings, the concerns raised, and the solutions requested (or demanded).

Ironically, an attempt by Ryerson in the summer of 1850 to promote a more "professionalized" form of teacher gathering—an "in-service" approach to training through the medium of "teachers' institutes" held in a number of towns—resulted in further grassroots backlash. Although conducted under tight control by education officials, teachers took these events as an opportunity to hold their own meetings as well. As a result, not only did the ensuing flurry of letters to Ryerson raise concerns about the top-down nature of the "institutes" themselves,[9] but many also berated the onerous conditions occasioned by the newly passed school acts, while others relayed demands expressed by their members, ranging from improved salaries and teacher certification procedures to the selection of more appropriate school superintendents.[10] Most poignant (or forceful), perhaps, was the petition sent directly by the Dumfries Teachers' Association to the colonial legislature, where it was read on July 11, 1850. After presenting requests for democratizing future teacher institutes and the replacement of the Department of Education's Council of Public Instruction with a structure that would be "composed in part of practical teachers, or persons who have been such," their missive ended with the following note:

> Resolved that this Meeting, having carefully examined the duties imposed on the Chief Superintendent by the late and present School Acts, is of the opinion that his Office is not necessary, as the duties may be performed at much less expense to the Country, by clerks connected with some other Department of the Government.[11]

By this point it must have become very clear to Ryerson and other education officials at the local and provincial levels that something more had to be done to curtail this mounting local resistance from classroom teachers across the province.

Founding the "Ontario Teachers' Association"

To be sure, Ryerson had always favored the existence of teachers' associations—but only those formed "under judicious arrangements" (that is, under the direct supervision of education officials).[12] In 1860, Ryerson's desires were finally realized, with the founding of the "Ontario Teachers' Association."[13] In spite of its name, and Ryerson's insistence that he was not associated with it in any way,[14] it was an organization that was very much initiated, promoted, and subsequently controlled by provincial and local state education officials. The founding meeting (held in the Toronto courthouse) was cochaired by Thomas Robertson (principal of the Department of Education's normal school), Reverend John Jennings (a member of Ryerson's Council of Public Instruction), and Archibald Macallum (a University of Toronto professor); at the end of the meeting, Robertson was elected the organization's first president.[15] Throughout many decades of its existence, the presidency and executive positions were controlled by the same stratum of male education officials.

There is no question that this organization, throughout its lifetime, very successfully fulfilled the goals intended by its founders. Its main public face throughout its entire existence was, in the words of one historian, an "annual talkfest" where "teachers go-to-meeting with their betters" and "where everyone applauded inspirational addresses."[16] "Inspirational" was probably an apt description of these events. Opening sessions invariably involved prayers by noted religious (Christian) leaders followed by welcoming speeches by important political, business, and academic officials. Most of the subsequent sessions over the three-to-four day event involved presentations by "experts" from various fields. While not all lectures were as stark sounding as the one in 1874 entitled "The Antiquity and Dignity of the Public School Teacher,"[17] four themes dominated over the years: professionalization, moral regulation, the national agenda, and centralization of the school system.

Another instance of where the educational elite used the Ontario Teachers' Association (OTA) to promote the increased bureaucratization, centralization, and professionalization of the school system occurred at the one or two "business" meetings scheduled each year. Here resolutions were considered, and great pains were taken to provide the appearance that "teachers" from across the province had participated in these debates and concurred with their outcomes—ones that invariably supported "progress" in the system. However, judging from the documented deliberations of these sessions, considerable discussion and acrimony often occurred regarding many of these resolutions—frequently pitting the elite against the relatively few classroom teachers who did attend. For example, at the second annual meeting in 1862, a motion from a Toronto teacher requesting that the province provide an alternative certification route for teachers unable to attend the official normal school in Toronto generated "long and spirited debate" but ultimately was "voted down by a small majority."[18] Three years later, a similar motion from a teacher—requesting changes in provincial regulation so that a neutral third party, rather than the local school superintendent, would adjudicate salary and tenure issues between teachers and employers—was defeated on the floor.[19] Understandably, the message was soon out to teachers about the real import of "their" organization. As one teacher noted, in a letter to *The Toronto Globe* following another raucous gathering at the 1868 conference, teachers are

> the least influential element in its [OTA's] composition . . . not a dozen [teachers'] names appear in the report of those who took any active part in the proceedings of the association . . . [It] does not represent their opinions and wishes; it is not under their control or guidance; but its chief offices are held, and its actions controlled, by others who have no personal or professional interest in their welfare. Teachers know that if they attend as silent spectators, their presence will give colour to the erroneous impression that their profession is represented by the association; and to attend for the purpose of protesting against the organization and management of the association would be worse than useless. Hence their absence.

The letter concluded with the comment that, in addition, school principals should "cease to meddle in the affairs" of common school teachers.[20]

In addition to status differences, maintaining traditional patriarchal relations was certainly another fundamental component of this project. Within the OTA itself, male education officials dominated both the presidency and the organization's executive for the following decades. Even at the founding meeting, as the official biographer of the OTA subsequently noted, the "proprieties" of gender division manifested themselves—"the females were segregated in the jury box."[21] No record appears among the many reports of the event of any contribution they may have made to the discussions—an interesting fact in itself, whether or not any of the women did actually find it possible, or worthwhile, to comment.[22] For many ensuing decades, the executive included virtually no women, and during its first 80 years of existence, only one woman served as president—Mrs. Ada Marean Hughes, wife of a longstanding Toronto school superintendent, in 1901. Patriarchy certainly underlay many of the motions passed (or defeated) over the years—as the increased bureaucratization and professionalization of the system, officially advocated by the OTA, certainly worked against the interests of women teachers.[23]

Teachers Respond—The Rise (and Unfortunate Fall) of the Perth County Conspiracy

Given the support provided by the "official" pronouncements of the OTA, during the ensuing two decades the Department of Education was able to introduce yet another series of edicts further bureaucratizing the school system. These included more onerous training and certification regulations and further enhancements of its control over local teacher institutes (which were treated by state officials as the only legitimate form of teachers' association, in their dealings with local teachers).[24] By 1884, the Central Committee of Examiners had been established to control (and ramp up) all teacher certification structures, standards, and procedures in the province; in addition, a provincial director of teachers' institutes was hired, with the requirement that he "shall attend the annual meeting of each Institute, and shall discuss at least three subjects on the program." Presumably, his presence was also important in order to ensure that regulations concerning these meetings were followed in every case, including a prescription that "all questions and discussions foreign to the Teachers' work should be avoided"—a clear indication that those in charge were to brook no talk of education politics or of mobilizing to improve teachers' material conditions. Also, the regulations included requirements stipulating the length of sessions and that local officials document and report on teachers' attendance at these compulsory, and highly scripted and controlled, meetings.[25]

However, in spite of (or precisely because of) these restrictions, and the efforts by the OTA officials to control the scope and activities, it is clear that local independent teachers' associations continued to meet, separately from the official gatherings, and to lobby for changes in provincial regulations and policies in regard to their material working conditions. These issues became even more pressing by the mid-1880s, as the province was hit by a deep economic recession that seriously affected teachers along with many others in the community[26]—to the extent that even the dominant educational press was publishing letters and editorials about teachers' plight. For example, commenting in a letter published in a November 1885 issue of *Educational Weekly* on the abuse he claimed he had received from his school board, a teacher from North Dumfries asked, "Is it not true that teachers are organizing themselves against such evils?" Perhaps in direct reply, a teacher from St. Mary's responded in a subsequent issue that "[teachers are] now agitating the movement and are only awaiting for [*sic*] a leader."[27]

In fact, during November of that same year, teachers from across Perth County, west of Toronto, had met, precisely to form a union. As a result of the "enthusiastic" gathering, "it was resolved that a union be formed," which would, among other things, provide material assistance, "protect [teachers] as regards salary," establish a benefit plan for sick teachers and aid in establishing unions in other counties. An executive consisting of two women and two men was elected, along with representatives from 16 different localities across the county.[28] This seemed to be the spark that ignited teachers across the province—over the ensuing months, local teachers' meetings were held in many locales, all of which endorsed the idea of forming an independent provincial teachers' organization.[29] Even the normally conservative editors of the *Canada School Journal* encouraged these plans in a series of editorials, not only wishing "success" for the movement but also expressing the hope that, once established, it would remain "free from all outside influence and dictation from the Education Department or any other quarter."[30] As one correspondent put it,

> A professional union is regarded as the only attainable and feasible method of overcoming the difficulty in question. Teachers have too long been mere playthings in the hands of departmental prestidigitators. It is high time that they should arise.[31]

In July of the following summer, the founding meeting of an independent teachers' association was held in Toronto, organized by a former teacher, David Boyle. As he had advertised, it would be "for the purpose of putting the scheme in shape . . . not [for] discussing its advisability, which will be taken for granted as having been already decided." At that meeting, "about sixty teachers" discussed various aspects of unionization; in the end, a resolution was overwhelmingly passed to form a new provincial teacher union charged with "improvement of their intellectual, social and material political conditions." As one participant noted, in direct reference to the OTA, "Even such loosely bounded organizations as are in existence have failed to effect that unity of purpose with its corresponding influence which ought to characterize us as teachers."[32]

Unfortunately for the founders of this new union, it was clear that their actions were not to be tolerated by the provincial authorities. At the annual meeting of the OTA held a few days later, a number of officials spoke out strongly against these events and the union concept in general. As one official noted, "Teaching is . . . more than a trade . . . it is, or should be, a real vocation or mission . . . a ministry." The depth of their opposition became clear when they announced to the gathering their own plans for the establishment of an alternative new organization, the "College of Preceptors"—one which, they claimed, would "hold the same relation to the state . . . that the Law Society holds to the state."[33] The assembly endorsed the plan in principle and ordered it sent out to all counties to be presented by provincial officials attending the official meetings of the teachers' institutes.

From a number of reports, it was clear that presenting these "official" plans across the province during the following school year also provided opportunities for schooling officials to denigrate the union plan.[34] In addition, the union movement suffered from a number of vicious editorials printed in the dominant press and in educational journals—even those that had initially been supportive of the union movement.[35] By the following summer, the actions of these officials had taken their toll, and a sparsely attended second annual meeting of the new union was its last. Ironically, as evidenced by the proceedings at the OTA conference that following summer, it became clear that these officials also had no real interest in supporting the "College of Preceptors" plan either, and it was quashed as quickly as it had been raised. Clearly, the concept had been devised and floated only to disrupt the flow of the teacher union movement.[36]

There is no doubt that, in spite of a burgeoning union movement across many trades in the province during this time,[37] a number of things stood in the way of an effective teacher union being organized—geographic separation, lack of access to effective communication, the inability of teachers, given their salaries, to support an effective organization, and so on. However, the power of the state apparatus[38] to counter these initiatives certainly became clear to the proponents and supporters of the movement—and these lessons were taken carefully into consideration, if not effectively overcome, in the ensuing decades of struggle.

Local Teachers' Organizations and the Rise of the Toronto Women Teachers' Association

As compared to teachers in rural areas of the province, teachers working in closer proximity in the larger centers were advantaged in forming their own organizations. In Toronto, for example, the Toronto Teachers' Association (TTA) came together in 1877. From the outset, however, even though the vast majority of teachers in the city were women, this group was dominated by male schooling officials; in many other ways it mirrored the structure and activities of the provincial OTA. Similar semiannual conferences were held, including opening sessions involving local dignitaries, prayers, and anthems. Two days of lectures and presentations then followed, based either on "inspirational" themes—like the 1882 talk entitled "The Moral Power and Duty of Teachers"—or on more practical topics, such as "Mental Arithmetic," "How to Direct the Private Reading of Scholars," and "Auzililiary [*sic*] Verbs of Mood."[39]

This male dominance of the organization clearly mirrored the structures of schooling systems in urbanized areas—a relatively small number of men, mainly principals, supervising a large number of much more poorly paid women.[40] Given these conditions, it is understandable why males were keen to control the affairs of the TTA, particularly in relation to dealing with their employers over the differentials in salaries and working conditions. This singular focus was certainly made clear to the women members of the organization. In their own words,

> Women's opinions were neither asked for nor heeded. Even on occasion when a deputation of men and women went before the Board, the (Board) members said they would hear from the men—and mark you, it was women's salaries which were under discussion.[41]

Not only were women teachers not listened to, but the hierarchical structures also placed them under continuous scrutiny and surveillance—particularly oppressive in an era when there was no protection of tenure and dismissals could be enacted without any provision of reason. For example, at a special meeting held in 1882, a number of women teachers signed a petition to the board asking it to reconsider their offer of a paltry raise. As a result, each of these teachers subsequently received a letter from the board "intimating that if her position was not to her liking, the board would accept her resignation."[42]

Finally, in 1885, once again rebuffed at a meeting where they were determined to raise the issue of salary inequalities, something new happened. In the words of the participants themselves,

> Realizing that our point of view would receive no consideration until we united in some definite way, some of us, eight in all, lingered after the meeting and discussed ways and means. The nucleus of the first association of women teachers in Canada was formed then.[43]

This Women Teachers' Association in Toronto took hold immediately—and certainly represented a new phase in the history of independent teachers' associations in the province. While the minutes for the first six years are no longer available, it is clear that their new organization had an almost immediate impact on their working lives. Within a year of the organization's founding, the Toronto board changed its long-standing method of determining salaries, from level of grade taught to seniority—a change that could only have benefited women teachers. Given the board's previous intransigence, this doubtless resulted from organized lobbying on the part of women themselves. By the next annual meeting of the TTA, they made sure that at least half of that association's executive consisted of women, presumably to help ensure that their issues would get proper hearing at meetings.

By 1891, confronted by growing opposition from board members to further requests for salary considerations (including a petition signed by virtually all of the women teachers in the city),[44] some women teachers became directly involved in the municipal elections that winter. In conjunction with the Women's Enfranchisement Association, they were successful in electing three women to the Toronto public school board for the first time. In spite of this support, and their continued lobbying and presence en masse at board meetings in 1892 to push for increased pay, it became clear that their opponents were formidable indeed. These requests were denied, amid attacks by at least one dominant Toronto newspaper that claimed that they had no "just ground for complaint" and that they had weakened their case "because of the gross indelicacy shown in attempting to terrorize the members of the board by attending the meetings en masse."[45]

However, not to be in any way daunted, they engaged during the ensuing months in further planning in regard to the municipal franchise for women, making arrangements to rent permanent space outside of board property for an office and meeting room, presenting a petition to the board requesting that teachers be given a copy of any report on them made by school principals, and criticizing (successfully, as it turned out) a board plan that had established another layer of "supervising principals" over them. In addition, organizing educational and social events became part of the association's activities, including travelogues provided by members themselves and a talk given by one of the three recently elected female board members.[46] These activities continued strongly, during the rest of the decade and into the new century; the fact that other urban centers in Ontario also saw the rise of similar women teachers' organizations suggests that the Toronto association served well as a precedent and example to follow.[47]

To be sure, the struggles were many for the organization. Generating adequate funds remained a problem, given the low salaries earned by women teachers throughout these decades. Annual membership fees, set at 50 cents in 1892, were lowered to 25 cents and then to 10 cents in 1894 and 1898. Given one report's indication that the ranks swelled "immediately" from 114 to 275 members after the second decrease, it is understandable that 14 years would go by before they were raised again—to only 25 cents. Clearly, finances remained an issue for the organization. For example, the meeting room leased in 1892 in an era of optimism had to be relinquished after only a few months, for lack of adequate funds.[48]

Ensuring membership involvement was also a continuing challenge. The executive learned very quickly, as the result of one ill-fated meeting that had been scheduled for an evening hour, that most members could participate only by going to meetings directly from school in the afternoon. While few married women were hired during this era, the stereotype of unmarried teachers being totally independent and responsible only for themselves was probably far from the reality of the situation. In 1907, a survey conducted by Toronto women teachers indicated that 76 percent of them had "more to do with their salaries than support only themselves." On many occasions, WTA minutes reported absences from meetings and even resignations from executive and committee positions as a result of illness and other pressures in the home. Toronto board minutes are also replete with requests for leaves of absence for similar reasons.[49] The magnitude of this evidence and the widespread need for single women teachers to support intergenerational family members suggest that the myth that being a "spinster" equated to personal independence was only that—a myth.

In addition, in spite of the gender-specific nature of the Toronto Women Teachers' Association, the organization often found itself dealing with inner conflict over other fundamental issues. While all members were presumably in favor of seeing improvements in their salaries and working conditions, the organization's minutes portray considerable friction over strategies to achieve this. For some, the solution was to bargain collectively and as strongly as possible, to achieve concessions from their employers. Others, however, eschewed such militancy and felt that their situation would be enhanced only when individual teachers demonstrated that they were worthy of such consideration; accordingly, they believed that their organization should primarily be concerned with the self-improvement of members, though self-study, lectures, social gatherings, and the like. Employers were to be consulted, not confronted, in their requests for material improvements.

As the early years of the new century progressed, these differences seemed to intensify. Realizing that they needed wider support in their bid to improve their material conditions, members soon began to differ on whether this support should be gained from organizations representing other workers in the city or from groups representing business and other professional interests. It would appear that initially they were able to successfully involve both the Toronto Trades and Labor Council (TLC) and the Toronto branch of the Manufacturers' Association in a petition to the board over salaries in 1901.[50] However, other efforts to reach out seemed to lead only to increasing friction, and to seemingly little overall resolution of the issue. Beginning in 1901, affiliation with the TLC was advocated at a number of meetings, resulting finally (over a decade later) in a special meeting in May 1913 to discuss the issue, to which James Simpson, Labor mayor of Toronto, was invited. Those advocating a more conservative stance arranged in the same year for speakers to talk on subjects such as "The Teachers' Work and Influence from a Business Point of View," and they promoted affiliation with the Women's Canadian Club. Ultimately, it was this "more professional" direction that seemed to take the upper hand. Soon after, a motion was passed insisting that the "interests of the WTA be broadened and the meetings take more the form of a social club, the social side being emphasized." Even a notice of motion by a dissenting member—"that women principals be ineligible to become members of the Association" (an entire page is torn out of the minutes book at this point)—did not seem to signal any substantive deviation from this new "professional" direction. At the next meeting, another committee was established "to look into the matter of promoting sociability among teachers."[51] Local women interested in different directions for teachers' associations would have to wait out the First World War before a new start could be made.

Summary

In contrast to an earlier location of attachment to and responsibility for a local community, by the 1840s Ontario teachers began experiencing a new, top-down, material and ideological state agenda. Maintaining paid employment required increasing adherence to state regulation of their training, certification, curriculum, and pedagogy. In addition, they were under increasing ideological pressure to become "professional," to place themselves above their communities, and to promote education for the purpose of ensuring that the nation's youth were schooled for meeting "the wants of the age."[52]

To be sure, some teachers resisted both these centralized controls and the ideology of professionalism, and they struggled throughout the second half of the nineteenth century to form associations that would be different—ones that would be controlled by members themselves. For the most part, however, these attempts—at both the provincial and the local level—were largely unsuccessful, certainly for women teachers. Educational officials were generally able to control the activities of local teachers' groups and prevent the establishment of independent associations, until well into the twentieth century.

In spite of their efforts in forming their own local organizations during these times, women teachers in particular suffered from these developments, as strong gender discrimination continued to dominate the workplace. At the end of the First World War, there were definite signs of change, as women teachers from across the province organized to form the first permanent province-wide teachers' association, the Federation of Women Teachers' Associations of Ontario (FWTAO). By the time of their first annual meeting, they had been able to gather an impressive 4,236 members—support that was engendered, one could surmise, by the continuing low state of their working conditions and by the declaration of their first president, Evelyn Johnson, that she stood for "putting the 'financial' first and 'professional' second." As she explained, "We are going to endeavour to raise the professional status, but we can do it only by raising the financial first . . . How in the world can those teachers raise their professional status on such salaries?"[53]

With these events, it is perhaps not surprising that leaders of the provincial male elementary school teachers, and secondary school teachers, moved quickly to form their own province-wide associations. Also, perhaps not surprisingly given their historically advantaged status in the system, even from the outset neither espoused any serious intention of challenging the bureaucracy. In fact, as exemplified in the words of one high official of the secondary teachers' federation just a few years after its founding, clearly in an attempt to quell concerns among his own members about lack of success in alleviating working conditions for teachers,

> The Departments of Education are cooperating with the teachers' representatives, that grievances may be remedied and reforms instituted. In Ontario, the Premier, who is Minister of Education, invariably grants a courteous interview to their deputations, displays a keen interest in their representations, and discusses them in a friendly and frank manner. This attitude tends to remove differences of opinion and promote harmony.[54]

Unfortunately, even before the end of the decade, things changed radically within the FWTAO as well, as the evolving leadership of the FWTAO turned in favor of accommodation with the provincial authorities. As the secretary general of the FWTAO reported in a 1929 lead editorial in the organization's journal, she was excited about "the splendid spirit existing on each occasion that the representatives of the [provincial school boards'] Trustees Association have met with us in an informal conference." As she claimed,

> This attitude, together with the friendly cooperation accorded us by the [provincial] Department of Education, makes us feel that much will be possible in the coming years that we have deemed impossible in the past. It behooves us to show our worthiness of the confidence we have gained. Let us work hard this year to strengthen our membership and to increase the professional spirit in all women teachers.[55]

As a number of historians have noted, by the end of the 1930s—in spite of the devastating effects on teachers of the economic depression as well as documented cases of local teachers' attempts to mobilize for improvements in their condition—officials of all three associations had sunk to promoting, in the words of one historian, "lukewarm professionalism."[56] To be sure, by midcentury, some progress had been made in relation to legislating province-wide standard contract templates and pensions.[57] Ironically, however, while the leaders of these organizations proved very active over the years in promoting the ideology of professionalism, they were clearly quite unable (or unwilling) to effect the one change that might have ensured an adequate supply of "proper" teachers for the task—overall improvement in the material conditions of teaching.

In summary, the history of teachers' associations during the nineteenth and early twentieth centuries could be portrayed as an unfortunate repeating cycle—classroom teachers suffering increased pressures on their work, leading to their increased resistance and attempts to form strong associations, leading to opposition by state officials and, increasingly, intervention and mediation by official teacher leaders. Given recent reports of the effects on teachers' work of the neoliberal restructuring of public schooling and their seeming inability to counter these changes effectively, one could suggest that this cycle continues today.[58]

Notes

1. Provincial Archives of Ontario, Record Group Two, Series C-6-C, Incoming Correspondence to the Department of Education (hereafter C-6-C), Graffe to Murray, March 27, 1843.
2. C-6-C, McKenzie to Murray, March 10, 1843.
3. While post-1830s "schooling reformers" who denigrated these earlier community-based educational forms, a number of scholars have documented their overall success in teaching subjects required at the time. Even Egerton Ryerson, the ultimate reformer, claimed in 1839 (in an earlier role) that "he did not know of a native of this province twenty years of age who cannot read" and remarked that the circulation of newspapers in Upper Canada that year was "four times as large in proportion to the population as in England itself," as quoted in Charles Bruce Sissons, *Egerton Ryerson: His Life and Letters*, vol. 1 (Toronto: Clarke, Irwin, 1937), 505. See also, for example, R. D. Gidney, "Elementary Education in Upper Canada: A Reassessment," in *Education and Social Change, Themes from Ontario's Past*, edited by Michael Katz and Paul Mattingly (New York: New York University Press, 1975).
4. Not the least of the upheavals were the popular insurrections against the colonial government in Upper and Lower Canada (Ontario and Quebec) from 1837 to 1838. However, there were certainly other reasons why colonial officials were anxious to put in place some system for "proper" socialization of the colony's youth—increasing immigration, bleak economic recessions, and the social effects of the expanding mercantile and capitalist economies. See, for example, Bruce Curtis, *Building the Educational State: Canada West, 1836–1872* (London: Althouse Press, 1988); Susan Houston, "Politics, Schools and Social Change in Upper Canada," in *Pre-Industrial Canada, 1760–1849*, edited by Michael Cross and Gregory Kealey (Toronto: McClelland and Stewart, 1982).
5. Quoted in J. G. Hodgins, *Documentary History of Education in Upper Canada*, vol. 4, 304. One early historian of education in Ontario interpreted this remark (probably quite correctly) as meaning that, in Murray's estimation, women teachers' "ability to pass that examination was clearly beyond the realm of possibility!" J. G. Althouse, *The Ontario Teacher: A Historical Account of Progress, 1800–1910* (PhD diss., University of Toronto, 1929, reprinted, Ontario Teachers' Federation, 1967), 47.

6. Wendy Bryans, "Virtuous Women at Half the Price: The Feminization of the Teaching Force and Early Women Teacher Organizations in Ontario" (MA thesis, University of Toronto, 1974); see also Greg Stott, "'In Reply to Your Advertisement . . .': Local Influences on the Hiring of Teachers, Arkona, Ontario, 1882–1884," *Historical Studies in Education/Revue d'histoire de l'éducation* 20, 2008.
7. C-6-C, Blake to Murray, October 16, 1843.
8. Ibid., Livesley to Murray, October 3, 1843.
9. Even the official in charge of these institutes had to admit to Ryerson that when he attempted to have teachers sign a sheet at the close of the program, several "were unwilling to enter their names without some guarantee that the local arrangements [for future sessions] would be in the hands of the members." C-6-C, Robertson to Ryerson, June 10, 1850.
10. See, for example, letters reprinted in Hodgins, *Documentary History*, vol. 9, 65. For a detailed account of these institutes and their aftermath, see Harry Smaller, "Teachers' Institutes: Instituting Proper Teaching," *Ontario History* 80, 1988.
11. Hodgins, *Documentary History*, vol. 9, 16, 64.
12. As he explained in an 1846 report, with such "proper" organizations, "the most accomplished minds would give a tone to the others; roughness and peculiarities of manner would be rubbed off . . . men would learn . . . the manner of keeping their position in society," *Annual Report of the Ontario Department of Education* (hereafter *Report*), 1846, 209–10. In 1850, in a province-wide circular, he continued with his promotion, stating that by these means "teachers themselves would assume responsibility for the purg[ing from their own ranks] of every inebriate, every blasphemer, every ignorant idler, who cannot teach and will not learn." *Journal of Education* 3, 1850, 181.
13. In fact, this organization had several interim name changes during its initial years, before arriving at "Ontario Teachers' Association." It changed again to the "Ontario Education Association" in 1893, and under this name it remained active until its final demise in the 1980s.
14. As he adroitly noted, "I think the objects and the usefulness of the Association might be impeded, if not defeated, by the possibility or suspicion of its deliberations being influenced in the slightest degree by any public officer," *Toronto Globe*, August 5, 1863. Regardless, it is difficult to imagine, given the politics of the times, that state officials had not consulted him, and gained his approval, for the founding of this "teachers' association." Thomas Robertson, principal of the Department of Education's normal school, was involved in drawing up the announcement of the founding meeting, which was well published in Ryerson's *Journal of Education*.
15. An official history of the organization was published at its centennial in 1960: Edwin Guillet, *In the Cause of Education: Centennial History of the Ontario Educational Association, 1861–1960* (Toronto: University of Toronto Press, 1960). For further details on the founding meeting and the organization's foundational role in maintaining traditional relations of gender and status in the larger provincial schooling system, see Harry Smaller, "Gender and Status: The First Meeting of the Teachers' Association of Canada West, January 25, 1861," *Historical Studies in Education/Revue d'histoire de l'éducation* 6, 1994.

16. J. M. Paton, *The Role of Teachers' Organizations in Canadian Education* (Toronto: W. J. Gage Limited, 1962), 23. As suggested here, and in the larger literature, very few classroom teachers, male or female, actually attended these events, in spite of innumerable efforts over the years to encourage their participation. The conferences were, however, widely publicized in both the dominant and educational press, providing the image of a teacher-engaged organization.
17. Guillet, *In the Cause*, 70. "There is no grander calling than that of the teacher," he concluded, "but it rests with us to see that its utility and nobility are recognized."
18. *Toronto Globe*, August 7, 1862.
19. Ibid., August 9, 1865. Even if the outcome of either of these motions had been different, it is highly unlikely that Ryerson would have acted on them. However, it was certainly to the benefit of schooling promoters to be able to claim that a "teachers' association" had spoken in favor of their ongoing bureaucratization efforts.
20. Ibid., August 7, 1868.
21. Guillet, *In the Cause*, 20.
22. Smaller, "First Meeting."
23. Ryerson's early record certainly made it clear that he was opposed to women becoming teachers, and the first session of his newly founded Toronto normal school excluded them. This policy changed quickly, however, when it became clear that they would have few registrants otherwise. See, for example, Alison Prentice, "'Like Friendly Atoms in Chemistry?'—Women and Men at Normal School in Mid-Nineteenth Century Toronto," in *Old Ontario: Essays in Honour of JMS Careless*, edited by David Keane and Colin Read (Toronto: Dundurn Press, 1990).
24. In fact, local and provincial officials used the terms "association," "institute," and even "teacher convention" interchangeably, and presumably for good reason. See, for example, reports and comments in the department's *Annual Report*, 1878, 128; 1880–81, 143; 1885, xxvi.
25. *Report* 1885, 39–40. In 1881, the superintendent from West Middlesex was able to report to Toronto that "the association consists of four sessions averaging three hours [each], during which the roll is called eight times," ibid., 1881, 143. Note the official's usage of the term "association" in this context.
26. "142 applications for a position in the Glencoe P[ublic] S[chool]," *Stratford Beacon Herald*, November 20, 1885; "Goderich . . . 150 applications for 6 positions," ibid., November 27, 1885.
27. *Educational Weekly*, November 12, 1885; January 7, 1886.
28. Ibid., January 7, 1886. For a more detailed discussion of these events, and those which followed, see Harry Smaller, "Teacher Unions, (Neo)liberalism and the State: The Perth County Conspiracy of 1885," *Pedagogica Historica* 40, 2004.
29. See, for example, reports in the *Canada School Journal*, May 15, June 1, July 1, 1886; *Canadian Statesman* (Bowmanville), May 28, 1886.
30. *Canada School Journal*, May 15, 1886.
31. *Toronto Mail*, June 29, 1886.
32. *Toronto Globe*, August 10, 1886.
33. *Toronto Globe*, August 12, 1886; even an attempt by some members to pass an amendment simply asking that the aims of the organization be clarified was "negativated by a large majority," *Toronto Mail*, August 11, 1886.

34. See, for example, reports in *Canada School Journal*, November 15, 1886, 264; March 16, 1887, 72; *Educational Journal*, July 15, 1887, 94.
35. For example, very soon after the union's founding meeting, *Educational Weekly* charged that "unions" have "become of late a very bad repute, and for very good reasons . . . Such a union attempts to gain higher salaries, not by raising the intellectual or social status of the teachers, but by coercion," *Educational Weekly*, August 12, 1886. It would appear that while the editors of these journals (themselves closely connected to the state schooling system) might have initially seen the movement's value in improving the poor material conditions suffered by teachers across the province, they were quick to be convinced of possible overall ramifications of such a movement.
36. In fact, the idea was probably taken from similar events that occurred in England in the early 1860s, also in order to disrupt any teacher reaction to the implementation of new teaching codes at that time. See Noel Parry and Jose Parry, "The Teachers and Professionalism: The Failure of an Occupational Strategy," in *Educability, Schools and Ideology*, edited by Michael Flude and John Ahier (New York: John Wiley and Sons, 1974).
37. See, for example, Charles Lipton, *The Trade Union Movement in Canada, 1827–1959* (Toronto: NC Press, 1975).
38. In the context of state intervention in this incipient unionization movement, it is certainly possible that the main organizer of the union's founding meeting, David Boyle, was "bought off" by the provincial government—if not from the very beginning, at least at some point following the founding meeting. See Smaller, "Teacher Unions," 89–90.
39. Taken from the minute books of the Toronto Teachers' Association (hereafter TTA Minutes), located in the archives of the Toronto District School Board.
40. In 1885, 196 of the 202 women teachers in the Toronto board had titles such as "female junior assistants" and "female teachers." By comparison, not one male teacher held a position below "master" or "assistant master." In 1881, salaries for women ranged from $200 to $600, and for men, $750 to $1100 (this disparity had actually worsened over the previous decade)—from Toronto Board of Education, *Toronto Board of Education Annual Report* (hereafter *TBE Report*), 1885, 49; 1881, 10–15; 1870, 65–57. In addition, females invariably taught the much larger and rambunctious primary-grade classes in the schools, while the males taught considerably smaller classes in the higher grades. See, for example, Marta Danylewycz and Alison Prentice, "Teachers' Work: Changing Patterns and Perceptions in the Emerging School Systems of Nineteenth and Early Twentieth Century Central Canada," *Labour/Le travail* 17, 1986; Eric Sager, "Women Teachers in Canada, 1881–1901: Revisiting the 'Feminization' of an Occupation," *Canadian Historical Review* 88, 2007.
41. Harriet Johnston, Jessie P. Semple, and A. A. Gray, *The Story of the Women Teachers' Association of Toronto* (Toronto: Thomas Nelson and Sons, 1932), 10; see also Bryans, "Virtuous Women." These events in Toronto were hardly unique among women teachers in many jurisdictions in Canada, in the United States, and beyond. See, for example, ibid.; A. M. Kojder, "The Saskatoon Women Teachers' Association: A Demand for Recognition," *Saskatchewan History* 30 (2), 1977; Kate

Rousmaniere, *Citizen Teacher: The Life and Leadership of Margaret Haley* (Albany: State University of New York Press, 2005); Margaret Nelson, "Vermont Schoolteachers in the Nineteenth Century," *Vermont History* 49 (1), 1981; B. K. Hyams, "The Battle of the Sexes in Teachers' Organizations: A South Australia Episode, 1937–1950," in *Australian Teachers*, edited by A. Spaull (Melbourne, Australia: Macmillan, 1977).

42. Johnston et al., *The Story*, 9.
43. Ibid.
44. Ibid., 133–34. It should be noted that, more recently, some scholars have questioned whether women teachers during these times, and/or into the twentieth century, were as poorly compensated or treated as has been suggested in these earlier accounts—as compared to other women, or men, in the paid working force. However, considering the firsthand accounts and statistical data noted above, I remain unconvinced. See, for example, Sager, "Women Teachers"; Rebecca Priegert Coulter, "'Girls Just Want to Have Fun': Women Teachers and the Pleasures of the Profession," in *History Is Hers: Women Educators in Twentieth-Century Ontario*, edited by Rebecca Priegert Coulter and Helen Harper (Calgary: Detselig, 2005).
45. *Toronto News*, February 25, 1892.
46. Minutes of the Women Teachers' Association general meetings (hereafter WTA Minutes), 1891, 2; 1892, 8.
47. Doris French, *High Button Bootstraps* (Toronto: Ryerson Press, 1968), 26–28; Bryans, "Virtuous Women."
48. WTA Minutes, 1892, 4; 1893, 21; 1894, 30–31; Johnston et al., *The Story*, 22.
49. WTA Minutes, 1892, 5–6; 1907, 209.
50. WTA Minutes, 1901, 118.
51. WTA Minutes, 1901, 114; 1911, 253; 1912, 274, 281; 1913, 276, 283–84, 289, 295. For further discussion of these tensions, see Harry Smaller, "A Room of One's Own: The Early Years of the Toronto Women Teachers' Association," in *Gender and Education in Ontario: An Historical Reader*, edited by Ruby Heap and Alison Prentice (Toronto: Canadian Scholars' Press, 1991).
52. Quote from the first volume of Ryerson's *Journal of Education*, 1848, 51.
53. FWTAO Minutes, April 23, 1919, 16.
54. Ibid., 3, 1925, 11–12. This text was also intended as a response to mounting criticism among Ontario teachers, based on their knowledge that their counterparts in western provinces—who adopted a much more radical approach, including strikes, during the 1920s and 1930s—had improved their working conditions considerably more as a result. Harry Smaller, "The Teaching Profession Act in Canada—A Critical Perspective," in *Labour Gains, Labour Pains: Fifty Years of PC1003*, edited by Cy Gonick, Paul Phillips, and Jesse Vorst (Halifax, Canada: Fernwood Publishing, 1996).
55. *FWTAO Bulletin* 7, 1929, 25.
56. French, *Bootstraps*, 115; see also Bryans, "Virtuous Women"; Elizabeth Graham, "Schoolmarms and Early Teaching in Ontario," in *Women at Work: Ontario*

1850–1930, edited by Janice Acton, Penny Goldsmith, and Bonnie Shepard (Toronto: Canadian Women's Educational Press, 1974). In 1943, at the behest of teacher federation leaders of the time, this "lukewarm professionalism" was formally established in provincial legislation. In spite of being entitled the "Teaching Profession Act," the legislation contained none of the traditional authority found in similar acts (those for lawyers, doctors, etc.). Its only two provisions were, first, the requirement of compulsory membership in official state-designated federations by all teachers in publicly funded schools, and second, that these organizations operate "relations and disciplines" panels to enforce the proper behavior of members—from Smaller, "Teaching Profession Act."

57. For the province, "low-cost" items that certainly benefited teachers in some ways, but also the system, for both measures encouraged teachers to remain in positions in spite of dissatisfaction with other conditions of work.
58. See, for example, Stephen Ball, *The Education Debate* (Bristol, UK: University of Bristol, 2013); Fazal Rizvi and Bob Lingard, *Globalizing Education Policy* (London and New York: Routledge, 2010); Peter Taubman, *Teaching by Numbers: Deconstructing the Discourse of Standards and Accountability in Education* (New York: Routledge, 2009).

References

Althouse, John George. 1967. "The Ontario teacher: A historical account of progress, 1800–1910." PhD diss., University of Toronto.

Ball, Stephen. 2013. *The education debate*. Bristol, UK: University of Bristol.

Bryans, Wendy. 1974. "Virtuous women at half the price: The feminization of the teaching force and early women teacher organizations in Ontario." MA thesis, University of Toronto.

Coulter, Rebecca Priegert. 2005. "'Girls just want to have fun': Women teachers and the pleasures of the profession." In *History is hers: Women educators in twentieth-century Ontario*, edited by Rebecca Priegert Coulter and Helen Harper, 211–29. Calgary: Detselig.

Curtis, Bruce. 1988. *Building the educational state: Canada West, 1836–1872*. London: Althouse Press.

Danylewycz, Marta, and Alison Prentice. 1986. "Teachers' work: Changing patterns and perceptions in the emerging school systems of nineteenth and early twentieth century central Canada." *Labour/Le travail* 17 (Spring): 59–82.

French, Doris. 1968. *High button bootstraps*. Toronto: Ryerson Press.

Gidney, Robert. 1975. "Elementary education in Upper Canada: A reassessment." In *Education and social change, themes from Ontario's past*, edited by Michael Katz and Paul Mattingly, 3–56. New York: New York University Press.

Graham, Elizabeth. 1974. "Schoolmarms and early teaching in Ontario." In *Women at work: Ontario 1850–1930*, edited by Janice Acton, Penny Goldsmith, and Bonnie Shepard, 165–87. Toronto: Canadian Women's Educational Press.

Guillet, Edwin. 1960. "In the cause of education: Centennial history of the Ontario Educational Association, 1861–1960." Toronto: University of Toronto Press.

Houston, Susan. 1982. "Politics, schools and social change in Upper Canada." In *Pre-industrial Canada, 1760–1849*, edited by Michael Cross and Gregory Kealey, 161–88. Toronto: McClelland and Stewart.

Johnston, Harriet, Jessie Semple, and A. A. Gray. 1932. *The story of the Women Teachers' Association of Toronto*. Toronto: Thomas Nelson and Sons.

Kojder, Apolonja Maria. 1977. "The Saskatoon Women Teachers' Association: A demand for recognition." *Saskatchewan History* 30 (2): 63–74.

Lipton, Charles. 1975. *The trade union movement in Canada, 1827–1959*. Toronto: NC Press.

Nelson, Margaret. 1981. "Vermont schoolteachers in the nineteenth century." *Vermont History* 49 (1): 5–30.

Parry, Noel, and Jose Parry. 1974. "The teachers and professionalism: The failure of an occupational strategy." In *Educability, schools and ideology*, edited by Michael Flude and John Ahier, 160–86. New York: John Wiley and Sons.

Paton, J. M. 1962. "The role of teachers' organizations in Canadian education." Toronto: W. J. Gage Limited.

Prentice, Alison. 1990. "'Like friendly atoms in chemistry?'—Women and men at normal school in mid-nineteenth century Toronto." In *Old Ontario: Essays in honour of JMS Careless*, edited by David Keane and Colin Read, 285–318. Toronto: Dundurn Press.

Rizvi, Fazal, and Bob Lingard. 2010. *Globalizing education policy*. London and New York: Routledge.

Rousmaniere, Kate. 2005. *Citizen teacher: The life and leadership of Margaret Haley*. Albany: State University of New York Press.

Sager, Eric. 2007. "Women teachers in Canada, 1881–1901: Revisiting the 'feminization' of an occupation." *Canadian Historical Review* 88 (2): 201–36.

Sissons, Charles Bruce. 1937. *Egerton Ryerson: His life and letters*, vol. 1. Toronto: Clarke, Irwin.

Smaller, Harry. 1988. "Teachers' institutes: Instituting proper teaching." *Ontario History* 80 (4): 270–91.

Smaller, Harry. 1991. "A room of one's own: The early years of the Toronto Women Teachers' Association." In *Gender and education in Ontario: An historical reader*, edited by Ruby Heap and Alison Prentice, 103–27. Toronto: Canadian Scholars' Press.

Smaller, Harry. 1994. "Gender and status: The first meeting of the Teachers' Association of Canada West, January 25, 1861." *Historical Studies in Education/Revue d'histoire de l'éducation* 6 (2): 201–18.

Smaller, Harry. 1996. "The Teaching Profession Act in Canada—A critical perspective." In *Labour gains, labour pains: Fifty years of PC1003*, edited by Cy Gonick, Paul Phillips, and Jesse Vorst, 341–60. Halifax, Canada: Fernwood Publishing.

Smaller, Harry. 2004. "Teacher unions, (neo)liberalism and the state: The Perth County conspiracy of 1885." *Pedagogica Historica* 40 (1–2): 75–91.

Stott, Greg. 2008. "'In reply to your advertisement . . .': Local influences on the hiring of teachers, Arkona, Ontario, 1882–1884." *Historical Studies in Education/Revue d'histoire de l'éducation* 20: 1–21.

Taubman, Peter. 2009. *Teaching by numbers: Deconstructing the discourse of standards and accountability in education.* New York: Routledge.

CHAPTER 3

Defending Teachers' Rights and Promoting Public Education: Evolving and Emerging Union Strategies within a Globalized Neoliberal Context

Wendy Poole

Teacher unions in Canada have been impacted by global recession, increasing competition from private schools, fiscal restraint that shrinks expenditure on education, and a neoliberal policy environment hostile to unions. What are the unique challenges teacher unions in Canada face, and what strategies are they utilizing to enhance their vitality? Canadian education is under provincial, not federal, jurisdiction (with the exception of aboriginal education), and the nature and extent of neoliberal education policy varies greatly from one province to another. To begin to address the question, I focus on a single case study—the case of the British Columbia Teachers' Federation (BCTF), the sole bargaining agent for public school teachers in the province of British Columbia. The BCTF has mounted particularly strong, consistent, and more or less successful resistance to neoliberal education policy. The BCTF case illustrates a variety of strategies teacher unions are employing to battle neoliberal education policy, to protect their collective rights as teachers and union members, and to defend public education.

Organization of the Chapter and Data Sources

The chapter begins with a synopsis of neoliberal education policies in British Columbia (BC) and then moves to a discussion of BCTF strategies for responding to those policies. Some of these strategies are traditional, while others are evolutionary forms of traditional strategies, and still others are relatively new dimensions of teacher union activism that have emerged since the 1980s and 1990s. The relative success of these strategies is examined, and the chapter concludes with a discussion of the implications for the future of the BCTF and possibly other teacher unions.

Data for this chapter come partly from previous studies I have conducted related to teacher unions in North America, labor relations in K–12 education in BC, identities of social activist teachers, and the history of K–12 education finance in BC, and from coauthored studies related to market-driven finance mechanisms in BC. I also draw from organizational studies of the BCTF conducted by other authors and from histories of education and labor in BC. In addition, I analyze government legislation, court decisions, online publications of the BCTF and its international and local community partners, and online documents of the BC Public School Employers' Association.

Neoliberal Education Policy in BC

Neoliberal education policy is not altogether new to BC. With the exception of two periods (1972–1975 and 1991–2001), a series of right-of-center political parties have formed the government of the province since 1952 (BC Government 2014). Market principles, including responsiveness and consumer choice, have been part of the education policy landscape of BC since 1977, when the Social Credit government began to subsidize faith-based schools and other private schools in the province (Crawford 2014; Poole 2014). Teachers also faced existential challenges to their union through government attempts to eliminate compulsory union membership in 1971 and 1987 (BCTF 2014a). Beginning in 2001, however, the right-of-center Liberal government has enacted an aggressive neoliberal agenda, now 13 years in duration, which has challenged teachers and their union in multiple ways.

BC teachers have experienced direct attacks as government takes action intended to limit the power of the union and the rights of teachers. Neoliberal education policy that emphasizes efficiency, accountability, and marketization of education has led to significant reductions in public funding, resulting in the closure of about two hundred schools across the province, the loss of thousands of teaching jobs,[1] and the intensification of teachers' work as class sizes have increased and special education, library services, and instruction for English language learners have been cut (BCTF 2014b; Poole 2007a). Accountability measures and pressure to assist with marketing their schools mean additional administrative work for teachers, further contributing to the intensification of their work (Martens 2012). Loss of teaching jobs reduces the capacity of the teacher union to collect dues at the same time that costs related to collective bargaining, political action, and legal challenges have risen. Teachers, parents, and the general public are weary of conflict between teachers and government.

Neoliberal discourse constructs the state as the guarantor of market liberalization and promotes the application of market principles to the public sector, including education (Ball 1998; Rizvi 2008; Robertson 2011). Neoliberal governments are committed to increasing the efficiency of public education and improving the quality of education, usually through standardized testing and accountability measures, with the aim of producing human capital for highly competitive global markets. School districts, educational administrators, and teachers are expected to do more with fewer resources. Teachers face deteriorating working conditions and stagnant salaries, and they look to their unions for support.

Not only must teacher unions respond to the real needs of their members, but they must also battle public discourse that discredits their activities and public policy that potentially threatens their existence. Teacher unions are discounted in the neoliberal mind-set as "special interest groups" that have little or no legitimate role to play in an education market. Teacher unions are perceived to be self-serving, bureaucratic oligarchies that operate separately from teachers (Moe 2006).

Government Policies Targeting the BCTF

From the beginning of its first term in office in 2001, the Liberal government has targeted the BCTF (Poole 2007a). One of its first measures was to declare education an essential service, hoping this would curb the power of teachers to conduct strikes. Legislation stripped hundreds of lines of contract language and many rights from the teachers' contract and removed certain domains, such as class size and composition and staffing levels, from the collective bargaining process. A "net zero" mandate was imposed on collective bargaining with all public sector unions, which meant that any contractual salary increases and other provisions with a monetary value would need to be offset by corresponding savings in other areas.

Concern about the BCTF's influence in the election of council members of the British Columbia College of Teachers led government to abolish the council in 2003 and replace it with government appointees who then developed Standards for the Education, Competence, and Professional Conduct of Educators in British Columbia (Poole 2007a). Later, in 2011, the college was eliminated entirely and replaced with a Teachers' Council with a mandate to set standards for teacher certification, approve teacher education programs, and address matters related to teacher discipline (Glegg 2013; Walker and von Bergmann 2013). Henceforth, disciplinary actions were to be reported publicly and teachers would have no right of appeal to the courts regarding disciplinary actions.

Collective bargaining in K–12 education has typically been protracted and unproductive throughout the four terms of the Liberal Party's rule since 2001 (with the exception of the 2006 collective agreement). Government has repeatedly used its legislative powers to extend or impose collective agreements, strip contract language deemed undesirable, win concessions, and remove certain working conditions (e.g., class size and composition, staffing ratios) from the scope of collective bargaining.

Union Response Strategies

In response to these challenges, the BCTF has employed a number of strategies, some of them traditional and others emerging or more intensive than evidenced in the past. The more traditional approaches will be examined first.

Job Action

The BCTF achieved full collective bargaining and the right to strike in 1987, decades after other teacher unions in Canada (Lawton, Bedard, MacLellan, and Li 1999). Before the mid-1990s, collective bargaining and strikes had occurred at the local (school district) level, but province-wide strikes were unheard of until 1971, when a dispute arose over teachers' pensions (BCTF 2014a). In 1983, teachers across the province engaged in a three-day strike to protest cuts to education funding and a set of 26 legislative bills that negatively impacted human and labor rights in the province (BCTF 2014a). A structure for province-wide collective bargaining was put in place by 1994, and since then collective bargaining has been a public power struggle. Collective agreements were imposed through legislation in 1998 (when the employers' association refused to ratify a tentative agreement), 2002, and 2012. An agreement was reached through the intervention of a mediator in 2005 after a two-week strike and a heavy fine for the union. Only one collective agreement was successfully negotiated (2006) without intervention (BCTF 2014c).

Prior to the latest round of collective bargaining, which began in 2013, the BCTF and the British Columbia Public School Employers' Association (BCPSEA) negotiated a framework agreement intended to improve the collective bargaining process. The framework agreement included the use of common data and a facilitator (BCPSEA 2013). However, government directly interfered when the premier issued a directive to the BCPSEA to seek a ten-year deal with teachers and when government dismissed the BCPSEA and appointed its own negotiator in July 2013 (BC Ministry of Education 2013). Collective bargaining failed to result in an agreement, teachers went on strike in June 2013, and the BCPSEA imposed a partial lockout. At the time this is being written, there is still no sign of an agreement. Summer school was disrupted and the school year will not begin as scheduled on September 2.

Job action does not always involve full-scale strikes. Limited job action is sometimes used to pressure the employers' association and government. Teachers withdrew administrative and voluntary services in the fall of 2001, again for several months in 2011–12, and for approximately one month in the spring of 2014 when the employers' association retaliated by docking teachers' daily remuneration by 10 percent (BC Labor Relations Board 2014).

Job action has not resulted in the achievement of teachers' collective bargaining goals over the past 12–13 years. However, the real story may be the solidarity of teachers across the province. Despite persistent efforts by government and the BCPSEA to thwart job action and the weariness that teachers feel about years of almost continuous conflict with government, teachers' support for their union has remained strong when it matters most. Evidence is found in the strong strike mandates that teachers have repeatedly provided to the union leadership. Recently (March 2014), 89 percent of participating teachers voted to endorse a staged approach to job action in the latest round of bargaining. Though many teachers are unhappy, solidarity is strong in BC, and this is the union's most important asset.

Protests and Demonstrations

The BCTF has engaged in a number of protests associated with collective bargaining and education policy. For example, a "day of protest" was held on January 28, 2002, in which thousands of teachers marched or rallied in local communities, including a large rally at the provincial legislature; another large rally was held at the legislature on October 17, 2005 (Poole 2007a). The BCTF typically is supported by the Canadian Union of Public Employees (CUPE) and by the BC Federation of Labor (BCFed), whose members or representatives attend protests and make public statements in support of the BCTF. In the fall of 2005, during the teachers' strike, the CUPE and BCFed unions walked off the job in some communities (Poole 2007a).

BC College of Teachers

Perhaps the most unique and prolonged protest by the BCTF began in 2003 when the government replaced the Council of the College of Teachers with an interim council composed of a majority of government-appointed members. Decrying government's action as an affront to self-regulation of the teaching profession, more than half of BC teachers refused to pay their professional dues to the college, despite threats that they might lose their teaching certificates and, therefore, their jobs. In 2004, the council was reconstituted once more, this time providing for a majority of elected members. Teachers voted to submit their fees to the college and resume participation in the election of council members. However, a review of the College of Teachers in 2010 concluded that elected teachers were unable to separate quasi-judicial responsibilities from teacher advocacy, and therefore the college was not fulfilling its mandate of protecting the public interest (Avison 2010). In 2011, the College of Teachers was replaced with the BC Teachers' Council and placed under the control of the Ministry of Education. This ended an experiment in teacher self-regulation in the province of British Columbia.

Foundation Skills Assessment (FSA)

The FSA is a test of literacy and numeracy skills administered each year to BC students in grades four and seven. The test results are available on the Ministry of Education's website. However, a right-of-center think tank, the Fraser Institute, uses the FSA results, together with provincial exam results at the secondary level and other school-based indicators, to produce a school report card that ranks every school in the province. These rankings are the subject of controversy regarding the Fraser Institute's claims that they represent "objective" measures: the inclusion of public and private schools in the same rankings; failure to consider variations in school and community contexts; the publication of the rankings by prominent newspapers in the province; and the tendency of some parents to use the rankings to make judgments about the quality of schools and decisions about where to enroll their children.

In 2008, delegates at the BCTF's annual general meeting decided to boycott teacher participation in preparing for, administering, and marking the FSA tests unless the ministry moved to a random sampling approach. In 2009, the BCTF held a membership referendum on this matter. The BCPSEA directed teachers to administer the tests, and when the BCTF failed to comply, the employers' association filed a complaint with the Labor Relations Board, which subsequently ruled that teachers are required to administer tests as directed by the Ministry of Education. Following another referendum regarding the Labor Relations Board ruling, BC teachers agreed to abide by the ruling, albeit under protest.

Despite legal restrictions on teachers' noncompliance with respect to administration of the tests, the BCTF gained considerable ground in their protest against the FSAs. First, the support of its members on this issue is indisputable and was noted by the BCTF president (at the time): "There is no doubt in anybody's mind now that teachers are fully behind the campaign against the FSA" (BCTF 2009). Additionally, the BC School Superintendents Association and the BC School Trustees Association openly criticized the use of FSA data for purposes of ranking schools, thus partially supporting the BCTF's position. Perhaps most importantly, a significant number of parents requested that principals excuse their children from FSA testing. Nonparticipation by considerable numbers of students in some schools further undermined the already questionable validity and reliability of the tests, thus limiting the credibility of their results.

Public Messaging

While communication with the public is not new for the BCTF, its use has intensified over the last decade. The emergence and abundance of social media have provided cost-efficient opportunities for the BCTF to reach a wide and diverse audience. The union has accounts with Facebook, Twitter (https://twitter.com/bctf), YouTube (https://www.youtube.com/user/BCTFvids), and Pinterest (http://www.pinterest.com/bctf). Press releases and seminars are aired via Livestream. Advertisements are placed in traditional venues as well, including newspapers, radio, television, and public transit. Some advertisements appear in nonofficial languages spoken by large segments of the population in BC—Mandarin, Cantonese, and Punjabi.

The BCTF often uses advertising to criticize provincial education policy and to promote investment in public education. For example, the "When will they learn?" campaign, launched in 2008, focused on government cuts to public school funding, increasing class sizes, and diminishing support for student learning. Other campaigns have focused on garnering public support for teachers' collective bargaining demands and buttressing the union's assertion that better teaching conditions lead to improved learning conditions.

Schools often serve as venues for BCTF's messaging. Teachers have been known to display posters in schools; wear black armbands, T-shirts, and buttons bearing slogans; and distribute pamphlets and flyers to parents, sometimes through students. Political messaging in schools has garnered negative responses from some school boards and has resulted in arbitration and court rulings.

Legal Challenges

Since 2002, the BCTF has engaged intensively in legal challenges to combat neoliberal education policy and attempts by the employer (BCPSEA) to limit teachers' protests.

Legal Challenges to Government Legislation

Legal challenges to government legislation abounded after 2001, when the newly elected Liberal government passed a series of legislative bills attacking teachers' rights and the power of the teacher union. Essential service legislation was passed in 2001, within the first 90 days of the government's mandate. As mentioned previously, the Liberal government has employed legislation to impose collective agreements on teachers on several occasions. While back-to-work legislation is not a new phenomenon, the frequency of its use since 2001 is remarkable.

Another new development is government's utilization of its legislative powers to attack collective bargaining rights. In 2002, the Liberals passed Bills 27, 28, and 29, marking the first time a Canadian government unilaterally rewrote collective agreements. Bills 27 and 28 imposed a collective agreement on teachers and struck from the teachers' collective agreement provisions on matters such as class size, class composition, staffing levels of specialist teachers, length of the school day, and hours of instruction in a school year. Future collective bargaining related to these matters was prohibited, and this significantly narrowed the scope of collective bargaining for teachers. The legislation also moved several local collective agreements into the province-wide agreement and, in the ensuing process, stripped hundreds of locally bargained provisions.

The BCTF appealed to the International Labor Organization (ILO), which condemned the BC government's actions as violations of international labor standards. Although Canada is a signatory to these standards, the ILO has no power to enforce its decisions, so while this ruling and three additional rulings throughout the first decade of the twenty-first century were moral victories for the BCTF, the BC government simply ignored the reprimands.

Bolstered by a 2007 ruling that the Charter of Rights and Freedoms protects collective bargaining, the BCTF launched a legal challenge. In 2011, ten years after the legislation came into effect, the BC Supreme Court ruled many parts of the legislation unconstitutional on the grounds that they violated teachers' Charter rights to the process (as opposed to the content) of collective bargaining. The BC government was given one year to revise its legislation. Then, in a surprise move, the government passed Bill 22 (Bill 22-2012), effectively reinstating the contents of Bills 27 and 28.

The BCTF challenged Bill 22, and in January 2014 the BC Supreme Court ruled this legislation unconstitutional.[2] The provincial government was ordered to pay the BCTF's court costs plus $2 million in damages. This was a tremendous legal and moral win for teachers. The BCTF could take the high ground, while government struggled to explain itself to the legislature and to the media. This contest is not over. The government has appealed the court's decision, and it has been granted a stay of proceedings until the appeal can be heard. The upcoming appeal will be an important case for labor relations in education because it will address the decades-old tension between teachers' rights to a voice in establishing working conditions and government's prerogative to set education policy.

Legal Challenges Regarding Teachers' Freedom of Expression

Several times over the past decade, employers (represented by the BCPSEA) have directed teachers to cease and desist in engaging in political messaging in BC schools. The BCTF has countered by filing grievances and using the arbitration process to make an argument for teachers' freedom of expression.

The BCTF has experienced mixed results through arbitration. The Munroe[3] decision favored the teachers' position, stating that "school boards unjustifiably infringed on teachers' rights to freedom of expression by restricting their ability to post and distribute information and engage parents in discussions during parent/teacher interviews." Kinzie[4] ruled that the employers' refusal to allow teachers to communicate concerns regarding FSA tests to parents, in sealed envelopes delivered by students, unjustifiably interfered with teachers' Charter right to freedom of expression.

In contrast to these favorable outcomes, Burke[5] ruled that the employer was justified in limiting freedom of expression when it disciplined a teacher for discussing messages critical of FSA tests with students, finding that this directly impacted statutorily mandated educational programs. Similarly, Thompson[6] determined that it is not permissible for teachers to introduce political messages "either in the form of printed matter or buttons worn on their garments into the classroom or the walls or doors immediately adjacent to classrooms." A court appeal of these decisions by the BCTF resulted in a ruling affirming teachers' right to freedom of expression in schools.[7] This decision is a major win for teachers and appears to grant teachers free rein to discuss their views on political issues. The limits to that freedom have yet to be determined. It is entirely possible, and even likely, that this issue will be revisited sometime in the future.

Labor Solidarity

The BCTF is broadening its solidarity engagement with a more comprehensive set of labor organizations, in both domestic and international contexts.

Domestic

It has long been the policy of the BCTF to demonstrate solidarity with education assistants and school support workers when their unions (CUPE) are on strike. During CUPE strikes, it is policy that teachers will not cross picket lines, although a few teachers sometimes do so. The BCTF moved to strengthen its relationship with noneducation unions in 2003 when it joined the BCFed. Affiliate unions in the BCFed represent a wide variety of both skilled and unskilled workers. The decision to join was a controversial one, since many teachers worried they would lose professional autonomy as part of a broader labor organization; however, the union president (at the time) made a convincing case about shared values and goals and the belief that there is strength in numbers.

The BCTF acted to affiliate with labor at the national level when it became a member of the Canadian Labor Congress (CLC) in 2006. The CLC is an umbrella organization for a wide variety of affiliated Canadian and international unions as well as provincial federations of labor and regional labor councils. The BCTF's move followed in the footsteps of other teacher unions in Ontario that had already joined the CLC.

Joining these organizations was a strategic move by the BCTF to ally itself with the labor movement as a means of expanding its influence and base of support. Ironically, the BCTF withdrew from membership in the Canadian Teachers' Federation in 2008 over conflicts related to the CTF's governance structure and expenditures. Budgetary issues associated with declining membership and revenue from dues (related to reductions of teaching staff across the province) played an important role in the BCTF's decision to withdraw from the CTF, and it would be inappropriate to interpret this decision as disengagement from other teacher unions in Canada.

International

Internationally, the BCTF engages in solidarity activities, primarily with other teacher unions and increasingly with nongovernmental organizations, student groups, and community groups. Some types of solidarity initiatives have been used since as early as the 1920s, while other types have emerged since the mid-1990s.

The more traditional approaches to international solidarity involve building alliances between the BCTF and teacher unions in other countries through teacher exchanges, professional development, and union capacity building. The BCTF has an active International Solidarity Program with stable funding at a rate (1.86 percent of annual dues) protected by policy.

BCTF's international solidarity efforts concentrate on Latin America, southern Africa, and the Caribbean. Some organizational projects focus on providing professional development in English-language-learning pedagogy to teachers in the host country through workshops conducted by teachers in BC and host countries. Other projects have focused on antisexist and inclusive pedagogy and support for the engagement of women in their teacher unions. In southern Africa, projects have aided teacher unions in several countries to organize or build their capacity. The BCTF funds the nongovernmental organization (NGO) Education Beyond Borders, supporting teachers engaged in professional development in Africa. Grants to international unions are sometimes provided to support teachers and students when schools are disrupted when natural disasters or conflicts, occur and to support union efforts to challenge neoliberal education policy and repression of democratic teachers' organizations.

Social Movement Unionism

Social movement unionism (SMU) is a concept that emerged in the 1980s in response to criticisms of institutionalized unionism. Sometimes drawing from Michels's (1911, 1915) critique of representative democracy and what he called the "iron law of oligarchy," critics argue that unions have become institutionalized and bureaucratic "business unions" and, in the process, lost their roots in, and commitment to, the labor movement. As Turner and Hurd (2001, 23) argue, unions may be shifting strategies:

> Unions are now shifting their strategic orientation and promoting a new social movement unionism. This is aimed at organizing the unorganized and taking political action to strengthen union influence. The ultimate objective is to reform labor laws with new protections for workers and unions and to reform the institutions of industrial relations.

This description suggests unions are reengaging with labor as a movement focused on the rights of workers, unions, and industrial relations, but with a greater emphasis on "member involvement and activism" (Turner and Hurd 2001, 11).

Most SMU scholars argue that it means not just reemphasis on labor as a movement and greater internal democracy, but a new unionism. For example, SMU extends to issues beyond the workplace:

> Social movement unionism recognises the new industrial working class is only part of a larger class movement for whom conditions have become intolerable. It reaches outside the workplace, is deeply democratic, militant, internationalist and political and is based on rank and file activists rather than official union structures. (Neary 2002, 166)

SMU engages with the community: "Broadly defined, SMU is a trend in contemporary unionism in which workers and trade unions are united in larger coalitions with an array of community organizations for achieving mutual goals in the furthering of economic and social justice" (Devinatz 2008, 205). Such community engagement may be local or international or both.

Does the BCTF engage with SMU and, if so, is this engagement strategic? Addressing these questions requires an examination of the BCTF's objectives—whether they have changed, in what ways, and why.

Teacher unions in Canada, from their inception in the late 1800s and early 1900s, have been spaces where social justice issues are discussed and union organizing intersects, to some degree, with social movements beyond that of labor. Since the 1970s, spurred by the social movements of the 1960s and 1970s, groups of social activist teachers have demanded space and resources within their unions to champion social justice and social justice education. The BCTF is a particularly strong example of this because social justice goals have been entrenched in the organization's constitution.

By the 1970s, social movement activism was beginning to influence the structure of teachers' organizations. The feminist movement raised awareness about women's rights and issues, and women teachers formed "status of women" committees and demanded a greater voice for women in their workplaces and unions in addition to curricula, policies, and collective agreements addressing gender issues in education. An antiracist activist group also formed within the BCTF in the mid-1970s.

By the 1990s, social activist teachers were advocating the use of BCTF resources to support initiatives addressing a greater variety of social justice issues. By 1998, when the BCTF reviewed its social justice governance structure, it was committing over $1 million annually to these initiatives (Watson 1998). A survey conducted in 2003 indicated that 85 percent of the BCTF's members believed it should advocate social justice (Turner 2005). Today, there are four social justice action groups within the organizational structure focused on antiracism, homophobia and heterosexism, poverty, and the status of women. These groups engage with community groups to develop social justice curricula for teachers and organize local workshops and conferences on social justice issues. In addition, the BCTF has organizational membership in and/or supports many local community action groups.

Social justice provides opportunities for teachers who are not interested in taking traditional leadership roles in the union (e.g., collective bargaining and member services) to engage with their union in meaningful ways. Rottman (2013) makes a convincing case that there are bidirectional links between social justice unionism and union vitality in the BCTF because social justice strengthens both the internal relevance of the union to its members (and therefore strengthens member engagement and participation in the union) and the external relevance of the union to the community.

Some forms of international solidarity work constitute social justice activism. Coteaching with teachers in international contexts, supporting the empowerment of women in international teacher unions, and supporting international teachers in the development of decolonizing curricula and pedagogy are, at the same time, acts of solidarity with fellow teachers and engagement with social justice activism. Teachers involved in international solidarity work may come to understand some of the complexities of and interconnections between social justice and unionism in education, and sometimes they become more deeply engaged in both forms of activism (Poole 2007a).

International partnerships extend beyond national teacher unions. The BCTF partners with the Vancouver-based nongovernmental organization Codevelopment Canada (CoDev), which facilitates and provides translation services and financial support for many of the BCTF's international solidarity projects in Latin America. CoDev builds partnerships between "like-minded organizations" in Canada and Latin America to foster mutual understanding, solidarity, community empowerment, and social change—to "ultimately improve prospects for a fairer global order" (http://idea-network.ca). Other international partners include Education International (EI), a federation comprising over four hundred educator unions and associations around the world, and Oxfam, which has provided financial support for projects in Africa.

A Social Movement to Protect and Promote Public Education

During the early developmental years, teachers used their union organizations to engage with a social movement for publicly funded education accessible to all children. In recent years, there has been a resurgence of interest and attention given to this objective by the BCTF. In response to neoliberal attempts to marketize education, many teacher unions in Canada and around the world have engaged in a new social movement to protect and promote public education.

Since the mid-1990s, the BCTF's International Solidarity Committee has coordinated the formation of strategic alliances with other teacher unions in the Western Hemisphere. The Trinational Coalition for the Defense of Public Education was formed by teacher unions in Canada, the United States, and Mexico in response to the signing of the North American Free Trade Agreement (NAFTA) in 1994. Teachers in the NAFTA countries share concerns about the influence of free trade agreements and transnational organizations such as the World Bank, the World Trade Organization (WTO), and the Organization for Economic Cooperation and Development (OECD) on education policy and practice. The coalition meets every two years to exchange information about education reform in member countries and discuss strategies for challenging reforms perceived as eroding commitment and equal access to free, quality public education.

A broader alliance, the Initiative for Democratic Education in the Americas (IDEA), was formed in 1998–99. Its representatives include teachers' organizations from Argentina (CTERA), Brazil (CNTE), Canada (BCTF), Ecuador (UNE), Mexico (Mexican Section of the Trinational Coalition), the United States (CUNY), regional teacher unions in Central America (FOMCA) and the Caribbean (CUT), as well as an organization representing students in Latin America and the Caribbean (OCLAE). The mission of IDEA is stated as follows:

> The IDEA network carries out research, establishes communication networks, publishes documents and organizes conferences and seminars related to neoliberalism, trade agreements and the defense of public education. It also organizes hemispheric campaigns to defend public education. The objective of these activities is to lay the groundwork for an understanding of the impact of neoliberal policies on education in the Americas and to develop alternatives to ensure inclusive, democratic and quality public education. (http://ideanetwork.ca/about-us)

Both alliances—the Trinational Coalition and IDEA—demonstrate a belief that it is not just teacher unions that are threatened, but the institution of public education itself. They object to the commodification and privatization of education and to an increasing emphasis on the role of schools in the development of "human capital." They propose the conceptualization of education as a human right.

There are challenges associated with the formation and operation of these coalitions. Language differences are an obvious challenge when unions from Canada (where the official languages are English and French) engage with Latin American unions that are predominantly Spanish speaking. The language translation services offered by CoDev have played crucial roles in these coalitions.

Differences may be ideational as well. For example, coalition members may have different political-economic perspectives that could present challenges to effective collective action. In my observations, representatives of the various unions are respectful of differences. With translation services to support dialogue, coalition members have developed an understanding that neoliberal education policy can and does emerge within a variety of political-economic contexts. Collective action is directed toward addressing the negative impacts of neoliberalism in education and creating a new social imaginary.

The BCTF's International Solidarity Committee coordinates international activities; however, this program faces financial challenges. Projects have been supported, in part, by grants from the Canadian International Development Agency (CIDA). However, the Canadian government made significant policy changes in 2011 that reoriented official development assistance toward the interests of private Canadian companies, particularly those in the extractive industries (Brown 2013; LeBlanc 2012). Refusal to partner with companies they believe to be contributing to environmental degradation as well as social and economic oppression in international contexts has disqualified BCTF partner nongovernmental organizations like CoDev from receiving CIDA funding. BCTF finances have been strained by a large number of legal cases and job actions, and many teachers are resistant to paying higher dues. A resolution to reduce funding for international solidarity activities was introduced at the 2014 annual general meeting, but it was defeated, and funding for this work continues to be protected.

Summary and Conclusion

The BCTF is a union under siege. It operates in a public sector targeted by government for reform, much of which has a neoliberal orientation. Government has demonstrated its intention to use legislative and other forms of power to curb the influence of the teacher union and impose its will in collective bargaining.

Labor relations in education are undergoing significant change. Rights and practices we long thought institutionalized are being tested. Through the case of the BCTF, we see how teachers' constitutional rights to freedom of association, in the form of collective bargaining rights, and freedom of expression are being challenged by their employers and by government. These are significant developments that have important implications with respect to interpreting teachers' rights. If the past 13 years are an indication, the union will need to dedicate more resources to collective bargaining and legal action to combat neoliberal reform. Even a change in government may not guarantee relief, since all governments feel pressure to conform to globalized neoliberal discourse and policy.

The success or failure of the BCTF's strategies is difficult to measure. The union has won some battles and lost others. Some of its wins, however, have great significance, most notably the court decisions in 2013 and 2014 that affirmed teachers' rights with respect to freedom of expression and collective bargaining. The 2014 decision regarding Bill 22, which declared unconstitutional the government's stripping of provisions of the teachers' contract, might have restored staffing, special services, and working conditions to 2002 levels and returned class size and composition to the scope of bargaining. However, government is appealing the decision and, at the time this chapter was written, has given little or no ground in the current round of collective bargaining. Despite the legal triumph, the union may not regain any of what was previously lost in their next collective agreement. Nevertheless, the legal case resulted in considerable criticism of government by members of the public, especially because the court proceedings revealed documents supporting the union's claim that the government failed to bargain in good faith. The moral victory is a significant one and may have payoffs in terms of public support.

The union continues to give a high level of priority to member welfare and union security. These objectives have led the BCTF to make formal connections with labor federations in BC and other Canadian provinces, creating greater strength in numbers. In this way, business unionism has loosened its grip and is evolving. The move is predominantly a strategic one. It means that teachers understand that they have much in common with other workers who have experienced similar struggles and who share an interest in public education, and that mutual benefits can be gained from solidarity. But if the relationship continues in the long term, it may have important implications for teacher identity. Whereas teachers once identified themselves as professionals, apart from labor, they may come to see themselves as part of the labor movement.

The BCTF has engaged in a struggle for the future of public education. Spurred by concerns about the impacts of free trade agreements and globalized neoliberal policy on education, the BCTF has broadened the scope of its international engagement, forming alliances with teacher unions in the Americas. These alliances are incrementally deepening connections with student and parent organizations. International solidarity work politicizes many of the teachers who participate, a process that could, as the allied unions hope, lead to increased teacher engagement with their respective unions.

A gradual evolution in the union's objectives has resulted in the entrenchment of social justice goals in the organization's constitution and budget. Social justice activism and international solidarity converge in some respects and take on characteristics of social movement unionism. Social movement unionism is evolving within the BCTF and for Canadian teacher unions in general, and its future trajectory is uncertain, especially at the international level. Social justice and environmental education are being addressed by teacher and leadership education programs in BC, which means that more teachers entering the profession are knowledgeable about these issues and may have a greater propensity to get involved in social justice education and social movement unionism. However, not all teachers are comfortable with the political nature of social justice activism (Poole 2007b) or with teacher activism that extends beyond the boundaries of education. There may be some backlash if social movement unionism becomes a stronger focus. Budgetary constraints may limit international solidarity and social movement unionism if resources continue to be consumed by legal and economic matters. Technological communication facilitates this work and generates efficiencies; however, face-to-face meetings are necessary to build strong relationships, and costs may limit work at the international level.

Despite being battered, the BCTF remains a vital organization. It has maintained the support of a majority of its members, as evidenced by strong strike mandates. Teachers are weary of conflict, and they want to focus on teaching and learning; while some are critical of specific union tactics, their anger with, and mistrust of, government sustains their resolve to fight. If current trends continue, teachers' salaries will fail to keep pace with inflation. As new generations of teachers struggle to pay for the rising costs of housing, child care, energy, and other necessities, they may become more militant. Working with more children whose families are also struggling and facing fewer resources to address their students' needs may also fortify teachers' militancy. There is no evidence that teachers are becoming more compliant.

Provincial governments have greater power than unions, through legislation, regulation, and election mandates. As a general rule, governments and employers act, and unions react. The next move will come from government. Government may very well continue its policy direction and move toward American and Australian style "fair workplace" or "right to work" legislation that could significantly limit union power. However, governments depend on a supportive electorate, and questions are being raised by the public about the fairness of government actions and the level of financial support for public education. In the short term, damning court decisions such as Griffin (2014) and the union's public messaging campaigns may sway public opinion enough to curb some of the aggressiveness of government. In the long term, global social movements and social movement unionism may be powerful equalizers if they can be sustained, broadened, and deepened.

Notes

1. Declining student enrollment in most school districts in BC in recent years has also contributed to the loss of teaching positions.
2. Griffin, S. 2014. British Columbia Teachers' Federation v. British Columbia, 2014 BCSC 121.
3. Munroe. 2004. 78 C.L.A.S. 6 2004 C.L.B.12478, 129 L.A.C. (4th) 245, [2004] B.C.C.A.A.A. No. 82.
4. Kinzie, J. 2008. 93 C.L.A.S. 277 2008 C.L.B. 2852, 172 L.A.C. (4th) 299, [2008] B.C.C.A.A.A. No. 51.
5. Burke, E. M. 2011. 105 C.L.A.S. 176 2011 C.L.B. 5917, 206 L.A.C. (4th) 165.
6. Thompson, M. 2011. 109 C.L.A.S. 123 2011 C.L.B. 29003, 214 L.A.C. (4th) 25.

7. Levine, J. A., Garson, J. A., and Hinkson, J. A. 2013. 228 A.C.W.S. (3d) 690 2013 C.L.B. 13313, 44 B.C.L.R. (5th) 261, 2013 BCCA 241, 2013 CarswellBC 1351, [2013] B.C.W.L.D. 4561, [2013] B.C.W.L.D. 4522, [2013] B.C.W.L.D. 4669.

References

Avison, Donald. 2010. *A college divided: Report of the fact finder on the BC College of Teachers*. Vancouver: British Columbia Teachers' Federation.

Ball, Stephen. 1998. "Big policies/small world: An introduction to international perspective in education policy." *Comparative Education* 34 (2): 119–31.

BC Labor Relations Board. 2014. "Letter decision BC LABOR RELATIONS BOARD No. 104/2014." Last modified June 4. http://www.bcpsea.bc.ca/documents/teacherpercent 20bargaining/Bargainingpercent20Bulletin/LABORRELATIONSBOARDpercent 20Decision percent20B104-2014.pdf.

BC Public School Employers' Association. 2013. *Teacher–public school employer collective bargaining 2013: A new approach in challenging times*. Retrieved from http://www. bcpsea.bc.ca/documents/Information percent20and percent20Insight/00-HJF-Rep percent20Council percent20Feb percent2016 percent202013-Teacher-Public percent20School percent20Employer percent20Collective percent20Bargaining percent202013.pdf.

Bill 22-2012. Education Improvement Act. 2012. "Legislative assembly of the province of British Columbia." https://www.leg.bc.ca/39th4th/1st_read/gov22-1.htm.

British Columbia Ministry of Education. 2013. *Working together for students: A framework for long term stability in education: Toward a 10 year agreement with public school teachers*. Victoria: British Colombia Ministry of Education.

British Columbia Teachers' Federation. 2009. "The campaign continues." *Teacher* (newsmagazine of the BCTF), March.

British Columbia Teachers' Federation. 2014a. *History of the BCTF*. Vancouver: British Columbia Teachers' Federation.

British Columbia Teachers' Federation. 2014b. *School closures*. Vancouver: British Columbia Teachers' Federation.

British Columbia Teachers' Federation. 2014c. *Bargaining history*. Vancouver: British Columbia Teachers' Federation.

Brown, Stephen. 2013. "Undermining foreign aid: The extractive sector and commercialization of Canadian development assistance." Accessed September 16. http://open canada.org/features/undermining-foreign-aid/.

Crawford, Kilian. 2014. "BC's private school boom." *The Tyee*, March 15.

Devinatz, Victor. 2008. "Introduction to symposium on 'The future of social movement unionism.'" *Employee Responsibilities and Rights Journal* 20 (3): 205.

Glegg, Alaistair. 2013. "The British Columbia College of Teachers: An obituary." *Historical Studies in Education* 25 (2): 45–64.

Government of British Colombia. 2014. "Premiers of British Columbia, 1871–today." Accessed August 1, 2014. http://www.gov.bc.ca/bcfacts/premiers.html.

Griffin, Susan. 2014. British Columbia Teachers' Federation v. British Columbia, 2014 BCSC 121.

Lawton, Stephen, George Bedard, Duncan MacLellan, and Xiaobin Li. 1999. *Teachers' unions in Canada*. Calgary, Alberta: Detselig.

LeBlanc, Daniel. 2012. "CIDA funds seen to be subsidizing mining firms." *Globe and Mail*, January 29.

Martens, Sherrie. 2012. "Teachers' perceptions of intra-school choice in secondary schools and its impact on professional interactions." Published master's graduating paper, University of British Columbia.

Michels, Robert. 1915. *Political parties: A sociological study of the oligarchical tendencies of modern democracies*. New York: Free Press.

Moe, Terry. 2006. "Union power and the education of children." In *Collective bargaining in education: Negotiating change in today's schools*, edited by Jane Hannaway and Andrew Rotherham, 229–56. Cambridge, MA: Harvard University Press.

Neary, Michael. 2002. "Labour moves: A critique of the concept of social movement unionism." In *The labour debate: An investigation into the theory and reality of capitalist work*, edited by Ana Dinerstein and Mary. Neary, 158–87. Brookfield, VT: Ashgate.

Poole, Wendy. 2007a. "Neo-liberalism in British Columbia education and teachers' union resistance." *International Electronic Journal for Leadership in Learning* 11 (24): 1–13.

Poole, Wendy. 2007b. "Teacher identity and social activism." Paper presented at the annual meeting of the Canadian Society for the Study of Education, Saskatoon, Saskatchewan, May 26–29.

Poole, Wendy. 2014. *A history of public school finance in British Columbia*. Unpublished work in progress.

Rizvi, Fazal. 2008. "Rethinking educational aims in an era of globalization." In *Changing education—Leadership, innovation and development in a globalizing Asia Pacific*, edited by Peter Hershock, Mark Mason, and John Hawkins, 63–91. Hong Kong: Comparative Educational Research Center.

Robertson, Susan. 2011. *The strange non-death of neoliberal privatisation in the World Bank's education strategy 2020*. Center for Globalization, Education, and Societies, Bristol, UK.

Rottman, Cindy. 2013. "Social justice teacher activism: A key to union vitality." *Our Schools/Our Selves* 23 (1): 73–81.

Turner, Jane. 2005. "An AGM vision comes to life: Social justice action groups are happening." *Social Justice Newsletter* 1 (1): 1–2.

Turner, Lowell, and Richard Hurd. 2001. "Building social movement unionism: The transformation of the American labor movement." In *Rekindling the movement: Labor's quest for relevance in the twenty-first century*, edited by Lowell Turner, H. C. Katz, and Richard Hurd, 9–26. Ithaca, NY: Cornell University Press.

Walker, Judith, and HsingChi von Bergmann. 2013. "Teacher education policy in Canada: Beyond professionalization and deregulation." *Canadian Journal of Education* 36 (4): 65–92.

Watson, Linda. 1998. "Social justice review." *Teacher* (newsmagazine of the BCTF), March.

CHAPTER 4

Remembering, Reimagining, and Reviving Social Justice Teacher Unionism

Cindy Rottmann, Larry Kuehn, Christine Stewart, Jane Turner, and James Chamberlain

Social Justice Teacher Unionism, What a Great Idea!

Union-active teachers in Chicago and elsewhere have recently fought to reform their organizations in the name of social justice. This growing movement is remarkable, but it is not new. Organizational histories commissioned or written by teacher union insiders (Chafe 1968; Cuff 1985; French 1968; Glass 1989; NUT 2008) and accounts of teacher unionism written by educational historians and sociologists (Danylewycz and Prentice 1986; Foley 1995; Gaskell 2008; Murphy 1990; Smaller 1991; Urban 1982) suggest at least five periods of social justice teacher union activism since the beginning of the twentieth century.

In the late 1800s, women teachers, many of whom were working-class immigrants, began to fight for fair representation. For example, in 1899, eight hundred Chicago school teachers led by Margaret Haley and Catherine Goggin of the Chicago Teachers' Federation made plans to interrupt the male, administrator-dominated leadership of the National Education Association by organizing a teacher-led National Teachers' Federation (Murphy 1990; Rousmaniere 2005). The NEA leadership blocked their efforts, but over the next few decades women teachers, influenced by labor and suffrage movements in Canada, the United States, and the United Kingdom, began advocating equal pay, the repeal of legislation prohibiting married women from teaching, and a vision of education based on classroom experience rather than university credits (Gitlin 1996; Kean 1989; Labatt 1993; Murphy 1990; Rousmaniere 2005; Smaller 1991; Urban 1982).

In the period leading up to the First World War, a small but vocal group of teachers affiliated with the American Federation of Teachers, and with left-leaning political parties within otherwise conservative teachers' organizations in Canada, fought for academic freedom for their members (Chafe 1968; Clarke 2002; Murphy 1990; Smaller 1998; Urban 1982). The central principle behind these struggles was to challenge dismissals of teachers perceived to be critical of the war effort. This fight for academic freedom has regularly resurfaced across space and time.

In the late 1960s and the 1970s, a growing group of mainly unionized teachers joined the feminist and civil rights movements, hoping to infuse activist potential into their organizations and their classrooms (Dewing 1973; McKenna 1999; Murphy 1990). They wrote antiracist and multicultural curricula, fought to desegregate unions in segregated states, and advocated increased leadership representation of racialized demographic groups in their unions and schools. At the same time, social justice teacher unionism experienced a major setback in New York City as tensions arose between predominantly white unionized teachers fighting for professional autonomy and predominantly black community members advocating community control over education (Kahlenberg 2007; Perlstein 2005).

Two and a half decades later, a group of activists and academics met in Portland, Oregon to advocate a new model of social justice teacher unionism that merged the antiracist concerns of community control advocates with the industrial and professional concerns of unionized teachers (NCEA 1994; Peterson and Charney 1999). While social justice initiatives have a long, piecemeal history among unionized teachers, these initiatives were organized into a movement with a name—"social justice unionism." While the movement has not radically transformed teachers' organizations in the two decades since this meeting, it has given union leaders an umbrella under which to highlight their equity-oriented initiatives.

Finally, from the 1980s to the present day, international solidarity networks between teacher unions in the global north and south have allowed organized teachers to learn from and support colleagues facing similar conditions across educational jurisdictions, resisting, where possible, the inclusion of educational services in international trade agreements (Kuehn 1996). This international movement with roots going back to the 1920s (Compton and Weiner 2008; Kuehn 2006) suggests that a few vocal teacher union activists worldwide have historically contributed to socially just change in schools and society. These solidarity networks have reduced teachers' isolation and allowed them to share activist strategies, but the networks remain tenuous because teachers' struggles occur on a markedly uneven political terrain. Teachers in Canada, the United States, the United Kingdom, the European Union, Australia, and New Zealand are struggling against a growing achievement gap and increasingly creative privatization strategies, while teachers in parts of Mexico, Namibia, rural China, and rural India, as well as poor, racialized, and indigenous communities in the United States and Canada, are facing eroding working conditions, inadequately financed schools, restricted mobility, incarceration, and in some cases, death (Compton and Weiner 2008).

These five activist periods demonstrate the historically persistent yet ephemeral nature of social justice unionism. The problem is not that a great new idea has failed to be considered. Rather, the oppressive conditions that make it such a great idea constrain our ability to institutionalize its goals. With this challenge in mind, our chapter investigates the opportunities and constraints faced by activist teachers fortunate enough to work in a self-defined social justice union—the BCTF.

Methodology

The idea for this chapter emerged from an institutional case study of social justice activism at the BCTF based on 25 career history interviews with elected officials, administrative staff, and full-time teachers (Rottmann 2011). In the years since the study was conducted, the primary investigator and four key participants have discussed ways to maximize the activist potential of this study. We decided to resist the ahistorical tendencies of educational reformers by drawing connections between four decades of teacher union activist experience and a strategically imagined, social movement inspired future. After reading the final report from the initial case study, four of the five authors constructed narratives in response to the following questions:

1. When and how did your social justice commitments first take hold in the BCTF?
2. What federation structures or practices supported or constrained your work?
3. What impact has your activist work had on the federation, on you, or on educational improvement?
4. What do you hope for the future?
5. What can we all do to transform your imagined hope into reality?

Our research questions and analysis are inspired by hooks's (1992, 5) assertion that "we are always in the process of remembering the past even as we create new ways to imagine and make the future." By remembering the past, social justice activists can build on the strategies of those who came before them. By imagining the future, they can interrupt and reframe hegemonic notions of improvement imposed upon them by educational reformers. In short, our conceptual framework highlights the frequently masked agentic role of social justice activists and allows us to recognize their work as the designers, drivers, and implementers of educational change.

Four Activist Narratives Based on 155 Years of Experience

Four of the 30 activists, elected officials, and staff interviewed for the initial study generated narratives in response to the five questions listed above. Please see table 4-1 for their entry points, years of union involvement, and leadership roles.

The four longitudinal, evidence-based narratives that follow constitute our central findings for this chapter.

Institutionalizing International Teacher Union Solidarity—Larry Kuehn

From the first annual general meeting of the BCTF I attended as a delegate in 1969, there were always international issues on the agenda. It just seemed that this was a regular part of the work of the union. It was only looking back

Table 4-1 Social justice activists/staff BCTF involvement

Activist/staff	*Entry point*	*Years of union involvement*	*BCTF leadership roles*
Larry Kuehn	Delegate to 1969 AGM	1969–present	BCTF president; director (research and technology); responsible for International Solidarity Program (10 percent of job description)
Jane Turner	S/W network via curriculum development	1974–2009	Coordinator, Status of Women program; assistant director (professional and social issues); responsible for Social Justice Committee
James Chamberlain	LGBTQ group organizing to pass motion at 1997 AGM	1995–2012	Assistant director (professional and social issues); responsible for Social Justice Committee
Chris Stewart	Delegate to 1997 AGM	1997–2012	Assistant director (professional and social issues); coordinator, Aboriginal Education Program; member-at-large, BCTF executive committee

that I realized that this normalization of international solidarity might be exceptional. When I was doing research for a dissertation I discovered that international connections had been a part of the union's work stretching back to the 1920s, in the years just after the formation of the union.

When I was BCTF president in 1981, we created a structure such that international work became embedded in the fees and business of the union. We set aside 1.86 percent of the fee revenue on an ongoing basis (more than $500,000 a year now) and created a committee of members to oversee the work.

My personal engagement and commitment grew out of participating in a delegation to Central America in 1985. Honduras and Guatemala had military governments, Nicaragua was fighting the contras, and El Salvador was in the midst of a civil war. Teacher unions in some cases were illegal or officially taken over by government forces, and all were engaged in the struggles in many ways. It was admiration for the resilience and commitment of these teachers that solidified my own commitment. I have been fortunate to have had international solidarity as part of my responsibilities as a staff member of the union for more than 25 years.

Because international solidarity is built into the structure of the union, we have been able to make long-term commitments to working with teacher unions in Latin America and southern Africa. Our programs have supported social justice activities paralleling the social justice programs of our own union. These have included promoting the engagement of women in union and school leadership, supporting the development of nonracial unions in South Africa and Namibia, and opposing neoliberal policies, including privatization and trade agreements.

The broad strategy of the program for the past 30 years has been one based on values and structures. The values are those of seeking more social equity—globally and in our own society, in social class and identity. The structural aspect is based on the collective strength of unions-supporting institutions that have the capability of pursuing the values over the long term and beyond particular individuals. In the gender work, for example, our union partners have been encouraged to create women's secretariat structures within the union that would be a vehicle for making space over the longer term for changing the gender makeup and impact of leadership in the union.

Although international solidarity is integral to the BCTF, it has a lower profile than many other aspects of union work. The extent of the BCTF program is only understood by a segment of the activists, particularly those who have been part of activities and colleagues with whom they have shared their experiences. Many teachers who have taken part in the international program talk about the impact on them in changing how they understand their own society and situation and increasing their commitment to social justice.

Many BCTF members participate in international work outside the union structure through international NGOs, global education in their classrooms, and personal projects they undertake. Some of these complement the international solidarity work of the BCTF. Some of them are based on charity rather than solidarity.

Looking forward, the challenge is bringing together the organizational work, the personal work, and the commitment of teachers to international solidarity. In the context of austerity and neoliberal attacks on unions, it is essential to consolidate and amplify solidarity as a response.

Weaving Women's Issues into Union Structures, Practices, and Norms—Jane Turner

As a student teacher at the University of British Columbia in 1974, I became involved in preparing an annotated bibliography for a women's studies curriculum commissioned by the government of the province. A few months later, as a newly employed teacher, I became part of the Status of Women Committee's provincial network of contacts. My work as a feminist activist in my union began.

The BCTF had created a Status of Women program in 1973. The program was democratically structured. Teachers in every local branch of the BCTF could create their own Status of Women Committee. The chair of the local committee would be the official BCTF Status of Women contact. Contacts were given training on how to run a committee, organize feminist events, raise issues regarding the status of women, and teach nonsexist pedagogy. Contacts discussed their local issues with members of the provincial committee, a group of nine geographically representative women appointed by the executive of the BCTF. Each provincial committee member was responsible for a geographic zone of contacts, which met twice a year zonally (according to geographic zones established by the union) and once a year at a provincial conference held for all contacts.

The most difficult nut for feminists in the federation to crack was in the area of negotiating union contracts. The bargaining structures of the federation were generally controlled and populated by men, men who had little interest in addressing "women's issues." Prorated benefits for part-time work, improved parenthood leaves, sick leave to take care of ill children, guaranteed access to part-time work and the right to return to full-time work, sexual harassment, and nonsexist work environment clauses were all issues that the women of the BCTF wanted to discuss. While we were successful in having them included in the bargaining package, they were usually the first ones to fall off the table when the hard bargaining began.

As a result, we began a campaign to get women elected to bargaining committees across the province. In 1976, there were only a handful of women at the tables discussing wages and benefits for teachers. A decade later, almost all local contracts had language addressing all of the issues previously mentioned. All curriculum review committees had to look at nonsexist pedagogy and learning resources. In addition, women were active members of all the major committees of the federation, not just the S/W committees. Women's voices were strong and their organizing capabilities legendary, and women's issues and concerns were part of every aspect of union life. Outside groups looked to the BCTF Status of Women program for leadership on feminist issues.

I was so fortunate to be part of the development of the Status of Women program. I learned more than I gave. I became a proficient public speaker and a credible writer, and I learned much about the principles of organizing and cooperative planning. I was able to teach women's studies to high school students for ten years.

I would like to think that the biggest impact I had in my feminist work within the BCTF was encouraging other women to become active and take on leadership roles within schools and local and provincial structures. I hope that they thought, "If she can do this, so can I."

Ironically, after the 25th anniversary of the Status of Women program in the BCTF, the program was disbanded. Amid calls for reduced spending on social justice programs within the federation, there was a small group of power brokers who recognized the competing power of the women's network that had been set up throughout the province. They too wanted the S/W program to be eliminated, so under the guise of fiscal constraints, all of the discrete social justice programs within the BCTF were rolled into one under the umbrella of "social justice."

While I would love to see a return to the discrete programs within the federation, my more realistic dream would be that no matter what the internal structure, teachers continue to speak out and take strong positions on women's issues, whether popular or not. When we speak out and organize to change the actions of governments, private and public institutions, and individuals within society to promote and extend the rights of women in our local and global communities, then I know we will be continuing the legacy of the early Status of Women program.

Collaborating with the BCTF to Build Safer Schools for LGBTQ Teachers and Youth—James Chamberlain

Between 1997 and 2004, the BCTF passed a series of motions establishing a program to actively address homophobia and heterosexism in schools. This resulted in a dedicated staff member at the BCTF and the beginning of education for members about the harm caused by homophobia to students, staff, and families. During this time, the BCTF worked closely with gay and Lesbian Educators (GALE-BC), now called the Pride Education Network, to develop resources for classroom use at the K–12 level. He/she also began to educate teachers through professional development workshops on LGBTQ (lesbian, gay, bisexual, transgender, queer) issues. In my view, this was the beginning of systemic change on LGBTQ issues in BC schools. As of 2013, 20 school districts in BC have discrete antihomophobia policies. Much of this change has been attitudinal and largely the result of education activists and the BCTF staff member who works on LGBTQ issues collaborating on a variety of projects.

The BCTF currently has two staff members dedicated to social justice work in six discrete areas—peace, environmental justice, status of women, antiracism, antipoverty, and LGBTQ issues. This is not enough to support significant systemic change. Ideally, every school district needs staff members who can support teachers in the field. The Vancouver School Board has an antiracism and diversity mentor and an antihomophobia and diversity mentor (both staffed at 80 percent time). These teachers help others to do this work. All other school boards in BC lack these skilled professionals. At the BCTF level, social justice programs should be funded as a percentage of members' union dues. They should not be subject to the political whims of individual leaders or executive committees. Budgets should be guaranteed in order to allow for sustainable funding over the long term. Finally, in a perfect world, all teachers would have mandatory professional development in all areas of social justice in order to build their knowledge of LGBTQ issues and of other forms of oppression.

Buoyed by Mentors While Drowning in a Sea of White Faces—Christine Stewart

My traditional name is Galksi' Gibaykwhl Sook'-Wilps Ksim Xsaan, and I am from the Nisga'a Nation. I am one of seven children. I was raised between my mother's home and my grandmother's home.

I came to the BCTF with very little teaching experience but a lot of life experience. At my first annual general meeting I was just visiting, and felt that I was drowning in a sea of whiteness. There were very few visibly different people and no aboriginal people.

As I became more involved in the aboriginal education program, I was fortunate to work with some wonderful teachers. We have together made a great difference for social equity in our work sites and the lives of children in BC public schools. We continue to work within BC labor to promote improved living conditions for the children we teach and the communities we live and work in. In addition, aboriginal teachers, trained by BCTF facilitators, are leading community workshops on Indian residential school reconciliation.

The greatest support I received while working at the BCTF was being listened to and having my ideas honored and respected. People I met through union work saw something in me and have encouraged and supported me. I have benefited a great deal from the mentoring of others. The training and mentoring I have received by being involved in numerous committees, both at the local level and the BCTF provincial level, has allowed me to listen to the voices of many members.

My hope for the future of this work is threefold: Within the federation my hope is for more aboriginal staff in every area of our organization. I hope for an aboriginal employment equity policy within the workplace of the BCTF offices. Within the membership, my hope is for all of the members to understand the complex and dynamic histories of all aboriginal people. They must understand that we want what they want for their children—a sense of belonging, high school completion, friends, and teachers who can really interact with our children. Finally, I want all aboriginal teachers to know that their union, both local and provincial, has set the table. There must be a place at the table for them.

Institutionalizing Activist Strategies and Accomplishments

BCTF-affiliated social justice activists have been instrumental in shifting the climate for equity issues in their union, making the federation more responsive to a larger cross section of teachers. The establishment of feminist and antiracist activist networks in the mid-1970s diversified possible entry points and demographics for union-involved teachers. The institutionalization of these networks with contacts in over 70 locals led to an expansion of union roles beyond school representative, grievance officer, and table officer positions, diversifying the range of ideas and motions at annual general meetings. While delegates' freedom to raise questions and motions from the floor has been restricted in recent years, there remains a place for critical dialogue driven by locally active teachers committed to an even wider range of activist issues.

As influential contributors to this institutional work, teacher activists acknowledged being changed by their federation involvement through deepened analyses and commitment, broadened horizons (Bascia and Young 2001), and leadership development. They improved their oral and written communication skills, learned how to collectively persuade individuals who stood above them in the educational hierarchy, found ways to reduce the isolation experienced by most classroom teachers, and began to self-identify as leaders.

Finally, at the levels of school and society, federation-sponsored initiatives have served students and teachers in communities at the local, provincial, national, and international level. First, social justice activists who have undergone personally transformative learning experiences through their union involvement have passed on their passion and commitments to K–12 students in BC schools. Beyond the passion of classroom teachers, the workshops, lesson plans, course offerings, and resource lists generated by union-active teachers for use by their colleagues in schools across the province could easily fill a library. Across the decades, teacher activists involved in the Status of Women program were instrumental in bargaining for the inclusion of maternity clauses and nonsexist working conditions in local contracts, thus shifting the climate for women teachers in provincial schools. More recently, aboriginal teachers have built on this important precedent by bargaining for the inclusion of employment equity language in many local contracts. Even more recently, teachers involved in the aboriginal education program have led community-based workshops on Indian residential school reconciliation. At the administrative level, antihomophobia activists involved in the Pride Education Network in partnership with BCTF staff have catalyzed the development of antihomophobia policies in 20 of 60 provincial school districts. Similarly powerful collaborations have occurred at the global level through international solidarity relationships between the BCTF and teacher unions in Latin American and southern Africa.

This list of local, provincial, and global accomplishments reveals only a small fraction of the educational improvement initiatives supported, incubated, and catalyzed by social justice teacher union activists in one Canadian teacher union (Rottmann 2012). Imagine what would happen if they were charged with the responsibility of setting the pace for educational improvement in the years to come.

Surmounting Obstacles through Concretely Imagined Futures

"We are always in the process of remembering the past even as we create new ways to imagine and make the future" (hooks 1992, 5)

When applied to the idea of educational improvement, bell hooks's quote acts as both a cautionary tale and a promise yet to be fulfilled. If elite decision makers with privileged histories become the educational architects of the future, oppressive forces in society will remain intact. In more concrete terms, if educational policy makers with privileged upbringings base early twenty-first-century school reform on an untroubled memory of a "golden era" in education, sociopolitical injustices will be preserved. If, on the other hand, multiple actors with a range of biographically diverse histories and school experiences build concretely imagined futures upon continually troubled past experiences, we may, as a society, begin to collectively surmount seemingly insurmountable educational obstacles. This is the promise of democratized school reform. On a smaller scale, it is also the promise of democratized union reform.

Our main objective in this chapter has been to interrupt the perpetual cycle of amnesia surrounding social justice teacher unionism. While the movement has yet to be mainstreamed, the principles driving it have been energetically practiced for nearly a century and a half by groups of committed activists working on the margins of the labor movement—in our case, a group of activists affiliated with the BCTF between 1967 and 2014. Please see table 4-2 for a summary of formalized activist strategies, barriers, and recommendations for the future.

Looking across the four narratives, Kuehn's, Turner's, Chamberlain's, and Stewart's hopes for the future emerge from five central barriers to social justice work: institutional isolation, an unsustainable resource base, organizational patterns of privilege, deficit mentalities held by teachers, and international

Table 4-2 Hopes for the future built on four generations of activist strategy

Social movement	*Institutionalized BCTF structure*	*Barriers*	*Imagined futures*
Labor	International Solidarity Program (1981–present)	Austerity context; persistent charity (not solidarity) perspective among members	Consolidation and amplification of solidarity
Feminism	Status of Women program and network (1973–1998)	Patriarchal norms → women's issues first to fall off the table in tough economic times	Ideally return to S/W networks; teachers take strong positions on women's issues even if unpopular
Anticolonialism	Aboriginal Education program and network (1999–present)	Unacknowledged deficit mentality of aboriginal children and families among members	Aboriginal employment equity policy in BCTF; pressure on all teachers to unpack colonial perspectives
LGBTQ rights	GALE-BC → Pride Education Network (1992–present)	Unreliable funding for BCTF social justice programming	All social justice programs funded as a percentage of union dues

relationships based on charity. We[1] believe the acknowledgment and surmounting of these barriers, rather than one-off neoliberal reform ideas, should drive educational change.

First, the expectation that any single organization can independently eliminate social injustice from schools and society sets teacher union activists up for failure. Thus, it is important to combine the efforts of union activists with community-based activists working on similar issues. Still, even if relationships between union and community-based activists are strengthened, they cannot lead to sustainable change until they are paired with social and economic policies addressing the disadvantages faced by low-income, primarily racialized communities.

Second, the negative repercussions of government-imposed and union-imposed austerity measures for social justice programming have upset social justice activists within the BCTF and have restricted the breadth and depth of new social justice initiatives. It makes sense for teacher unions to prioritize members' working conditions over other organizational functions. They are, after all, legislatively obligated to represent teachers' occupational interests. There is no reason, however, why this legitimate set of priorities should result in the erosion of social justice infrastructure, as occurred with the feminist and antiracist networks in the late 1990s. One way to stabilize funding for social justice programming without shifting union priorities away from teachers' working conditions is to allocate a fixed percentage of union dues to all union programs and divisions—including social justice. Decisions about the best vehicle for bargaining, campaigns, professional development, governance, and social justice will be left in the hands of the activists and staff responsible for each of these programs. It takes far more money and initiative to rebuild a demolished social justice network than to keep these programs going with reduced funds until the economic tide turns. The resulting retention of programmatic diversity has important implications for member engagement, organizational democracy, and union contributions to educational improvement—all of which contribute to union vitality.

The third and fourth barriers—organizational patterns of privilege and deficit mentalities held by teachers—are integrally related. The former is a product of patriarchal, heterosexist, colonial norms within the union, while the latter is a product of similarly unacknowledged patterns of privilege in schools. Union leaders and district administrators would be well advised to adopt employment equity policies within their respective jurisdictions so that teachers, school administrators, union activists, and union leaders reflect the demographic diversity of children in every kindergarten classroom. Finally, it is imperative that educators at all levels acknowledge and unlearn their implicit assumptions about "other people's children" (Delpit 1995).

It is important for union-involved educators to collectively overcome social justice models based on charity. In the current economic climate of austerity, it has become increasingly important for networks of antioppression activists to consolidate and amplify local, provincial, national, and international solidarity relationships between labor activists, community-based activists, and educators. To the extent that we can collectively realize the imagined futures of diverse groups of social justice activists, we will be able to collectively counter the erosion of public education at the local and global levels.

These five conceptual bridges connecting surmountable barriers to concretely imagined futures provide teacher union insiders with a platform to discuss productive and unproductive internal tensions in their organizations. We hope and believe that these conversations will build the foundation of an increasingly resilient social justice teacher union movement—a movement that will not have to be revived, because it has been remembered and reimagined.

Note

1. The five authors of this chapter have not achieved consensus on the recommendations that follow.

References

Bascia, Nina, and Young, Beth. 2001. "Women's careers beyond the classroom: Changing roles in a changing world." *Curriculum Inquiry* 31 (3): 271–302.

Chafe, Jane. 1968. *Chalk, sweat, and cheers: A history of the Manitoba Teachers' Society commemorating its 50th anniversary 1919–1969*. Saskatchewan, Canada: Hunter Rose Company.

Clarke, Frank. 2002. "Keep communism out of our schools: Cold war anti-communism at the Toronto Board of Education, 1948–1951." *Labour/Le travail* 49 (Spring): 93–119.

Compton, Mary, and Lois Weiner (eds.). 2008. *The global assault on teaching, teachers, and their unions: Stories for resistance*. London: Palgrave.

Cuff, Harry. 1985. *A history of the Newfoundland Teachers' Association 1890–1930*. St. John's, Canada: Creative Publishers.

Danylewycz, Marta, and Allison Prentice. 1986. "Teachers' work: Changing patterns and perceptions in the emerging school systems of nineteenth and early twentieth century central Canada." *Labour/Le travail* 17 (Spring): 59–80.

Delpit, Lisa. 1995. *Other people's children: Cultural conflict in the classroom*. New York: New Press.

Dewing, Robert. 1973. "The American Federation of Teachers and desegregation." *Journal of Negro Education* 42 (1): 79–92.

Foley, Janice. 1995. *Redistributing union power to women: The experiences of two women's committees*. PhD diss., University of British Columbia.

French, Doris. 1968. *High button boot straps: Federation of Women Teachers' Associations of Ontario 1918–1968*. Toronto: Ryerson Press.

Gaskell, Jane. 2008. "Learning from the women's movement about educational change." *Discourse: Studies in the Cultural Politics of Education* 29 (4): 437–49.

Gitlin, Andrew. 1996. "Gender and professionalization: An institutional analysis of teacher education and unionism at the turn of the twentieth century." *Teachers College Record* 97 (4): 588–624.

Glass, Fred. 1989. *A history of the California Federation of Teachers 1919–1989*. San Francisco, CA: CFT/Warren's Waller Press.

hooks, bell. 1992. *Black looks: Race and representation*. Boston: South End Press.

Kahlenberg, Richard. 2007. *Tough liberal: Albert Shanker and the battles over schools, unions, race, and democracy*. New York: Columbia University Press.

Kean, Hilda. 1989. "Teachers and the state 1900–30." *British Journal of Sociology of Education* 10 (2): 141–54.

Kuehn, Larry. 1996. "Teachers, NAFTA and public education in Canada: Issues for political action." In *Teacher activism in the 1990s*, edited by Susan Robertson and Harry Smaller, 27–34. Toronto: James Lorimer and Company Ltd.

Kuehn, Larry. 2006. "Intercambio: Social justice union internationalism in the B.C. Teachers' Federation." PhD diss.,University of British Columbia.

Labatt, Mary. 1993. *Always a journey: A history of the Federation of Women Teachers' Associations of Ontario 1918–1993*. Toronto: Federation of Women Teachers' Associations of Ontario.

McKenna, Tom. 1999. "Confronting racism in British Columbia." In *Transforming teacher unions: Fighting for better schools and social justice*, edited by Robert Peterson and Michael Charney, 52–57. Milwaukee, WI: Rethinking Schools.

Murphy, Marjorie. 1990. *Blackboard unions: The AFT and the NEA, 1900–1980*. Ithaca, NY: Cornell University Press.

National Coalition of Educational Activists. 1994. "Social justice unionism: A call to education activists." *Rethinking Schools* 9 (1): 1–4.

National Union of Teachers. 2008. "NUT history." Accessed February 1, 2010. http://www.teachers.org.uk/node/8515.

Perlstein, Daniel. 2005. *Justice, justice: School politics and the eclipse of liberalism*. New York: Peter Lang.

Peterson, Bob, and Michael Charney. 1999. *Transforming teacher unions: Fighting for better schools and social justice*. Milwaukee, WI: Rethinking Schools.

Rottmann, Cindy. 2011. *Organized leadership for equitable change: Union-active teachers dedicated to social justice*. PhD diss., University of Toronto.

Rottmann, Cindy. 2012. "Forty years in the union: Incubating, supporting, and catalyzing socially just educational change." *Journal of Educational Change* 13 (2): 191–216.

Rousmaniere, Kate. 2005. *Citizen teacher: The life and leadership of Margaret Haley.* Albany: State University of New York Press.

Smaller, Harry. 1991. "'A room of one's own': The early years of the Toronto Women Teachers' Association." In *Gender and education in Ontario: An historical reader*, edited by Ruby Heap and Alison Prentice, 103–24. Toronto: Canadian Scholar's Press.

Smaller, Harry. 1998. "Canadian teacher unions: A comparative perspective." *Contemporary Education* 69 (4): 223–27.

Urban, Wayne. 1982. *Why teachers organized.* Detroit, MI: Wayne State University Press.

PART II

Discourses

CHAPTER 5

Fragility and Volatility in Teacher Union–Governmental Relations

Nina Bascia and Pamela Osmond-Johnson

A primary function of teacher unions is to bring teachers' concerns about educational practice to the attention of policy makers (Bascia and Rottmann 2011). But in much of the world, teachers have little formal authority to directly influence policy decisions, and educational policy makers have limited knowledge about the dynamics of schooling. Governmental policy makers and teacher unions operate according to different priorities, the former focused on large-scale effects on educational practice and the latter on the conditions of teaching and learning. Often established after, and even in reaction to, formal educational systems (Murphy 1990; Smaller 1991; Urban 1982), teachers' organizations are not often viewed as legitimate decision makers. Most of the research on teacher union–governmental relationships characterizes them as perennially conflictual and working at cross-purposes (Bascia and Osmond 2012).

There are, however, some collaborative relationships between unions and government. Notable examples include the Scandinavian countries (Bascia and Osmond 2013); the social partnership in England through much of the first decade of the twenty-first century (Carter, Stevenson, and Passey 2010); and the relationship between the Alberta Teachers' Association and the Alberta government in Canada (Bascia and Osmond 2012, 2013). In these cases, teachers have sat at the policy-making table, and there has been a greater flow of information between the realities of practice and the making of policy.

Researchers who study teacher unions tend to emphasize either union–policy maker antipathy or, more rarely, collaboration. Hardly ever does research capture cases of these relationships in flux, moving from antagonism to cooperation or vice versa. Yet results from an international survey of teacher unions suggest that these relationships are typically complex and fragile (Bascia and Osmond 2013; Bascia et al. 1997). By examining this variation in union–decision maker relations over time, we are able to recognize a different sense of union-governmental dynamics than is possible with research that focuses on brief periods of time.

This chapter explores the phenomenon of teacher union–governmental relations where changing political and economic forces have led to changeable interorganizational dynamics, emphasizing how the reform discourses employed by teacher unions and governments also shift from antipathy to cooperation, or vice versa. The chapter seeks to understand how teacher union–government relationships relate to the reform discourses each of these entities espouses at different points in time.

To illustrate the phenomenon of shifting union-governmental relations, we present two case studies where relations between teacher unions and government have changed sharply over time: England and Alberta, Canada. The cases are derived from a study (Bascia and Osmond 2013) commissioned by Education International, a global federation of teacher unions that focuses on relations between teacher unions and governments. The cases were constructed on the basis of interviews with involved participants, available literature about these jurisdictions, and a survey of Education International's teacher union member organizations.

This chapter describes the relative power and the discourses at play in relations between teacher unions and governments, and then it provides context by describing the current reform environment in which teacher union–government relationships take place. Two case studies describe how teacher union–governmental relations can be transformed from cooperative to antagonistic and vice versa. The chapter then situates the two cases in relation to reform discourses and broader educational trends.

Discourses of Reform

Because of the difference in decision-making authority between government and teacher unions, the dynamics of union-government relations are fundamentally struggles over power. These struggles, the assertion of dominance, and the maintenance of power structures often occur through the use of language. Corson (1995, 3) argues, "All kinds of power are directed, mediated or resisted through language. For most everyday human purposes, power is exerted through verbal channels: Language is the vehicle for identifying, manipulating, and changing power relations between people." For educational researchers, discursive patterns serve as evidence of the nature of power relations between governments and teacher unions, demonstrating those relations' stability, variability, or contested nature.

Discursive dynamics are in play, for example, when people participate in their own subordination by unconsciously adopting and using discourses that reflect unequal power relations. For example, in the 1990s in Ontario, Canada, when the provincial government switched its discursive practices to characterize teacher federations as "unions," intended pejoratively, teachers' organizations started using the new name. But people and organizations can also challenge dominant ideologies by coming to new understandings and by introducing counterdiscourses (Bascia 2008).

Governments and teacher unions engage in the definition and redefinition of their relative power positions in the public domain through discourses about teaching and schooling, through policy positions, and through statements made in the press. In recent decades, political leaders have increased their use of "bully pulpit" discourses, asserting that their ideas about how the educational system ought to change are logical and inevitable (Jung and Kirst 1986). During the same time period, teacher unions have stepped up their efforts to engage discursively on the public stage, convinced that they are uniquely situated to persuade the public toward greater respect and support for education (Bascia and Osmond 2012).

Changes in discursive patterns are related to changes in relationships between government and teacher unions, but this is not simple. Discursive changes often forge new kinds of relationships, and changes in relationships can lead to the adoption of new discursive practices. In the cases presented here, we see evidence of both.

Teacher Union–Governmental Relations in an International Context

The context in which teacher unions currently engage with governments is characterized by the adoption of substantial policies focused on improving educational outcomes in order to secure a competitive advantage in an increasingly globalized and integrated economic world order (Steiner-Khamsi 2004; Stevenson 2007).

In a period of worldwide economic volatility, governments have been reducing their allocation of expenditure for public education. Many countries have seen increases in governmental support for educational privatization (Ball and Youdell 2008), including the diversion of funds from public to private schools. Many educational reforms emphasize centralized evaluation and control while at the same time devolving managerial control to schools.

The convergence of these tendencies has resulted in less programmatic diversity and experimentation, an emphasis on traditional roles and activities for teachers and school administrators, reporting systems that emphasize surveillance rather than bidirectional or lateral informing, and an infrastructure that is thin on support for teaching (Bascia 2005).

Teachers are at the center of most current educational policy efforts: many reforms focus directly on changing teachers, while other proposals directly affect teachers' work. For example, new curriculum and student assessment schemes place greater controls on what teachers teach and how teaching is carried out and require more time and energy spent by teachers on administrative tasks (Carter, Stevenson, and Passey 2010). New inspection practices affect teachers in terms of "workload, bureaucratization, stress, demotivation, alienation and feelings of insecurity" (Verger, Altinyelken, and De Koning 2013, 149; also Robertson 2012).

Within this context, fundamental tensions between teacher unions and governments become more explicit. In many jurisdictions, teacher union purview is narrowed to a shrinking range of issues because of both reduced funding and legislation (Bascia 1994, 1998, 2008).

In much of the world, teacher unions have been viewed by governments and in the press as "at best benign or irrelevant but frequently obstructive, rarely visionary, and tending to promote mediocrity" (Bascia 2003, 3). Unions have attempted to forge a persuasive image of themselves as educational reformers, but this has been an uphill battle. Antiunion rhetoric and legislative fiat are global phenomena. In Canada, the British Columbia Teachers' Federation attempted to publicly counteract attacks on unionization by the Campbell government, including contract stripping, imposed contracts, and the removal of teachers' right to strike (see the chapter by Poole in this volume). In Alberta, the Alberta Teachers' Association adopted a strategy to challenge the intense governmental pressure applied to education and teacher unions, in particular during the Klein years (Flower and Booi 1999; Bascia 2009). Teacher unions in many parts of the United States have been embroiled in what Lipman (2011) refers to as a deliberate attempt to weaken public sector unions. Carter, Stevenson, and Passey (2010) detailed the ongoing rapprochement and resistance of teacher unions in England in response to the neoliberal reforms of merit pay, league tables, and school inspections (see also Stevenson and Mercer's chapter in this volume).

In some jurisdictions, however, teacher unions and governments engage in collaborative decision-making practices at national, state/provincial, and/or local levels. In these locales, teacher unions have frequent, often daily, contact with members of government. Shared decision making, or at least a strong influence on decision making from teacher unions, may be a matter of structural arrangements. Frequent and substantive interactions may arise out of long-term cultures of collaboration. While teacher unions may not always agree with government, they are used to "sitting at the same table." Yet common ground and mutual discourses between governments and teacher unions are fragile, demonstrated through and within the volatile nature of relationships.

In the next section of the chapter, we present two cases—England and Alberta—that illustrate the dynamic nature of teacher union–government relations and the ways the two parties' discursive strategies reflect, reinforce, or challenge the status quo.

The Cases

England has had a checkered history of teacher union–government relations, with long periods of labor strife alternating with shorter periods of relative labor harmony. In their book *Industrial Relations in Education*, Carter, Stevenson, and Passy (2010) described how the national Labor government, elected in 1997 on a platform of "education, education, education," developed a strongly top-down approach to educational reform that alienated teachers who, in turn, were criticized for their resistance to "modernization." A study on teacher workload undertaken in 2001 reported that teachers spent about one-third of their time on nonteaching tasks. A decline in the perceived attractiveness of educational careers resulted in a shortage of teachers and principals. Teachers were unable and unwilling to manage the government's reforms, and teacher unions took industrial action.

It became evident that reform efforts were plateauing. England's teacher unions were invited to undertake discussions with the government to examine the possibility of interacting in a less antagonistic way. These discussions eventually resulted in a "social partnership," modeled after the collaborative relations between government, local employers, and teacher unions typical of Scandinavian countries, particularly Sweden. The resulting collective agreement restored teacher unions' rights to national level negotiations, which had been nonexistent since the mid-1980s.

The social partnership began by addressing concerns about teachers' workload and then extended the discussion to focus on teacher pay and performance management. Out of the social partnership came increases in per pupil funding and strategies intended to increase teachers' capacity to manage classroom change. By 2010, the social partnership was meeting on a weekly basis, with frequent phone calls and discussions among union and government officials between meetings.

The social partnership lasted from 2002 until 2010. Participants suggest that efforts were made to build trust by delineating the scope of the issues that could be discussed and by negotiating in such a way that both teacher unions and government could achieve satisfactory results. Perhaps as a consequence, the social partnership did not evolve past a focus on traditional union-employer labor issues regarding salaries and working conditions. It nonetheless became a body that discussed a wide range of educational issues.

When a Conservative government came into office in 2010, however, the power dynamic quickly shifted. The new government unilaterally passed a new education act that rescinded policies negotiated through the social partnership. Funding of local educational authorities was reduced and with it the support for school reform. The new education act also abolished the social partnership.

In the first two years of the Conservative government, nearly every teacher union voted to engage in national industrial action. The media, taking the government's side, claimed that teachers were motivated by their own vested interests. A union official said,

> Every day you can pick up any newspaper and there'll be a story about schools that blames teachers, or something which says that the root cause of the problem in our society is teachers. The government's "no excuses" mantra means you can't have serious discussions around the factors that impinge on educational performance, like poverty. This government has offended the majority of teachers.

* * *

Alberta, on the other hand, represents an instance of union renewal. In the 1990s, Albertans experienced severe cutbacks in government spending coupled with the downsizing of the public enterprise. The Alberta Teachers' Association (ATA), which represents all teachers and administrators in the province, was particularly concerned with underfunding for education and large class sizes. These issues were sticking points for teachers and the ATA, eventually resulting in a two-week province-wide strike in 2002.

After that strike, however, the ATA's relationship with the Alberta government was dramatically transformed, a process that began with collaboration on the Alberta Initiative for School Improvement (AISI). Placing teachers in the "driver's seat of educational change" through localized, teacher-led research projects, the program represented a sharp contrast from the events of the previous two decades in terms of heavy investment in educational funding and a collaborative spirit. Several additional collaborations evolved as offshoots of the trust that was built during the AISI. In some instances, the

ATA has sought funding from the government to support specific initiatives. In other cases, the government has directly sought the services of the ATA, for example, to take responsibility for part of the teacher certification process. According to one official, in 2012 the government viewed the ATA as "a valued partner in the development of different projects . . . Someone who adds value to those conversations and brings something to the table in terms of our expertise, our networking, our infrastructure."

The evolution of this relationship did not happen in spite of the adversity of prior years; it happened *because* of those challenging circumstances (Bascia 2008). In Alberta, in response to government hostility, the ATA became a strong advocate for improved public education on a broad scale. Seeking support for its members and political advantage for itself, the ATA worked in whatever arenas were available. For instance, when the government released a position paper, "Meeting the Challenge," the ATA released its own report, "Challenging the View." The ATA also established a Public Education Action Center to develop an ongoing, proactive campaign to mobilize teachers in grassroots activities, build effective coalitions, and employ ATA members in schools and local union branches to publically promote the idea that public education *does* work (Flower and Booi 1999, 127, 129).

In addition to these public and political activities, the ATA attempted to fill substantive gaps in educational practice resulting from the decimated educational infrastructure. While other teachers' organizations have argued that it is the school system's responsibility to support teachers' work, the ATA has perceived such gaps as opportunities to assert its own orientation toward teaching and schooling. For example, when the government legislated school councils in 1995, the ATA chose to support the plan. With the assistance of other stakeholders, it developed the official resource manual and provided training for school council participants, essentially managing to determine the shape of this reform (Bascia 2009; Flower and Booi 1999, 130).

The positive working relationship between the ATA and the Alberta government has been made possible also by the relatively small size of the province's educational community. Relationships between unions and their governments are often a product of personal connections between individuals (Bascia and Osmond 2012). ATA officials are interested in building relationships with government, regardless of the context of their work or their particular portfolio. An ATA official commented,

> Sometimes other teacher unions stand outside and around the perimeter and make a lot of noise. Meanwhile, the meeting is happening inside a room and they're not included . . . People have to value what you do and they have to do that by seeing what you do. And we believe that has to happen through collaboration.

But as demonstrated in the England case, the power differentials inherent in such relationships make them volatile. Recent interviews reveal that, after a collaborative deal with teachers could not be reached, the new government has legislated a contract, and the ATA has been left out of decision making once again. Despite its imposed nature, the contract does insert the ATA into various facets of educational policy over which it had not previously had influence. The AISI, the most innovative example of partnership between the province and the ATA, is now defunct.

Discourses of Teacher Union–Government Relations

Discourses "constitute part of the resources which people deploy in relating to one another—cooperating, separating, challenging, dominating—and seeking to change the ways in which they relate to one another" (Fairclough 2003, 124). In this way, teacher union organizations and governments position themselves in relation to one another through discourses of reform. A shared discourse is a way of indicating, and reinforcing, that these organizations are in agreement on what constitutes high-quality education. Alternatively, teacher unions or governments introduce and enforce new discourses to indicate their desire to alter the terms of engagement.

In England and Alberta, through changes in discursive patterns, the connection between discourses and relationships is clearly visible and reciprocal. In the England case, when the social partnership was in full swing, weekly meetings and conversations about substantive issues helped forge a common language. Conversely, changes in the terms of a preexisting partnership led to the subsequent adoption of competing discourses. A comparable situation unfolded in Alberta, where collaboration on the AISI and other projects jump-started a new cooperative relationship between the union and the government; over time, the government adopted the ATA's discourse regarding quality education.

In England during the social partnership, discussions occurred about "how you bring about reform in education, how you raise standards, how you address workforce concerns and how you make the workforce feel secure, valued, empowered, respected" (interview with union president, 2013). Elevating the position of teacher unions through the social partnership led to the development of a negotiated agenda, a shared set of understandings, and a shared discourse of the "new professionalism."

After the dissolution of the social partnership, the subsequent Conservative government's discourse shifted markedly, to criticizing teachers as "shirkers." A teacher union official described the first meeting of the social partnership after the election, at which it was announced that the government was ending the partnership. According to the official, the government's stance was "we've got our agenda, we'll let you know what that agenda is." This official articulated his union's efforts on behalf of teachers as

> reasserting or reclaiming the professionalism of our members. Teachers have been concerned that little by little their professionalism and their integrity is being chipped away at by a government that claims that teachers are just not up to the job.

He linked teachers' professional commitment to a sense of

> strong moral purpose . . . Teachers are saying, "We want to get on with the job of teaching and not to be diverted by unnecessary accountability and assessment protocols." That's what we're about in terms of looking to reclaim our professionalism.

In contrast to England, the Alberta government and teacher union have moved away from adversarial and opposing discourses related to teacher professionalism and have come to a negotiated agreement about what constitutes good teaching. In the 1990s and the early years of the twenty-first century, the provincial government's discourse emphasized the "sorry" state of the education system and equated the inadequacies with teachers' insufficiencies. Teachers were dismissed as a special interest group, and the relationship between the ATA and the government became increasingly hostile (Mackay and Flower 1999) as the organization endured what one official described as "government by ministerial choice, rather than the concept of public policy."

The ATA responded to teacher bashing by asserting its own voice and deliberately challenged this discourse, replacing it with one that characterized teachers as "trying to teach" and the problem as residing with the inadequacy of teaching conditions. ATA staff members were successful in persuading the government that they could serve as partners, and the government ultimately adopted the union's discourse.

Perceiving their mandate regarding educational reform as "thoughtful structuring of how education fits into the broader context of what we want in our society," undertake work that could be described in terms of "opening a conversation" between the association, its members, and government. Within this context, however, the discourse of collaboration and partnership has been stopped in its tracks by governmental positions that prevent the ATA from participating in provincial decision making.

Conclusion

Relationships between teacher unions and governments are complex and precarious. One way to demonstrate the volatile nature of these relationships is through an analysis of shifts in the reform discourse employed by one or both of these organizations. In this chapter, we have highlighted two instances of changing discourses; in one there has been a disruption of a negotiated discourse, and in the other the union has strongly influenced the prevailing discourse about quality public education. The shift and evolution of discourses in these cases demonstrate both the variability and the fragility of such relationships, despite contextual differences.

Where collaborative relationships and compatible discourses exist, teacher unions have an opportunity to participate in educational decision making on a more substantive level. The Alberta case, in particular, also illustrates that teacher unions are capable of creating environments that support the promotion of cohesive discourses and positive working relations with government. This portrayal of unions is very different from the one typically found in either the media or much of the educational literature.

Whether attempting to minimize harm or playing a significant role in shaping educational practice, teacher unions provide an important counterweight to the influence of neoliberal reform (Compton and Weiner 2008). It is critical that teacher unions recognize the power of discourse to influence policy directions, and it would be wise to consider the capacity they actually have in shaping the wider discourse about education and educational policy. To sustain or to shift the dynamic relationship between unions and government, however, both policy makers and unions themselves must recognize the important role teacher unions can play. Given the current policy context, however, this is often a difficult endeavor.

References

Apple, Michael. 2008. "Curriculum planning: Content, reform, and the politics of accountability." In *The SAGE handbook of curriculum and instruction*, edited by F. Michael Connelly, Ming Fang He, and JoAnn Phillion, 25–44. Thousand Oaks, CA: Sage.

Bangs, John, John MacBeath, and Maurice Galton. 2010. *Reinventing school, reforming teaching: From political vision to classroom reality*. London: Routledge.

Bascia, Nina. 1994. *Unions in teachers' professional lives*. New York: Teachers College Press.

Bascia, Nina. 2000. "The other side of the equation: Teachers' professional development and the organizational capacity of teacher unions." *Educational Policy* 14 (3): 385–404.

Bascia, Nina. 2005. "Triage or tapestry: Teacher unions' contributions to systemic educational reform." In *International handbook of educational policy*, edited by Nina Bascia, Alister Cumming, Amanda Datnow, Kenneth Leithwood, and David Livingstone, 593–609. Dordrecht, Netherlands: Kluwer Academic Press.

Bascia, Nina. 2008. "What teachers want from their unions: What the literature tells us." In *The global assault on teaching, teachers, and their unions*, edited by Mary Compton and Lois Weiner, 95–108. New York: Palgrave Macmillan.

Bascia, Nina. 2008. "Learning through struggle: How the Alberta Teachers' Association maintains an even keel." In *Learning through community: Exploring participatory practices*, edited by Kathryn Church, Nina Bascia, and Eric Shragge, 169–86. Dordrecht, Netherlands: Springer.

Bascia, Nina, and Cindy Rottmann. 2011. "What's so important about teachers' working conditions? The fatal flaw in North American educational reform." *Journal of Education Policy* 26 (6): 787–802.

Bascia, Nina, and Pamela Osmond. 2012. *Teacher unions and educational reform.* Washington, DC: National Education Association.

Bascia, Nina, Susan Stiegelbauer, Noreen Jacka, Nancy Watson, and Michael Fullan. 1997. *Teacher associations and school reform: Building stronger connections*, an external review of the NCI Learning Laboratories Initiative, Washington, DC: National Education Association.

Carter, Bob, Howard Stevenson, and Rowena Passy. 2009. *Industrial relations in education.* London: Routledge.

Compton, Mary, and Lois Weiner (eds.). 2008. *The global assault on teaching, teachers, and their unions.* New York: Palgrave Macmillan.

Corson, David. 1995. "Discursive power in educational organizations: An introduction." In *Discourse and power in educational organizations*, edited by David Corson, 3–15. Toronto: OISE Press.

Fairclough, Norman. 1992. *Discourse and social change.* Cambridge, UK: Polity Press.

Flower, David J., and H. Larry Booi. 1999. "Challenging restructuring: The Alberta Teachers' Association." In *Contested classrooms: Education, globalization, and democracy in Alberta*, edited by Trever Harrison and Jerrold Kachur, 123–35. Edmonton: University of Alberta Press.

Hayhoe, Ruth, and Karen Mundy. 2008. "Introduction to comparative and international education: Why study comparative education?" In *Comparative and international education: Issues for teachers*, edited by Karen Mundy, Kathy Bickmore, Ruth Hayhoe, Meggan Madden, and Katherine Madjidi, 1–22. New York: Teachers College Press.

Jung, Richard, and Michael Kirst. 1986. "Beyond mutual adaptation: Into the bully pulpit: Recent research on the federal role in education." *Educational Administration Quarterly* 22: 80–109.

Kerchner, Charles, and Julia Koppich. 1993. *A union of professionals: Labor relations and educational reform.* New York: Teachers College Press.

Lipman, Pauline. 2011. "Neoliberal education restructuring: Dangers and opportunities of the present crisis." *Monthly Review* 6 (3): 114–27.

Loveless, Tom. 2000. *Conflicting missions? Teachers unions and educational reform.* Washington, DC: Brookings Institution Press.

Murray, Christine. 2004. "Innovative local teacher unions: What have they accomplished?" In *Teacher unions and education policy: Retrenchment or reform?*, edited by Ronald Henderson, Wayne Urban, and Paul Wolfman, 1–22. New York: Elsevier.

Organization for Economic Cooperation and Development. 2011. *Preliminary proposal for a comparative study on the role of teacher unions in educational reform across selected OECD countries.* Brussels, Belgium: Organization for Economic Cooperation and Development.

Poole, Wendy. 2007. "Neo-liberalism in British Columbia education and teachers' union resistance." *International Electronic Journal for Leadership in Learning* 11 (24).

Pringle, Rebecca. 2010. *Teachers unions as agents of change.* Toronto: Canadian Education Association.

Ravitch, Diane. 2010. *The death and life of the great American school system: How testing and choice are undermining education.* New York: Basic Books.

Robertson, Susan. 2012. "Placing teachers in global governance agendas." *Comparative Education Review* 56 (4): 584–607.

Rottman, Cindy. 2008. "Organized agents: Teacher unions as alternative educational sites for social justice activism." *Canadian Journal of Education* 31 (4): 975–1014.

Smaller, Harry. 1991. "A room of one's own: The early years of the Toronto Women Teachers' Association." In *Gender and education in Ontario: An historical reader*, edited by Ruby Heap and Alison Prentice, 105–26. Toronto: Canadian Scholars' Press.

Steiner-Khamsi, Gita. 2004. *The global politics of educational borrowing and lending.* New York: Teachers College Press.

Stevenson, Howard. 2007. "Restructuring teachers' work and trade union responses in England: Bargaining for change?" *American Educational Research Journal* 44 (2): 224–51.

Urban, Wayne. 1982. *Why teachers organized.* Detroit, MI: Wayne State University Press.

Urban, Wayne. 2004. "Teacher politics." In *Teacher unions and education policy: Retrenchment or reform?*, edited by Ronald Henderson, Wayne Urban, and Paul Wolfman, 103–23. New York: Elsevier.

Verger, Antoni, Hulya Kosar Altinyelken, and Mireille De Koning (eds.). 2013. *Global managerial education reforms and teachers.* Brussels, Belgium: Education International.

Whitty, Geoff, and Sally Power. 2003. "Making sense of educational reform: Global and national influences." In *The international handbook on the sociology of education: An international assessment of new research and theory*, edited by Carlos Torres and Ari Antikainen, 305–24. Lanham, MD: Roman and Littlefield.

CHAPTER 6

Model Citizen or Bad Influence? The Contested Nature of Teachers' Public Activism

Katy Swalwell

On February 11, 2011, Wisconsin governor Scott Walker unveiled his controversial Budget Repair Bill, which proposed legislation calling for budget cuts despite evidence that public sector unions were not to blame for state deficits (see Allegretto, Jacobs, and Lucia 2011; Delisle 2010). In a state with a long history of organized labor and moderate politics, many Wisconsinites were shocked to discover a provision within the bill that would severely restrict collective bargaining rights for public sector unions above and beyond demands for immediate concessions in benefits and pay. In response, hundreds of concerned citizens began sleeping in the rotunda as they waited to testify against the legislation, with thousands more participating in weekend rallies that garnered international attention; news reports estimated that such crowds had not been seen since protests against the Vietnam War (Simmons 2011).

Aside from testifying against the bill, petitioning to stop the legislation, and gathering signatures to recall elected officials, teachers across the state risked sanctions by coordinating "sick-outs" (absences) that shut down schools for several days (DeFour 2011b; Hetzner 2011; York 2011). These actions were hotly contested among union members and within the state more broadly. The debate intensified as reports emerged of doctors issuing sick notes for protesting teachers and when nearly one thousand students participated in walkouts to join in the rallies at the capitol (DeFour 2011a).[1]

In what ways did the public frame teachers' actions vis-à-vis the coordinated absences as conflicting or congruent with their pedagogical responsibilities? Were teachers disregarding their obligations to schools and abusing the public's trust, or were they demonstrating character by taking a stand? What were public perceptions about these teachers' political actions, and what does that say about teachers' obligations to balance their civic rights and professional responsibilities?

This chapter explores competing notions of the "good teacher" in relation to public, political activism as revealed through a purposeful sample of online newspaper article readers' comments responding to the Wisconsin teacher sick-outs. By framing these coordinated absences as a discursive event (Fairclough 1992a, 1995) that constitutes a rhetorical public sphere (Hauser 1999), critical discourse analysis helps examine the ways in which teachers' civic actions were framed as either conflicting or congruent with their pedagogical responsibilities. The data reveal that the majority of public discussants found the protesters to be "bad teachers" for their participation in the sick-outs, their support of unions, and what was perceived as general incompetence. The "good teacher" was one who stayed in school, rejected union influence, and sacrificed his or her own benefits for what was perceived to be good for children. The public debate during the Wisconsin protests offers insights into the contested expectations for teachers as they struggle to be citizens, union members, and public employees in an era in which these roles are under attack.

Historical Public Perceptions of "Good" Teachers

While community expectations of teachers have evolved since the nineteenth century, how much and in what way teachers ought to be involved in the public sphere has been a persistent question. This is a deeply gendered debate, with "good" teachers being praised in the nineteenth century for their "innate feminine qualities" (Albisetti 1993) such as "feminine affections" and "moral feelings" (Enoch 2008) rather than their intellect or activism on behalf of a rapidly feminizing profession. The fact that the schoolhouse, modeled after parlor rooms, was considered to be a private, domestic space reflected the public's expectations of teachers—to be sheltered from and not active in public life (Enoch 2008).

There are important examples of women activist teachers throughout American history who challenge this mainstream, homogenizing narrative (see Crocco, Monroe, and Weiler 1999) and of other historical and contemporary instances that shed light on the importance of educators (and particularly teachers of color) exercising their rights as citizens to influence policies related to schooling and to the lives of their students (e.g., Buras

2010; Johnson 2002, 2004; Perillo 2012; Siddle Walker 2005; Street 1996). My purpose here is not to contribute to the empirical evidence that teachers have been politically active but to reveal public expectations that shape and constrain those actions.

With that in mind, it is useful to note how remnants of nineteenth-century gendered norms still linger. In a US study on the images of teachers from 1963 to 1993, for example, Judge (1995, 261–62) found a general conception of the good teacher to be that of a polite hostess who must "everywhere and always be amiable and welcoming . . . The teacher cannot ever be the agent of government, nor belong to some kind of national force: responsibility must lie with the local community, and with the elected school board." Whether one interprets this to mean that teachers do not have any civic responsibility or that their civic responsibility is to be apolitical, these ideas leave little space for teachers to be "transformative intellectuals" (Giroux 1985), "activist citizens" (Kennedy 2011), or "activist professionals" (Sachs 2000, 2003) who engage the public regarding issues related to their work (Apple 2011).

The sanitization of teachers' interactions with the public goes beyond debates about the disclosure of teachers' political views (see Goldstein and Benassi 1994; Hess and McAvoy 2009; Zhang et al. 2009) and is complicated by events like the protests in Wisconsin, when the hot topics impact teachers so directly. Public perceptions of teachers' activism are particularly vexed when connected with labor union activity: according to a 2011 Phi Delta Kappa/Gallup poll on the public's perceptions of public schools and teachers, 47 percent of respondents believed that the unionization of teachers has diminished the quality of public school education in the United States (Bushaw and Lopez 2011).

Identifying the Public Sphere

In order to examine how "good" teachers are framed in relation to current controversial teacher activism and what that means for teacher activists, we must first define the "public sphere." One of the hallmarks of a healthy, deliberative democracy is that citizens engage in "public reasoning" (Sen 2009)—that they are able to express their opinions and engage in discussions about a range of social and political matters (Hess 2009). This idea is often connected to Habermas's (1962) utopian ideal of the "public sphere" in which members of society can participate in discussions in order to make rational, informed public policy decisions that serve the common good.

The study that informs this chapter builds upon Habermas's conception of the public sphere but also takes into account critiques of his work like those of Fraser (1990), who highlights the ways in which this "ideal" space often masks the exclusion of voices from society's marginalized groups and helps to transform formerly repressive bourgeois political power into hegemonic control. Hauser (1999) also challenges Habermas' work by contending that public spheres form around people who are actively engaged in issues-based dialogue rather than existing a priori with regard to any particular identity group. A "rhetorical public sphere" is thus the

> discursive space in which strangers discuss issues they perceive to be of consequence for them and their group. Its rhetorical exchanges are the bases for shared awareness of common issues, shared interests, tendencies of extent and strength of difference and agreement, and self-constitution as a public whose opinions bear on the organization of society. (Hauser 1999, 64)

Since colonial times, an especially important rhetorical public sphere has been the letters sections of newspapers. These voices of "regular citizens" are seen to represent true public opinion (Wahl-Jorgensen 2007), paralleling opinion polls (Sigelman and Walkosz 1992) and influencing public views through wide readership (Pritchard and Berkowitz 1991). Nonetheless, the rhetorical public sphere of the traditional letters section remains restrictive, given that editorial boards often act as gatekeepers, rejecting letters based on a variety of factors (Wahl-Jorgensen 2001; Reader 2005) and often requiring identification of participants that limits participation (Reader, Stempel III, and Daniel 2004).

The recent adoption of online comment sections on which readers can post their responses to articles presents the opportunity for a more ideal public sphere in the spirit of Fraser's Habermasian critiques, given that these sites permit unlimited posts, allow ongoing discussion about a topic, and are open to anyone who registers as a user. In contrast to posts on blogs that tend to reach an ideologically narrow audience, online posts to mainstream news sources appear to represent a wider range of views from people interested in particular topics (McCluskey and Hmielowski 2011). The fact that these posts can be anonymous tends to both expand the range of views expressed (Reader 2005) and decrease the inhibition of participants (McDevitt, Kiousis, and Wahl-Jorgensen 2003). It also challenges researchers to determine who is posting comments, though they are likely politically active as there appears to be a positive correlation between informational Internet use and civic engagement (Shah, Kwak, and Holbert 2001). While this study certainly does not represent every rhetorical sphere, the historical and current popularity of letters to the editor makes the comments section a compelling site for collecting data that allow us to understand the arguments that floated around the community in response to teachers' political actions.

Data for this project were collected by conducting an Internet search for online news stories published by Wisconsin newspapers serving communities directly affected by the sick-outs. These communities were rural, suburban, and urban and represented a range of political viewpoints. Articles were included in the study only if they had elicited reader comments. The total collection included 40 articles with 3,074 reader posts from 11 newspapers ranging in date from February 14 to March 12, 2011. All of the comments as well as the original articles to which they responded were saved as pdf files and stored in a database. From the collection of articles, a purposeful sample was drawn from the day with the highest number of online comments—February 17, with over eight hundred comments responding to five articles from five newspapers (see table 6-1).

Six hundred forty-four of these comments were identified as being from distinct posters. Each of these articles was (and is) freely accessible to anyone with Internet access. In order to post comments, however, readers must register with the site at no cost. The posts are distinguishable by reader-selected pseudonyms and a small thumbnail icon. Each comment is time-stamped with the date and time of the post and appears in reverse chronological order below the article.

Table 6-1 Articles in Wisconsin newspapers documenting the teacher sick-outs, February 17, 2011

Article title	*Article type*	*Newspaper source*	*Community type*	*Number of comments*
"Teachers say unions prompted members to call in sick"	News story	*Journal Times* (Racine, WI)	195,000 people; leans Republican	343
"Madison schools, others closed amid calls for demonstration"	News story	*Wisconsin State Journal* (Madison, WI)	233,000 people; majority Democrat	291
"Protests against Walker plan set"	News story	*Janesville Gazette* (Janesville, WI)	62,000 people; leans Republican	63
"The budget showdown: Teachers set wrong example"	Opinion (opposed to sick-outs)	*Milwaukee Journal Sentinel* (Milwaukee, WI)	948,000 people; leans Democrat	42
"Why one teacher is protesting"	Opinion (supportive of sick-outs)	*Capital Times* (Madison, WI)	233,000 people; strongly Democrat	32

Critical Discourse Analysis

There are theoretical, methodological, historical, and political reasons for social scientists to consider discursive texts like online newspaper readers' comments to be an important source of data (Fairclough 1992b). Theoretically, texts play an important role as both resources for and products of the dialectical relationship between social structures and social action. As direct references to teachers' actions in response to Governor Walker's Budget Repair Bill, these online comments are clear examples of such a process. Methodologically, texts can provide empirical evidence for claims about social structures, relations, and processes. These comments both explicitly and implicitly express such ideas. Historically, texts are "sensitive barometers" of social change and, politically, are used as a form of social control as well as resistance that ought to be examined and critiqued.

By framing the sick-outs as a "discursive event" (Fairclough 1992a, 1995) and examining the online comments as textual artifacts of an inclusive rhetorical public sphere, discourse analysis allows us to examine the ways in which they function historically and politically to shape public perceptions about the teachers' protests.

Newspaper articles and editorial comments are common texts for critical discourse analysis (CDA) (Teo 2000). This analytic approach can highlight how discourse serves to reproduce or resist social and political inequalities (Rogers 2003). In fact, CDA takes language as the primary instrument through which ideology is transmitted, enacted, and reproduced. Its purpose is to uncover the ideological assumptions within the words of oral speech or written text and to push beyond mere descriptions of text. To do so, researchers examine its syntax and word choice; the ways in which the text is produced, distributed, and consumed; and the social context in which the text is embedded (Fairclough 2000).

Using CDA to analyze the data in this study involved several steps. At the microlevel, online comments were coded for the type of post they represented, the tone of the comment, the author, and the author's position. At the meso- and macrolevel, a second round of coding paid attention to emergent themes, particularly those related to posters' ideological assumptions related to the context of the Budget Repair Bill and other legislative reforms. These codes were collaboratively generated and individually applied by both members of the research team to ensure reliability.[2] Other analyses included a word count for key terms connected with the emergent themes and a cross-variable analysis of the authors, their positions, the newspaper source, and the themes within their comments.

Findings

The overwhelming majority of online comments posted in response to the news stories about the teacher sick-outs were *opinion statements*, followed closely by comments that can be classified as *insults*. A small portion of comments included *tangents*, *questions*, and *shared resources*. For the most part, resources included links to other articles and historical references about labor history. Roughly the same number of posts responded to others' comments as those that expressed stand-alone opinions.

Intriguingly, one chain of posts in relation to the *Wisconsin State Journal* article could be categorized as a *metadiscussion*, in which two commenters began to police the insider/outsider status of other posters. A few hours after a commenter (ObamaLied) negatively assessed the protests, fellow reader daycd posted this response: "ObamaLied wrote: 'I also notice that the hate, rage, and propensity towards violence was a lot more intense.' Then obviously you were not there." At 1:01 a.m., tomg added, "Obamalied has been registered on this site since Feb 17, 2011. Clearly does not have a long standing interest in Madison civic affairs." Five minutes later, she posted, "Likewise Tiger164, Revolutionary and Phocus registered on this site in the last day. It is hard to believe any of these people have a longstanding interest in Madison's schools. I think comments should not be anonymous. It is too easy for outside interests to warp the debate." She then posted her name and address, urged others to do the same, and "outed" other users who had only recently registered on the site. At 3:46 a.m., MylesGarson criticized her approach after expressing disdain for the teacher union:

> Now I fully realize that my comments are without merit since I do not reside in Madison, AND I recently registered. Two strikes and you're out according to the Self-Appointed Monitors of Madison (AKA Thought Police) who carefully monitor this site like good little liberals.

At 4:02 a.m., Kathy posted that Myles Garson had registered four hours before and continued to out other recent registrants posting particularly virulent comments.

Few posters were willing to identify themselves as Kathy did. The most frequent self-identifications were as anonymous parents or teachers. Of those, 71 percent of parents opposed the sick-outs. Nearly half the self-identified parents wrote that they homeschooled or sent their children to private school. Fifty percent of the teachers, half of whom identified as retired, opposed the sick-outs. Mr_V wrote, "I am teacher who have [*sic*] proudly gone to work today and now can't have a chance because of union lemmings. I apologize to all the parents who are now scrambling for day care." Another, Ms_S, suggested that "many teachers are intimidated into silence!" In general, the comments revealed that a two-to-one majority of all posters found the sick-outs to be conflicting with their conceptions of a "good" teacher: 69 percent of all commenters made oppositional comments while 31 percent made supportive comments. Almost no one was neutral.

It became clear that readers used the online comment space to express their opinions not just about the sick-outs but also about both public sector unions and public school teachers more broadly. In general, if someone found the sick-outs to be conflicting with their understanding of "good" teachers, they opposed public unions, and if someone found the sick-outs congruent with their understanding of "good" teachers, they supported public unions. A smaller portion of those opposed to the sick-outs also expressed disgust with *all* public school teachers, though others made it clear that they supported the "good" teachers who stayed in school. For example, Advocatus_Diaboli wrote, "Most teachers are not like the lying, sniveling, greedy, scum that turned out at the Capitol today."

Public Perceptions of the Sick-Outs

Commenters expressed multiple reasons why they found the protests in conflict with what a "good" teacher would do: the perceived deleterious effects on students given the length of time the schools were closed for the sick-outs, the legality of sick-outs as a form of protest, the futility of protests in the wake of an election, the exploitation of teachers by larger special interest forces (like unions) for their own purposes, and what was considered an undue influence on the hundreds of students who walked out in solidarity with their teachers. These commenters were clear that protesting teachers should be punished for "skipping" work, "not teaching students," and "brainwashing" kids. "Do not drag my child into your problems," NK324 posted,

> I want him to spend his days learning long division and about the constitution. THAT is what school is for, not teachers abusing their power and using my children as tools. Shame on all you teachers out there who put your political agendas ahead of the kids.

Some believed that, as Equitas noted, they were "doing the right thing at the wrong time . . . The real teachers stayed in their classrooms to teach. The posers jumped ship to go to madison." While some expressed gratitude for the teachers who refused to protest ("To all of the teachers & staff that showed up, THANK YOU for being mature and responsible. You set a great example for our kids," said Personal_Rights _= _ Personal _ Responsibility), others focused on the protesters by calling them "pigs," "thugs," "rapists," "extortionists," "parasites," "thieves," "kidnappers," "slugs," "roaches," "money hungry clowns," and "scum." A significant number of posts painted an infantilizing picture of protesting teachers as spoiled, ungrateful, selfish, unreasonable, overdramatic, and sheltered individuals who needed to "stop crying" and "grow up." "This whole situation reminds me of the proverbial 'I am taking my ball and going home because I don't like it!' Grow up and act like the RESPONSIBLE adults you are supposed to be," said malim2184. "There are right and wrong ways to express yourself," said Ezoner, "but affecting the education of our children by basically leaving to protest is not an acceptable answer. They must be fired immediately."

Commenters mentioned how sick-outs did little to elicit sympathy from those who were struggling in the recent economic downturn. Posts included references to teachers needing a "reality check" about the economy and private sector pain. For these readers, protesting teachers "don't get it." The views posted by Hammerman were commonplace:

> Welcome to the real world, honey. There is a lot of pain going on right now. If you worked in the private sector and blew off your job responsibilities you would be out on your rear. Be thankful you have a government job that awards you protection when you blow off your job duties. Thanks for screwing our kids over by not being in the classroom. As a taxpayer your actions disgust me. Take it out on the kids, you teachers are real gems.

These commenters emphasized the exploitation of taxpayers and suggested that if teachers did not like the reduced benefits and pay or union restrictions, they should find another job. "Let them go into the private sector and see what they pay in pension and benefits. The issue to me is that we, the taxpayers, are paying the exorbitant costs," said toehead.

For those who found the sick-outs congruent with their understanding of a "good teacher," the protests were seen as drawing attention to the teachers' cause and inconveniencing parents in order to make them take note of the proposed legislation. These commenters framed protesting teachers as "getting it" in that they were fighting larger threats to public education, the middle class, and democracy.

> I'm a parent of two kids in Madison schools. Teachers have my 100 percent support. Walker is using the economic crisis as an excuse to destroy unions. Wisconsin's hard-working public servants did not cause this crisis. Eliminating collective bargaining will not fix it. Spewing up divisions between private and public sector middle class families will not help the state solve problems

> and move forward. Working families should come together in opposition to this bill, which is a transparent attempt to undermine the very foundations of public education in Wisconsin.

Some commentators praised these teachers as strong examples of the "real" Wisconsin and criticized the opposition as ignorant (or "inbred," in the most extreme case). According to Fattigman, "There are no thugs. There are no tantrums. These are your neighbors, family people. Above all workers in the great tradition of Wisconsin working to stop radical change in five days."

These commenters extolled the ways they saw teachers exercising their rights to free speech and public assembly. To them, these teachers were role models, educating students about the democratic process by taking action. Said KWB24,

> What the kids are learning is civic responsibility, to look out for the common good. They are learning how to take political action, they are learning how to speak up on not only their behalf but on the behalf of other members of their community. They are learning that when your basic rights, rights that people fought and died for, rights guaranteed by law are threatened, when the security of your family and your neighbors is threatened, you don't stand around, you take action. One of the best life lessons that a teacher can impart.

Lastly, rather than seeing the protests as an illegal job action, these readers claimed that the budget bill and the governor's actions were illegal.

One point both sets of commenters seemed to agree upon was the need for teachers to be honest about the fact that they were protesting; there was almost unanimous disgust with the doctors who issued sick notes to protesting teachers. The difference between the two sets of commenters, however, was that those who supported the sick-outs explained the historical and logistical constraints preventing teachers from officially going on strike as somewhat of a justification for those teachers who called in sick, while those at the other end of the spectrum demanded that the teachers be fired immediately for their dishonesty.

Public Perceptions of Teacher Unions

For many readers, the online forum presented an opportunity to articulate their support or disrespect for public sector unions in addition to specific tactics of protesting teachers. For those who did not support the sick-outs, there was much to say: that unions were outdated and obstructionist, that they were intended for private not public workers, that they protected incompetence, that they had no fundamental right to collective bargaining, and that they were to blame for the state's economic woes. According to Randman, union members were the "aristocrats of the working class living off the sweat of other workers in the private sector."

These comments invariably highlighted the spoiled public unions' "cushy" benefits for their members at the expense of overburdened taxpayers. According to Oldtime,

> Along with most everyone I talk to these days, I am filled with disgust by the teacher's union. Yes, there are plenty of good, honest teachers who actually do care about kids . . . but almost all of them are still supporting the corrupt union that is about everything but kids. They support the same union that has helped to bankrupt this state, and bullies every single community into submission. The same union that protects the incompetent, the lazy, the crazy, and the truant. It was past time to open the doors of our schools to free the hostages.

According to six,

> Really? This isn't about wage and benefits? Come on, let's get honest here. Of course it is. Unions had their place, but now often times to more harm than good. They demand excessive wage/benefit packages in an awful economy. The parasite devours the host here. Companies are left having to shift their operations overseas.. or in the case of teachers etc.. the taxpayer is held hostage. Most non union workers would love to receive the pay/benefits that you're getting. Stop with the sense of entitlement. Be thankful you are gainfully employed. If you don't like it.. get a non union job. See how that works out for ya.

In addition to "parasite," the union leadership was described as "thugs," "extortionists," "crooks," "tyrants," "bullies," "a pestilence," "mafia," "weasels," and "rabblerousers." "These are NOT citizens protesting," said madcityjesse, "these are UNIONS protesting . . . so they can benefit."

Those who supported the sick-outs frequently expressed support for teacher unions, but there were some who supported the protest against the Budget Repair Bill while acknowledging flaws in the union system in general, demanding that unions should "do their fair share" in tough times. In general, supporters of protesting teachers recounted a proud union history, highlighted the ways in which teacher unions are valuable institutions that protect school quality, and encouraged all struggling workers to see unions as a solution rather than a problem. "Ultimately, the vast majority of the private sector should be attempting to emulate unions, rather than push for a race to the bottom that is largely driven by jealousy," said Jack 1126. These posts also challenged the fundamental premise upon which the Budget Repair Bill was based by declaring there to be no actual budget crisis. They pointed to the hyperaccumulation of wealth and an overzealous governor as the real emergency and bully.

Public Perceptions of Public School Teachers

Perhaps most startling was the viciousness with which many of the commenters attacked public school teachers in general. Though most posts explicitly distinguished between "bad" teachers who protested and "good" teachers who stayed in the classroom, many framed *all* teachers as incompetent and replaceable. "I think they should fire every teacher we have and replace them . . . That will show them union jerks. We can do much better hiring teachers for less pay and less benefits. Dumb #### teachers here anyways," posted WisLiferfromMadison. "All Wisconsin teachers have lost the respect and trust of the children and parents. These unions have been extorting the taxpayers long enough. To hide this cowardly behavior behind a veil and call it democracy is insulting," said westwilly.

In response, there were defenders of teachers from both ends of the spectrum. Khassy defended the good teachers against the bad: "It's a shame that ~75 percent of teachers/staff are being tarred and feathered because of the selfish, contract-violating, lying acts of ~25 percent." ADhah, on the other hand, defended all teachers by asking,

> What has happened to public opinion of teachers? I'm sorry if people think teachers are not performing well, if people think their kids are not gaining a good education from public teachers, but inspect what role you play in your child's education. Teachers were never meant to replace parents. Teachers were meant to serve an institution which was set up to make society a better place. Granted, I'm going a bit Emmerson and Locke here, but that is what public education was about. School is not a daycare or a prison. Teachers are not public SERVANTS, they are public employees.

Similar comments lionized teachers as underpaid and undervalued, challenging the notion that teachers ought to be endlessly self-sacrificing. Interestingly, most of these characterized public schools as dangerous places where students are lazy and teachers deserve "hazard pay." "Teachers are NOT greedy bums, screw you, the kids are spoiled brats," said snowfeather. "The majority of people have no idea what these teachers are subjected to on a daily basis with these little 'darlings' in the public school," said ajus1968; "the abuse these teachers are expected to endure is ridiculous." Mr_B shared his thoughts: "Parents fail their kids and expect teachers to do miracles with the messes they send there."

Discussion

What can online forums tell us about public perceptions of political issues? These comments, while part of a genre known for anonymous rants rather than measured debate, have the potential to function as dialogic public spaces where politically active and passionate community members express a range of views about controversial events. The chain of comments where readers began to identify themselves as Wisconsin residents and to "out" others who had only recently registered as "outsiders" indicates that this space was taken seriously as a rhetorical public sphere where community members could discuss and debate issues pertinent to local citizens.

What can online forums tell us about public perceptions of teachers' political activism? Those who framed the "Wisconsin uprising" protesters as "bad" teachers (which was the majority of posters) saw their civic actions as incongruent with their obligations to students and taxpayers. This focus on the difference between taxpayers and teachers underscored a distinction between a pragmatic/sacrificing private sector and an unrealistic/greedy public.

Even deeper was the belief that strikes and sick-outs are *never* acceptable because they hurt kids. For posters who saw protesting teachers as bad teachers, activism was not educative, nor did it expose students to good models of citizenship. Rather, their actions brainwashed kids, modeled juvenile behavior, or abandoned the students who needed teachers most. To not accept what was framed as the majority voice was petulant and childish; instead of "whining," unhappy teachers should simply choose another job. This emphasis on choice was quite strong throughout the oppositional commentary. The good teacher complies with policies that come from above, or leaves.

What accounts for these findings? This focus on choice, self-identification as a taxpayer rather than a citizen, disregard for grassroots social mobilizations, and the privileging of private over public institutions reveals a deeply rooted neoliberal ideology that undermines organized labor and public services and upholds a thin conception of democracy. It also indicates diminished expectations of the middle/working class for any social safety nets and the successful pitting of middle and working-class people against one another. And though there were no explicitly gendered comments in the series of posts, the idea that a good teacher should stay in the classroom without voicing complaints and put the children first seems consistent with the nineteenth-century understanding that respectable women should selflessly steer the domestic sphere rather than engage in public controversy.

There were posters who saw teachers' public activism as compatible with and even essential to their professionalism. Within this framework, good teachers had an obligation to speak up and were providing a model of good citizenship by doing so. Teachers' advocacy for better working conditions and pay were not in conflict with their support for kids—rather, the two were one and the same. Ultimately, however, the voices of community members who support unions and who believe activism to be an important part of teachers' professional identities were few and far between. And even those who believed that teachers had the right and duty to speak up debated about which tactics were most strategic. For example, there were serious questions about whether or not engaging in sick-outs crossed an ethical or professional line. Most readers, however, believed that if teachers were to make their voices heard, they ought to do so before or after school hours rather than shut down schools.

CDA of online comments as rhetorical public spheres makes clear that teachers who opted to participate in the Wisconsin sick-outs faced a community mostly unsupportive of their activism, their union membership, or even their teaching. Though there were some commenters who valued teachers' work and supported the rights of public sector unions to collectively bargain, there were many more who condemned their political strategies and, by extension, questioned their professionalism. Such a context presents a clear challenge for those civically active teachers who, regardless of their political affiliations, see their obligations as citizens, union members, and public school educators as inextricably intertwined.

Notes

1. Among those who protested, 84 teachers submitted fraudulent sick notes and 38 received suspensions for failing to rescind those notes by the April deadline (DeFour 2011b).
2. The research team included the author and her research assistant, Samantha Spinney.

References

Albesetti, James. 1993. "The feminization of teaching in the nineteenth century: A comparative perspective." *History of Education* 22 (3): 253–63.

Allegretto, Sylvia, Ken Jacobs, and Laurel Lucia. 2011. *The wrong target: Public sector unions and state budget deficit*. Berkeley, CA: Institute for Research on Labor and Employment.

Apple, Michael. 2011. "Democratic education in neoliberal and neoconservative times." *International Studies in Sociology of Education* 21 (1): 21–31.

Buras, Kristen. 2010. *Pedagogy, politics, and the privatized city: Stories of dispossession and defiance from New Orleans*. New York: Teachers College Press.

Bushaw, William, and Shane Lopez. 2011. "Betting on teachers: The 43rd annual Phi Delta Kappa/Gallup poll of the public's attitudes toward the public schools." *Kappan* 93 (1): 253–63.

Cooper, Michael, and Katharine Sleeye. 2011. "Wisconsin leads way as workers fight state cuts." *New York Times*, February 19. Accessed July 1, 2011. http://www.nytimes.com/2011/02/19/us/politics/19states.html.

Croco, Margaret Smith, Petra Munro, and Kathleen Weiler. 1999. *Pedagogies of resistance: Women educator activists, 1880–1960*. New York: Teachers College Press.

DeFour, Matthew. 2011a. "Madison schools closed Wednesday due to district-wide teacher sickout." *Wisconsin State Journal*, February 16. Accessed July 1, 2011. http://host.madison.com/wsj/news/local/education/local_schools/article_e3cfe584-3953-11e0-9284-001cc4c03286.html.

DeFour, Matthew. 2011b. "Two-thirds of Madison teachers joined protests, district says." *Wisconsin State Journal*, April 29. Accessed July 1, 2011. http://host.madison.com/wsj/news/local/govt-and-politics/article_86781fb4-7288-11e0-92c8-001cc4c03286.html.

Delisle, Elizabeth Cove. 2010. *Economic and budget issue brief: Fiscal stress faced by local governments*. Washington, DC: Congressional Budget Office.

Enoch, Jessica. 2008. "A woman's place is in the school: Rhetorics of gendered space in nineteenth-century America." *College English* 70 (3): 275–95.

Fairclough, Norman. 1992a. *Discourse and social change*. Malden, MA: Blackwell Publishing.

Fairclough, Norman. 1992b. "Discourse and text: Linguistic and intertextual analysis within discourse analysis." *Discourse and Society* 3 (2): 193–217.

Fairclough, Norman. 1995. *Critical discourse analysis: The critical study of language*. London: Longman Group.

Fraser, Nancy. 1990. "Rethinking the public sphere: A contribution to the critique of actually existing democracy." *Social Text* 25 (26): 56–80.

Giroux, Henry. 1985. "Teachers as transformative intellectuals." *Social Education* 49 (5): 376–77.

Goldstein, Gary, and Victor Benassi. 1994. "The relation between teacher self-disclosure and student classroom participation." *Teaching of Psychology* 21 (4): 212–17.

Greenhouse, Steven. 2014. "Wisconsin's legacy for unions." *New York Times*, February 22. Accessed March 22, 2014. http://www.nytimes.com/2014/02/23/business/wisconsins-legacy-for-unions.html?_r=0.

Habermas, Jurgen. 1962. *The structural transformation of the public sphere*. Boston: MIT Press.

Hauser, Gerard. 1999. *Vernacular voices: The rhetoric of publics and public spheres*. Columbia: University of South Carolina Press.

Hess, Diana. 2009. *Controversy in the classroom: The democratic power of discussion*. New York: Routledge.

Hess, Diana, and Paula McAvoy. 2009. "To disclose or not to disclose? A controversial choice for teachers." In *Controversy in the classroom: The democratic power of discussion*, 97–110. New York: Routledge.

Hetzner, Amy. 2011. Protesting teachers force some schools to cancel class. *Milwaukee Journal Sentinel*, February 18. Accessed July 1, 2011. http://www.jsonline.com/news/education/116452478.html.

Johnson, Lauri. 2002. "Making democracy real: Teacher union and community activism to promote diversity in the New York City public schools, 1935–1950." *Urban Education* 37 (5): 566–87.

Johnson, Lauri. 2004. "A generation of women activists: African American female educators in Harlem, 1930–1950." *Journal of African American History* 89 (3): 223–40.

Judge, Harry. 1995. "The images of teachers." *Oxford Review of Education* 21 (3): 253–64.

Kennedy, Kerry. 2011. "Teachers as active citizens—Can teacher education prepare them?" *Teacher Education and Practice* 24 (3): 348–50.

McCluskey, Michael, and Jay Hmielowski. 2011. "Opinion expression during social conflict: Comparing online reader comments and letters to the editor." *Journalism* 13 (3): 303–19.

McDevitt, Michael, Spiro Kiousis, and Karin Wahl-Jorgensen. 2003. "Spiral of moderation: Opinion expression in computer-mediated discussion." *International Journal of Public Opinion Research* 15 (4): 454–70.

Pérez-Peña, Richard. 2010. "News sites rethink anonymous online comments." *New York Times*, April 11. Accessed March 1, 2012. http://www.nytimes.com/2010/04/12/technology/12comments.html.

Perillo, Jonna. 2012. *Uncivil rights: Teachers, unions, and race in the battle for school equity*. Chicago: University of Chicago Press.

Pritchard, David, and Dan Berkowitz. 1991. "How readers' letters may influence editors and news emphasis: A content analysis of 10 newspapers, 1948–1978." *Journalism Quarterly* 68 (3): 388–95.

Reader, Bill. 2005. "An ethical 'blind spot': Problems of anonymous letters to the editor." *Journal of Mass Media Ethics* 20 (1): 62–76.

Reader, Bill, Guido Stempel III, and Douglass Daniel. 2004. "Age, wealth and education predict letters to the editor." *Newspaper Research Journal* 25 (4): 55–66.

Sachs, Judyth. 2000. "The activist professional." *Journal of Educational Change* 1 (1): 77–94.

Sachs, Judyth. 2003. *The activist teaching profession*. Philadelphia, PA: Open University Press.

Sen, Amartya. 2009. *The idea of justice*. Cambridge, MA: Belknap Press of Harvard University Press.

Shah, Dhavan, Nojin Kwak, and Lance Holbert. 2001. "'Connecting' and 'disconnecting' with civic life: Patterns of Internet use and the production of social capital." *Political Communication* 18 (2): 141–62.

Siddle Walker, Vanessa. 2005. "Organized resistance and black educators' quest for school equality, 1878–1938." *Teachers College Record* 107 (3): 355–88.

Sigelman, Lee, and Barbara Walkosz. 1992. "Letters to the editor as a public opinion thermometer: The Martin Luther King holiday vote in Arizona." *Social Science Quarterly* 73 (4): 938–46.

Simmons, Daniel. 2011. Anatomy of a protest: From a simple march to a national fight. *Wisconsin State Journal* special report, February 27. Accessed July 1, 2011. http://host.madison.com/wsj/news/local/govt-and-politics/article_3c7f9cd2-4274-11e0-8f25-001cc4c002e0.html.

Street, Susan. 1996. "Democratization 'from below' and popular culture: Teachers from Chiapas, Mexico." *Studies in Latin American Popular Culture* 15: 261–78.

Teo, Peter. 2000. "Racism in the news: A critical discourse analysis of news reporting in two Australian newspapers." *Discourse and Society* 11 (1): 7–49.

Wahl-Jorgensen, Karin. 2001. "Letters to the editor as a forum for public deliberation: Modes of publicity and democratic debate." *Critical Studies in Mass Communication* 18 (3): 303–20.

Wahl-Jorgensen, Karin. 2007. *Journalists and the public: Newsroom culture, letters to the editor, and democracy.* Cresskill, NJ: Hampton Press.

York, Bryon. 2011. "WI school district: 'Sick' teachers docked pay, other discipline." *Washington Examiner*, February 18. Accessed July 1, 2011. http://washington examiner.com/blogs/beltway-confidential/2011/02/wi-school-district-sick-teachers-face-docked-pay-other-discipline.

Zhang, Shaoan, Qingmin Shi, Stephen Tonelson, and Jack Robinson. 2009. "Preservice and inservice teachers' perceptions of appropriateness of teacher self-disclosure." *Teaching and Teacher Education* 25 (8): 1117–24.

CHAPTER 7

The Formal and Informal Contexts of Union Socialization

Ben Pogodzinski

Several US states in recent years have moved to hinder teacher unions' ability to recruit and retain members by restricting the scope of bargaining and/or removing agency-shop protections. For example, in Michigan, teacher evaluation and performance pay are no longer subject to collective bargaining, seniority provisions in teacher assignments have been substantially reduced, and teacher tenure has been significantly weakened. The weakening of union power likely raises questions for some teachers regarding the relevance of unions in teachers' work lives. This may be particularly true of novice teachers; the newest generation of teachers has been shown to be more supportive of controversial reforms such as pay for performance systems (traditionally opposed by the National Education Association (NEA) and American Federation of Teachers (AFT)) (Goldhaber, DeArmond, and DeBurgomaster 2007; Jacob and Springer 2008; Johnson 2004; Johnson and Papay 2009).

Teachers' beliefs and attitudes regarding their union are based upon their evaluation of the costs/benefits of membership as well as their own ideological orientation toward unionism in general (Etzioni 1975; Newton and Shore 1992). These beliefs and attitudes are likely also shaped in part by teachers' disposition toward their professional community of colleagues whom they rely on for resources and support (Bascia 1994). In other words, the professional community within which novice teachers work *communicates* the priorities and values of the organization, which may or may not reflect the values and priorities of the union leadership. As put by Bascia (1994, 7),

> By identifying, reinforcing, or responding to issues and values around which teachers find their common identity, teacher unions may contribute to the formation, composition, and boundary setting of professional communities. A union may speak for, or diverge from, particular teachers' understandings of their group identity.

Therefore, novice teachers are largely socialized into the teaching profession through their daily interactions with their colleagues. Through socialization the norms and values of an organization or group are transmitted to individuals and define the expectations for professional behavior (Allen and Meyer 1990; Fullagar et al. 1995; Jones 1986; Van Maanen and Schein 1979). For socialization into teacher unions, this would relate to the ways in which teachers come to understand the norms and values of the union as an organization and the expectations for teacher roles and involvement in supporting the union within the broader district context.

In previous work (Pogodzinski 2012; Pogodzinski and Jones 2012; Pogodzinski and Jones 2013), I drew upon theoretical frameworks of union membership (Newton and Shore 1992) and new structuralism (e.g., Lounsbury and Vantresca 2003; Powell and Colyvas 2008) to identify multiple dimensions of novice teacher socialization into teacher unions and the potential influence this had on novice teacher union attachment. In a school context, union attachment relates to the beliefs and attitudes a teacher has regarding the role of the union in his or her work life (Newton and Shore 1992). More specifically, I analyzed data from interviews with local teacher union presidents to identify formal efforts that union leaders employed to socialize novice teachers into teacher unions (Pogodzinski 2012). Furthermore, with my colleague, I analyzed survey data collected from novice teachers and their more senior colleagues to (1) identify the association between novice teachers' desire for union effort in their work lives and the organizational context (e.g., relational trust among colleagues and manageability of workload), (2) identify the extent to which novice teachers' desire for union effort in their work lives deviated from that of veteran teachers, and (3) examine possible influence that veteran teachers had on novice teachers' desires for union effort in their work lives over one year (Pogodzinski and Jones 2012; Pogodzinski and Jones 2013).

With regard to formal union-sponsored socialization, it became clear that the socialization efforts enacted by union leaders were limited in both scope and duration, raising questions about their utility in encouraging union attachment among novice teachers (Pogodzinski 2012). Union-sponsored socialization efforts were primarily delivered through initial contact between union leadership and new teachers at district-sponsored orientation sessions, and occasionally through brief one-on-one meetings with new teachers at the beginning of the school year. The primary focus was on recruitment (i.e., officially signing up) and explaining the benefits associated with union membership. Overall, union leaders spent little time communicating the specific functions the union performs in the district or expressing the expectations for teacher involvement in union activities.

With regard to informal socialization, Pogodzinski and Jones (2013) reported that novice teachers had significantly different beliefs regarding the role of teacher unions in their work lives compared to their more senior colleagues, particularly related to the amount of effort the union should make toward securing better fringe benefits and negotiating standards for teacher evaluations and how those evaluations are to be used. In both examples, veteran teachers on average desired greater union involvement compared to the novice teachers. Further, Pogodzinski and Jones (2012) showed that important elements of the school context were significantly associated with novices' desire for union work effort in their work lives. Specifically, through estimating a series of logistic regressions, they reported that novice teachers who reported a manageable workload desired lower levels of union effort in their work lives, while those who reported high levels of relational trust among teachers desired more union effort in their work lives. Both findings make intuitive sense: (1) novices who are struggling with their work and job responsibilities likely desire more union effort in shaping the work environment and mediating work expectations, and (2) high levels of relational trust among teachers suggests high levels of solidarity and if well aligned with union leadership may promote higher levels of union attachment.

In this chapter, I further examine the association between the organizational context and novice teachers' beliefs and attitudes regarding teacher unionism by estimating a series of regressions to identify the association between differences in novice and veteran union attitudes and beliefs and novices' reported levels of relational trust, professional fit, and collective responsibility. It is important to investigate the association between measures of the broader school context and teachers' beliefs and attitudes regarding unionism because it is the everyday reality of work that is most salient for teachers in terms of their identifying with the school organization (Bascia 1994). Furthermore, as unions represent a collective of teacher professionals (at least in theory), it is important to identify associations between novices' perceptions of the quality of school-level collegial relations and union attachment, and how this union attachment may differ from that of their more senior colleagues.

Organizational Socialization

In order to facilitate commitment to organizational goals and processes, organizational leaders seek to communicate the values, norms, and work expectations to new members, a process defined here as formal socialization (Allen and Meyer 1990; Fullager et al. 1995; Jones 1986; Van Maanen and Schein 1979). In other words, this type of socialization is often highly structured in nature to provide new members with a common experience and distinguish newcomers from veteran colleagues, and it is directly targeted toward achieving organizational goals (Fullager et al. 1995; Van Maanen and Schein 1979). This formalized element of socialization is marked by specific time frames, ranges of topics, and methods of delivery, thus often eliciting a standardized response from those being socialized into the organization (Fullager et al. 1995; Jones 1986). With regard to union socialization, it is often through formal socialization that new teachers come to be made aware of the structure of union leadership, a tertiary understanding of what the union does, and the direct benefits of union membership. This type of socialization is often limited in scope and duration; typically it occurs through initial orientation sessions or brief one-on-one interactions between union leaders and new teachers and is focused on recruitment of new teachers into the union (Pogodzinski 2012).

Novice teachers also encounter socialization through relationships with their colleagues. Compared to formal socialization, "individual socialization practices are idiosyncratic and informal. Each newcomer is exposed to a different set of learning experiences that allow greater variation and innovation in the new members' responses" (Fullager et al. 1995, 147). Through regular everyday interactions, colleagues may express their own beliefs and attitudes regarding the role of teacher unions in their work lives (Ostroff and Kozlowski 1992; Schein 1968; Van Maanen 1976), thus expressing collegial expectations to which novice teachers are to adhere as teachers in a unionized school. These informal relationships also express the more subtle norms and expectations regarding labor-management relations and teachers' work within the school and district (Feldman 1981; Louis et al. 1983; Ostroff and Kozlowski 1992). Additionally, teacher relationships have the potential to mediate the policies and expectations put forth by union leadership (Bryk and Schneider 2002; Coburn 2001; Coburn and Russell 2008; Granoveter 1978).

Novice teachers, though, are not empty vessels; teachers enact personal agency and often self-select into groups within the work environments that reflect their own values and preferences, thus arbitrating their openness to influence (Frank 1998; Macy 1990). Teachers likely enter into relationships that reinforce their assumptions rather than challenge them. Additionally, novice teachers' experience of their working environment and their attitudes and beliefs regarding teacher unionism and their work in general are shaped by the organizational culture and climate within which they work. Therefore, union socialization goes beyond formal union-teacher or informal teacher-teacher interactions, specifically focused on issues related to unionism but encompassing novice teachers' broader experiences within their schools.

The analysis presented in this chapter builds upon these previous findings by delving deeper into differences in average union attitudes and beliefs of novice teachers and their veteran colleagues at the school level, and the association of these differences with measures of the school context. As more states move to limit the scope of collective bargaining and remove agency-shop protections (e.g., Michigan, Wisconsin, and Indiana), it is ever more important to understand the processes through which novice teachers evaluate their school environment, how this relates to their attitudes and beliefs regarding teacher unionism, and how these attitudes and beliefs may diverge from those of their more senior colleagues. Ultimately, the ways through which teachers are socialized into their schools and therefore experience teacher unionism have implications for the strength and direction of teacher unions in the future.

Michigan-Indiana Early Career Teacher Study

The analysis presented in this chapter utilizes data collected as part of the Michigan-Indiana Early Career Teacher Study, a multiyear mixed-methods study primarily aimed at understanding the ways in which mentoring experiences influenced the beliefs and practices of novice teachers. As part of this study, data were collected to identify teachers' beliefs and attitudes regarding the appropriate role of teacher unions in their work lives. Data were collected during the 2007–08 school year in ten districts across Michigan and Indiana (see table 7-1 for more information regarding districts) derived from surveys of novice teachers and their close veteran colleagues.

Table 7-1 2007–08 enrollment and demographic information for participating districts

Student enrollment	*District*	*Free/reduced lunch (approximate)*	*Nonwhite (approximate)*
20,000–23,000	District A (IN)	60–65%	55–60%
	District B (MI)	10–15%	10–15%
15,000–19,999	District C (MI)	50–55%	10–15%
	District D (IN)	40–45%	55–60%
10,000–14,999	District E (IN)	60–65%	45–50%
	District F (IN)	55–60%	55–60%
	District G (IN)	45–50%	80–85%
	District H (MI)	25–30%	15–20%
7,000–9,999	District I (MI)	40–45%	45–50%
	District J (MI)	35–40%	45–50%

Novice Teacher Sample

Across the ten districts, novice teachers were invited to complete two surveys during the course of the 2007–08 school year, one in the fall (October/November) and another in the spring (April/May). To be eligible, the novice teachers had to be in the first three years of the profession and teaching general education (core content courses) at the elementary or middle school level. Overall, 184 novice teachers completed both the fall and spring surveys for a total response rate of approximately 50 percent. Based on data made available from the participating districts, the teachers included in the analysis were not significantly different from initial responders (those who only completed the fall survey) with regard to observable characteristics such as grade level taught, years of experience, gender, or race. In the final sample, 72 percent of the teachers were teaching at the elementary level, and the respondents were overwhelmingly white and female (88 percent and 83 percent, respectively). Additionally, 27 percent were in their first year of the profession, 44 percent in their second year, and 29 percent in their third year.

Colleague Sample

In addition to surveys from novice teachers, surveys were administered to a group of more senior teachers across the ten districts. In the fall survey, the novice teachers were asked to name their mentor and up to eight colleagues who were provided resources and support. These teachers were then invited to complete a survey in the winter (January/February) of 2008. Overall, 351 of the novice teachers' more senior colleagues completed the survey for a response rate of approximately 60 percent. Although not necessarily representative of the overall population of senior teachers within the schools, they likely represented the most influential group of teachers for the novice teacher sample and therefore were an appropriate group to survey when concerned with issues of socialization and the quality of teacher relations. For the group of more senior teachers, 61 percent were teaching at the elementary level, and the respondents were overwhelmingly white and female (92 percent and 83 percent, respectively).

Variables of Interest

Both novice and veteran teachers were asked to indicate the amount of effort (1 = *no effort at all* to 4 = *a lot of effort*) that they felt their union should put forth in securing various benefits. For this analysis, I focused on the following specific items: (1) giving teachers more say in teaching assignments,

(2) giving teachers more say in how they do their jobs, (3) improving job security, (4) negotiating standards for teacher evaluation and how evaluations are used, and (5) giving teachers more say in how the school system is run. Additionally, a composite measure termed "overall effort" was created by taking the mean response across all five items (Cronbach's $\alpha = 0.80$). At the school level, novice teachers' responses for each item and the composite measure were then deviated from the group mean for more senior teachers. This deviation measure is aimed at capturing the extent to which novice teachers differed in their union attachment from their more senior colleagues within a specific school context. As shown in table 7-2, at the school level the deviations are relatively small.

To gauge particular elements of the school context, novice teachers were asked to indicate the extent of relational trust, professional fit, and collective responsibility among colleagues within their school. As a whole, these constructs of the school context are aimed at identifying important working conditions that relate to the quality of relationships among teachers within a school. The quality of relationships relates to novice teachers' understanding of their working environment, including elements of teacher unionism. In other words, socialization into teacher unionism likely occurs not only through interactions with union leaders and other teachers regarding issues directly related to teacher unions (e.g., collective bargaining, expectations for participation in union activities, costs/benefits of membership) but more subtly through regular interactions in a given school context.

I focus on three specific aspects of collegial relations: (1) relational trust, (2) professional fit, and (3) collective responsibility. Relational trust as a construct refers to the extent to which teachers in a school trust and respect one another both personally and professionally, including the extent to which they perceive that as a group they are reliable, honest, and open (Bryk and Schneider 2002; Tschannen-Moran and Hoy 2000). In the fall 2007 survey, the novice teachers were asked to indicate their level of agreement (1 = *strongly disagree* to 4 = *strongly agree*) with four survey items aimed at measuring this construct. A composite variable was calculated by taking the mean response across the four items (correlation $\alpha = 0.89$). Professional fit relates to the extent to which teachers share similar preferences for practices and dispositions related to the profession and their specific school, including sharing goals, values, and work expectations (Chan et al. 2008; Kristof-Brown, Zimmerman, and Johnson 2005). The novice teachers were asked to indicate their level of agreement (1 = *strongly disagree* to 4 = *strongly agree*) with six survey items (correlation $\alpha = 0.89$), from which a composite measure was created by taking the mean response.

Finally, collective responsibility relates to the extent to which teachers are committed to achieving the goals of the school (Bryk and Schneider 2002;

Table 7-2 Descriptive information for variables

Variable	*Description*	*n*	*M*	*SD*
Effort	Composite of desire for union effort	154	0.339	0.331
Job security	Improving job security	149	0.522	0.418
Job duties	Getting teachers more say in how they do their jobs	149	0.494	0.463
Evaluation	Negotiating over standards for teacher evaluation and how the evaluations are used	149	0.490	0.418
System management	Getting teachers a say in how the school system is run	143	0.465	0.413
Assignments	Getting teachers more say in their teaching assignments or transfers	146	0.478	0.447
Fit (α = 0.89)	Composite measure of professional fit	177	3.294	0.506
Teaching fit	Approach to teaching fits with others	174	3.391	0.605
Interest fit	Professional interests fit with others	164	3.152	0.652
Identify	Identify with others	173	3.295	0.665
Goal fit	Professional goals fit with others	158	3.101	0.697
I matter	I matter to other teachers	165	3.376	0.578
Others matter	Other teachers matter to me	175	3.474	0.576
Trust (α = 0.89)	Composite measure of relational trust	177	3.118	0.645
Discuss	It's OK to discuss feelings with others	174	3.333	0.708
Teacher trust	Teachers trust one another	170	2.918	0.741
Respect leaders	Teachers respect others who are leaders	172	3.035	0.801
Respect experts	Teachers respect others who are experts	174	3.190	0.700
Collective (α = 0.91)	Composite measure of collective responsibility	177	3.602	0.740
Discipline	Help maintain discipline	177	3.520	0.930
Help teachers	Take responsibility for helping others	175	3.457	0.895
Improve quality	Take responsibility for improving quality	176	3.438	0.960
Help students	Feel responsible for helping students	177	3.621	0.838

Table 7-2 (*Continued*)

Variable	*Description*	*n*	*M*	*SD*
Expectations	Set high expectations for academic work	176	3.750	0.852
Ensure learning	Feel responsible for ensuring that students learn	176	3.818	0.869
Middle school	Teaches middle school (1 = *middle school*, 0 = *elementary school*)	184	0.282	0.451
Percent white	Percent of students in school who are white	183	0.486	0.279
Percent lunch	Percent of students eligible for free/reduced-price lunch	178	0.549	0.216
District size	Total district K–12 student population/1,000	184	15.625	5.689

Note: All union variable measures were deviated from the school group mean. Items were based on a four-point scale (1 = *no effort at all*, 2 = *a little effort*, 3 = *some effort*, 4 = *a lot of effort*).

Penuel et al. 2009). This construct differs from professional fit in the sense that *fit* is more focused on similarities among individuals and their personal professional goals, values, and expectations, whereas collective responsibility is more focused on collaboration to promote organizational success. As such, this construct may be seen as a precursor to collective action within a school as individuals gauge others' level of commitment and effort and adjust their attitudes and behavior accordingly (Granovetter 1978; Macy 1990). The measure of collective responsibility was based on novices' responses to six survey items in which they were asked to indicate the proportion of teachers (1 = *none*, 2 = *less than half*, 3 = *about half*, 4 = *most*, 5 = *all*) who participated in school-wide activities (correlation $\alpha = 0.91$); a composite variable was created by taking the mean response across the items. Table 7-2 provides descriptive information about each of the focal variables of interest, as well as additional variables used in the analysis.

Analytic Approach

In addition to reporting correlations between the measures of the school context and the measures of novices' desire for union effort in their work lives deviated from the school mean, I estimated a series of linear regressions in order to control for confounding effects of the variables. More specifically, I estimated the following regression model:

$$\bar{Y}_j - Y_i = \beta_0 + \beta_1 T + \beta_2 F + \beta_3 C + \beta_4 M + \beta_5 \mathbf{S} + e \quad (1).$$

In this model, ($\bar{Y}_j - Y_i$) is a specific measure of a novice teacher's desire for union effort deviated from their school group mean, modeled as a function of novice teachers' perceptions of relational trust (T), professional fit (F), and collective responsibility (C). I also control for whether or not the teacher was teaching at the middle school level (M) and three characteristics of the school environment (**S**): (1) percent of students eligible for free or reduced-price lunch, (2) percent of students who were white, and (3) district size. The error term is assumed to be normally distributed.

Findings

As shown in table 7-3, the correlations among the measures of school context and the union measures are relatively small in magnitude, with only a few reaching statistical significance, though most of the signs are in the expected direction. For example, lower perceptions of school-wide collective responsibility were associated with larger deviations in desire for union effort in negotiating standards for teacher evaluations and improving job security. Somewhat surprisingly, higher ratings of professional fit were associated with larger deviations in desire for union efforts in giving teachers more say in how the school system is run.

To further examine these associations, I estimated the regressions for each outcome as well as the composite measure of desire for union effort and included all three measures of the school context; the results are reported in table 7-4. As shown in the first column, the measure of perceived professional fit was positively associated with deviation in overall union effort and statistically significant ($p < 0.10$), suggesting that novice teachers who perceived higher levels of fit with their colleagues were more likely to diverge from their colleagues with regard to desire for union effort in their work lives, ceteris paribus. As shown in columns 2, 3, and 4, there were no statistically significant coefficients for any of the focal variables, though the coefficient

Table 7-3 Correlations among focal variables

	Trust	*Fit*	*Collective responsibility*
Overall effort	0.003	0.084	−0.097
Assignment	0.009	0.038	−0.018
Job duties	−0.112	−0.018	−0.119
Job security	−0.073	−0.003	−0.162*
Evaluation	−0.038	−0.004	−0.235***
System management	0.1123	0.200**	0.023

*p < 0.05 **p < 0.01 ***p < 0.001

Table 7-4 Regression estimates

	Overall effort	*Assignment*	*Job duties*	*Job security*	*Evaluation*	*System management*
Intercept	0.03	0.28	0.65	0.94**	0.44	−0.02
	(0.31)	(0.40)	(0.44)	(0.39)	(0.40)	(0.40)
Trust	0.01	−0.07	−0.13	−0.03	0.12	0.02
	(0.07)	(0.09)	(0.10)	(0.09)	(0.09)	(0.09)
Fit	0.13*	0.10	0.12	0.10	0.08	0.22**
	(0.07)	(0.09)	(0.11)	(0.09)	(0.10)	(0.09)
Responsibility	−0.08	0.03	−0.03	−0.11	−0.20***	−0.06
	(0.05)	(0.07)	(0.08)	(0.07)	(0.07)	(0.07)
Middle school	0.13**	0.35***	0.20**	0.02	0.08	0.11
	(0.07)	(0.09)	(0.09)	(0.08)	(0.09)	(0.08)
Percent free/reduced lunch	0.13	0.001	0.07	−0.14	0.11	−0.09
	(0.18)	(0.23)	(0.26)	(0.23)	(0.24)	(0.23)
Percent white	0.18	−0.04	0.09	−0.15	−0.03	0.10
	(0.15)	(0.19)	(0.22)	(0.19)	(0.20)	(0.19)
District size	−0.003	−0.01	−0.01	−0.01	0.005	−0.01
	(0.01)	(0.01)	(0.01)	(0.01)	(0.01)	(0.01)
R-squared	0.08	0.14	0.07	0.05	0.10	0.09

*p < 0.05 **p < 0.01 ***p < 0.001

for collective responsibility approached statistical significance at a lower threshold ($p = 0.11$) in relation to the measure of union effort in improving job security.

The coefficient for collective responsibility was in the expected direction and statistically significant ($p < 0.01$) in relation to the union measure of effort toward negotiating the standards for teacher evaluation and how those evaluations should be used. This indicates that, on average, novice teachers who perceived higher levels of collective responsibility among teachers within their school were likely to be more aligned with those colleagues with regard to desire for union effort in negotiating teacher evaluations. Finally, the coefficient for perceived professional fit was positive and statistically significant ($p < 0.05$) in relation to union effort to give teachers more say in how the school system is run. Again, at face value this appears counterintuitive.

Discussion

Although on their own the findings may not be earth-shattering, they do suggest that researchers and practitioners should take a closer look at the association between the broader school context and novice teachers' perceptions of teacher unionism. The analysis presented here builds upon previous findings related to the school context and novice teachers' perceptions of teacher unionism (Pogodzinski and Jones 2012, 2013) by more specifically identifying the relationship between novices' perceptions of the school context and their perceptions of desired union effort compared to those of their school-based colleagues. Therefore, although at the school level the average difference between novice teachers' desire for union effort in their work lives did not deviate much from that of their more senior colleagues, this analysis showed that at least part of that deviation is likely related to the general school context, particularly relationships among teachers. In other words, novices' perceptions about the appropriate role of the union in their work lives (and how those may differ from the views of their more senior colleagues) is partially shaped by their general perceptions of their working environment and not solely by their specific experiences with the union or management or their own personal ideologies regarding unionism.

The findings regarding the association between novices' perception of collective responsibility and the union role in negotiating teacher evaluations reflect this. The findings suggest that the greater the sense of collective responsibility, the more likely novices and their more senior colleagues will be aligned with regard to critical elements of how unions help shape teachers' work. If teachers work together and show collective effort in working toward achieving school-wide goals, they are more likely to be aligned with respect to their beliefs regarding teacher evaluation reform and the role of their local union in negotiating for standards of teacher evaluation. As an example, this has important implications for the extent of solidarity among teachers in supporting or resisting changes to traditional forms of teacher evaluation.

More broadly, it suggests that if novice teachers perceive that they work in a collegial environment where teachers work together for a common purpose, this perception might translate into specific novice teacher action. For example, research into novice teacher induction has repeatedly shown that being in a collaborative and caring professional environment that includes veteran teachers has positive impacts on novice teacher development and retention decisions (Achinstein et al. 2004; Grossman and Thompson 2004; Kardos et al. 2001; Smith and Ingersoll 2004). It is likely that these attitudes and beliefs would carry over to attitudes and beliefs regarding teacher unionism. In other words, if the veteran teachers within such school environments support their union leaders' initiatives, it is more likely that novice teachers will follow their lead. Conversely, if the veteran teachers provide lukewarm support for union initiatives, this may guide novice teacher attitudes and beliefs as well.

The findings regarding the association between perceptions of professional fit and union measures are not as straightforward. One might expect that the more aligned professionally novices and their veteran colleagues are, the more likely that they would align with regard to union attachment. The findings from this analysis do not support this assertion, and additional research is warranted to unpack these findings.

Limitations of Analysis and Future Research

There are some significant limitations with the analysis presented in this chapter that should be addressed by future research. First, when considering the socialization of novice teachers into teacher unionism, it is important to distinguish between their ideological and instrumental evaluation of teacher unionism (Newton and Shore 1992). In other words, teachers have a particular ideological stance toward unionism based on a host of factors, including their political leanings, past exposure to unionism, and attitudes regarding individuality and independence. Additionally, teachers make instrumental evaluations regarding unionism, specifically, weighing the costs and benefits of membership in a teacher union. Socialization into teacher unionism relates to both constructs, but it is not clear how ideological and instrumental evaluations of teacher unions change over time or are mediated by direct and indirect socialization into teacher unionism.

It should be noted that across all six estimated regressions, there were relatively small R-squared values. As a set of models, the focus was on identifying possible associations between the measures of the social context and the outcome variables, rather than explicitly trying to account for as much variation in the outcome variables as possible. This relates to the need for further data collection aimed at measuring novice teachers' ideological and instrumental evaluation of teacher unionism.

Secondly, the veteran colleague sample used in this analysis was not necessarily representative of the general population of teachers across the schools used in the analysis. Owing to limited resources for administering surveys, data collection was limited to egocentric social networks with a cap of eight teachers per novice teacher. Thus, this analysis identified the extent to which novice teachers' beliefs and attitudes deviated from their close colleagues rather than veteran teachers throughout their school. It is likely that novice teachers and their close colleagues are more aligned in their views regarding teacher unionism if they share other professional similarities and dispositions; the deviation from veteran teachers across the school may be understated in this analysis. Therefore, it would be beneficial in future research to collect data from all teachers within a particular school.

Finally, the data used in this analysis were from one school year. For studies of teacher socialization, it is preferred to collect data over a longer period of time to investigate how teachers' beliefs and attitudes regarding teacher unionism change as a function of formal socialization directed by union leaders, informal socialization by teacher colleagues, and teachers' personal experiences within a particular school context.

Conclusion

Novice teacher socialization is essential for the future of teacher unionism, as socialization has been shown to increase member commitment and participation in union activities (Fullager et al. 1995; Kelloway and Barling 1993). The future of teacher unionism may be more reliant on member attachment as state policies restrict the scope of collective bargaining and exacerbate the problems of free ridership by removing union membership (or fair share dues) as a condition of employment. Such state-level policies alter the costs and benefits of union membership in real terms, and such policies promote a particular ideological stance regarding public sector unions that undoubtedly will resonate with a significant number of teachers. For example, under Wisconsin's Act 10, teacher unions must conduct recertification elections on a yearly basis, and in the 2013 election cycle over 20 teacher unions in Wisconsin were decertified (MacIver 2013). Although this represents a small percentage of the teacher unions in the state, it highlights the challenge facing union leaders in Wisconsin and in other jurisdictions across the United States.

Such challenges should encourage union leaders to seek further engagement from veteran teachers, particularly with regard to communicating the goals and values of the union in meaningful ways (Kerchner and Koppich 2004). It should not be taken for granted that the goals and values of the union are shared by the majority of teachers, though, nor should it be taken for granted that members are wholeheartedly supportive of their union just because they signed their union cards. Socializing novice teachers into teacher unions and cultivating union attachment require more than promoting the benefits of union membership; they also depend on communicating the goals and values of the local teacher union within the broader context of particular schools and the teacher profession.

Although there are limitations to this analysis, the findings point to the need to further consider the extent to which novice teachers' beliefs and attitudes regarding teacher unionism are shaped not only by their interactions with union leaders and through less formal communications with their teacher colleagues, but more broadly by their perceptions of their school context—specifically related to the quality of relations among teachers. While union leadership is primarily concerned with specific elements of teachers' working environments, including teacher-administrator relationships, it is important to not ignore teacher-to-teacher relationships. In other words, as an organization that is theoretically about solidarity among members, union leadership needs to help cultivate that solidarity in day-to-day teacher interactions and routines.

Additionally, these collegial interactions likely mediate the formal socialization efforts directed by local union leaders (Coburn and Russell 2008). Depending on the veteran teachers' own union attachment, these interactions may either enhance union socialization efforts or undermine such formal efforts. It is imperative to better understand the degree to which official union positions and activities are broadly supported among teachers within a district, and how this is reflected through teachers' day-to-day interactions.

In order for local union leaders to do this, they must be willing to adapt to the changing external environment as well as to the varying needs and ideologies of their members. Therefore, it is necessary for union leaders to relay to all teachers the necessary professional elements for succeeding as a teacher within the local context, the structure of the union, and how the goals and values of the union support teacher professionalism (Chao et al. 1994; Tetrick 1995). This would help ensure that a more thorough understanding of teacher unionism is consistently reinforced across schools within a district and is reflected in everyday practices. The training of building representatives could aid in the building of school culture supportive of unionism and the professionalism that such unionism supports, as would targeted interventions by local union presidents in schools and departments that have low levels of union attachment. All of this is essential because, ultimately, new teachers are the future of teacher unionism. If socialization efforts fail to promote union attachment in the long run, then challenges to teacher unionism will come not only from state legislatures but also from within the union itself.

References

Achinstein, Betty, Rodney Ogawa, and Anna Speiglman. 2004. "Are we creating separate and unequal tracks of teachers? The effects of state policy, local conditions, and teacher characteristics on new teacher socialization." *Educational Evaluation and Policy Analysis* 41 (3): 557–603.

Allen, Natalie, and John Meyer. 1990. "Organizational socialization tactics: A longitudinal analysis of links to newcomers' commitment and role orientation." *Academy of Management Journal* 33 (4): 847–58.

Bascia, Nina. 1994. *Unions in teachers' professional lives: Social, intellectual, and practical concerns.* New York: Teachers College Press.

Bryk, Anthony, and Barbara Schneider. 2002. *Trust in schools: A core resource for improvement.* New York: Russell Sage Foundation.

Chan, Wai-Yen, Shun Lau, Youyan Nie, Sandy Lim, and David Hogan. 2008. "Organizational and personal predictors of teacher commitment: The mediating role of teacher efficacy and identification with school." *American Educational Research Journal* 45 (3): 597–630.

Chao, Georgia, Anne O'Leary-Kelly, Samantha Wolf, Howard Klein, and Phillip Gardner. 1994. "Organizational socialization: Its content and consequences." *Journal of Applied Psychology* 79 (5): 730–43.

Coburn, Cynthia. 2001. "Collective sensemaking about reading: How teachers mediate reading policy in their professional communities." *Educational Evaluation and Policy Analysis* 23 (2): 145–70.

Coburn, Cynthia, and Jennifer Russell. 2008. "District policy and teachers' social networks." *Educational Evaluation and Policy Analysis* 30 (3): 203–35.

Etzioni, Amitai. 1975. *A comparative analysis of complex organizations*. New York: Free Press.

Feldman, Daniel Charles. 1981. "The multiple socialization of organization members." *Academy of Management Review* 6 (2): 309–18.

Frank, Kenneth. 1998. "Quantitative methods for studying social contexts in multilevels and interpersonal relationships." *Review of Research in Education* 23: 172–216.

Fullagar, Clive, Daniel Gallagher, Michael Gordon, and Paul Clark. 1995. "Impact of early socialization on union commitment and participation: A longitudinal study." *Journal of Applied Psychology* 80 (1): 147–57.

Goldhaber, Daniel, Michael DeArmond, and Scott DeBurgomaster. 2007. *Teacher attitudes about compensation reform: Implications for reform implementation*. Seattle: Daniel J. Evans School of Public Affairs, University of Washington.

Granovetter, Mark. 1978. "Threshold models of collective behavior." *American Journal of Sociology* 83 (6): 1420–43.

Grossman, Pamela, and Clarissa Thompson. 2004. "District policy and beginning teachers: A lens on teacher learning." *Educational Evaluation and Policy Analysis* 26 (4): 281–301.

Jacob, Brain, and Matthew G. Springer. 2008. "Teacher attitudes on pay for performance: A pilot study." Paper presented at the National Center on Performance Incentives, Nashville, TN, October.

Johnson, Susan Moore. 2004. *Finders and keepers: Helping new teachers survive and thrive in our schools*. San Francisco, CA: Jossey-Bass.

Johnson, Susan, and John Papay. 2009. "Redesigning teacher pay: A system for the next generation of educators." In *EPI series on alternative teacher compensation*, vol. 2, edited by Sean Corcoran and Joydeep Roy. Washington, DC: Economic Policy Institute.

Jones, Gareth. 1986. "Socialization tactics, self-efficacy, and newcomers' adjustments to organizations." *Academy of Management Journal* 29 (2): 262–79.

Kardos, Susan, Susan Moore Johnson, Heather Peske, David Kauffman, and Edward Liu. 2001. "Counting on colleagues: New teachers encounter the professional cultures of their schools." *Educational Administration Quarterly* 37 (2): 250–90.

Kelloway, Kevin, and Julian Barling. 1993. "Members' participation in local union activities: Measurement, prediction, and replication." *Journal of Applied Psychology* 78 (2): 262–79.

Kerchner, Charles, and Julia Koppich. 2004. "Organizing around quality: The struggle to organize mind workers." In *Teacher unions and education policy: Retrenchment or reform?*, edited by Ronald Henderson, Wayne Urban, and Paul Wolman, 187–221. Oxford, UK: Elsevier.

Kristof-Brown, Amy, Ryan Zimmerman, and Erin Johnson. 2005. "Consequences of individuals' fit at work: A meta-analysis of person-job, person-organization, person-group, and person-supervisor fit." *Personnel Psychology* 58 (2): 281–342.

Louis, Meryl, Barry Posner, and Gary Powell. 1983. "The availability and helpfulness of socialization practices." *Personnel Psychology* 36 (4): 857–66.

Lounsbury, Michael, and Marc Ventresca. 2003. "The new structuralism in organizational theory." *Organization* 10 (3): 457–80.

MacIver Institute. 2013. "Workers dismantle over 70 unions in Wisconsin." Last modified December 19. http://www.maciverinstitute.com/2013/12/workers-shoot-down-unions-in-wisconsin/.

Macy, Michael. 1990. "Chains of cooperation: Threshold effects in collective action." *American Sociological Review* 56 (6): 730–47.

Newton, Lucy, and Lynn Mcfarlane Shore. 1992. "A model of union membership: Instrumentality, commitment, and opposition." *Academy of Management Review* 17 (2): 275–98.

Ostroff, Cheri, and Steve Kozlowski. 1992. "Organizational socialization as a learning process: The role of information acquisition." *Personnel Psychology* 45 (4): 849–74.

Penuel, William, Margaret Riel, Ann Krause, and Kenneth Frank. 2009. "Analyzing teachers' professional interactions in a school as social capital: A social network approach." *Teachers College Record* 111 (1): 124–63.

Pogodzinski, Ben. 2012. "The socialization of novice teachers into teacher unions." *Labor Studies Journal* 37 (2): 183–202.

Pogodzinski, Ben, and Nathan Jones. 2012. "Exploring novice teachers' attitudes and behaviors regarding teacher unionism." *Labor Studies Journal* 37(2): 183–202.

Pogodzinski, Ben, and Nathan Jones. 2013. "Examining novice teachers' socialization into unions." Available online at *Education and Urban Society* November 21, 2013: 0013124513510733.

Powell, Walter, and Jeannette Colyvas. 2008. "The microfoundations of institutional theory." In *The SAGE handbook of organizational institutionalism*, edited by Royston Greenwood, Christine Oliver, Kerstin Sahlin, and Roy Suddaby, 276–99. London: Sage.

Schein, Edgar. 1968. "Organizational socialization and the profession of management." *Industrial Management Review* 9: 1–16.

Smith, Thomas, and Richard Ingersoll. 2004. "Reducing teacher turnover: What are the components of effective induction." *American Educational Research Journal* 41: 681–714.

Tetrick, Lois. 1995. "Developing and maintaining union commitment: A theoretical framework." *Journal of Organizational Behavior* 16 (6): 583–95.

Tschannen-Moran, Megan, and Wayne Hoy. 2000. "A multidisciplinary analysis of the nature, meaning, and measurement of trust." *Review of Educational Research* 70 (4): 547–93.

Van Maanen, John. 1976. "Breaking in: Socialization to work." In *Handbook of work, organization, and society*, edited by Robert Dubin. Chicago: Rand McNally.

Van Maanen, John, and Edgar Schein. 1979. "Toward a theory of organizational socialization." In *Research in organizational behavior*, vol. 1, edited by Barry Staw. Greenwich, CT: JAI Press.

PART III

Renewal

CHAPTER 8

Classroom, Community, and Contract: A New Framework for Building Moral Legitimacy and Member Activism in Teacher Unions

Kara Popiel

The face of the teacher union has changed. In many countries today, teacher union members are less active than ever before. After sustained growth in union membership and activism and subsequent expansion of benefits and bargaining rights in the early 1900s through the 1990s, teacher union membership has remained relatively fixed in the past 20 years, and member engagement in the United States, Canada, England, Australia, and other countries has been jeopardized by policy decisions that limit collective bargaining, privatize public schools, and standardize educational programs (Boyd et al. 2000; Buras 2010; Compton and Weiner 2008; Cooper 2000; Farber 2006; Hargreaves and Fullan 2012; Hypolito 2008; Murphy 1990; Rincones 2008; Robertson 2008; Rousmaniere 1997, 2005; Urban 1982). Teachers who have recently entered the profession tend to favor nontraditional and market-based policies opposed by teacher unions, such as the elimination of tenure and seniority, using student test scores to evaluate teachers, and enacting nontraditional salary structures such as pay for performance or bonus pay (Farkas et al. 2003; Feistritzer 2011; Yarrow 2009). Newer teachers are also less likely to be active in the union, owing, in part, to their lack of connection to union values, lack of understanding of the role collective bargaining has played in securing better working conditions, and questioning of the union's moral legitimacy in its protection of teachers and teachers' rights (Bascia 2008; Chaison and Bigelow 2002; Popiel 2013). Now more than ever it is important for teacher unions to reconnect with members in meaningful and relevant ways and to engage members *as teachers* by addressing and advocating issues that directly affect teaching and learning.

This chapter explores how teacher unions can play a more meaningful and relevant role in teachers' professional lives by developing their capacity to support teachers in three fundamental ways:

- in the classroom, by advocating policies that directly affect teachers' work, by offering more opportunities for collaborative decision making, and through better communication and dissemination of professional information for their professional growth
- in the community, by developing partnerships with community organizations, addressing issues that directly affect students, and linking union work with broader social justice issues
- through contract negotiations, by reconnecting with members' needs so they can continue to bargain effectively and protect teachers' rights and by publicizing how the contract supports, rather than impedes, teaching and learning in the classroom

This chapter draws on the qualitative data from a mixed-methods study conducted in 2009 that explored how elementary, middle, and high school teachers in Yonkers, the fourth largest school district in New York State, described their beliefs about the teacher union and the factors that influenced their decisions to be active or inactive in the union. The full study included survey responses from 304 teacher union members and in-depth interviews with 30 teacher union members (15 active union members and 15 inactive union members)[1] in the Yonkers public school district (Popiel 2010, 2013).[2] Table 8-1 summarizes the conceptual framework and three major themes explored in the study: (1) professional values and beliefs about professionalism, (2) contextual or external factors, and (3) teachers' conceptions of their professional communities.

This chapter focuses on the core findings from the 30 interviews. These interviews enabled me to analyze the initial survey data in greater depth, to explore other influences on teacher union activism and nonactivism in greater detail, and to gain a deeper and clearer understanding of participants' beliefs about the union and how these beliefs influenced their decisions to be active or inactive in the union. The data reveal that the degree to which interview participants valued the union's support for contractual and professional issues and the degree to which they believed the union to be effective or ineffective in providing these supports were related to their decisions to be active or inactive in the union. The quotations presented in this chapter are representative of the responses of other participants who held similar beliefs.

Table 8-1 Teacher union activism and nonactivism: Beliefs about teacher unions and motivational factors suggested by previous research and literature

	Professional values and beliefs about professionalism (internal factors)	*Contextual and workplace factors (external factors)*	*Conceptions of professional communities (social factors)*
Active members	Material factors are linked to "occupational respectability" (Urban 1982, 139) and dignity (Murphy 1990) Union activism (via collective bargaining) increases professionalism by increasing teacher autonomy and voice (Casey 2006; Murphy 1990; Rousmaniere 2005) Unions are a form of involved citizenship and democratic voice for teachers (Casey 2006; Rousmaniere 2005)	Higher salaries, job security, better working conditions, and benefits are important (Boyd et al. 2000; Farkas et al. 2003; McDonnell and Pascal 1988; Moe 2006; Murphy 1990; Rousmaniere 2005; Urban 1982) Workplace setting necessitates or supports union involvement (Bascia 1994; Farkas et al. 2003; Johnson 1984) Past experience supports the need for union activism (Farkas et al. 2003)	The union supports and protects what members value most (Bascia 1994, 2008; Farkas et al. 2003) Conceptions of professional community include a role for the union or are predicated on union ideals (Bascia 1994, 2008; Farkas et al. 2003)
Inactive members	Unions address material concerns, not professional competence, quality, or responsibility for student achievement (Casey 2006; Koppich 2006) Labor unions' radical ideology is inappropriate for professionals; working-class affiliation is too narrow (Murphy 1990; Urban 1982) Adversarial relationships, job actions, and political strategies are not appropriate for professionals (Casey 2006; Kerchner and Caufman 1993; Koppich 2006)	Higher salaries, job security, better working conditions, and benefits are the union's most important functions (Farkas et al. 2003), and these do not require active personal involvement Workplace setting does not necessitate or does not support union involvement (Bascia 1994, 2008; Johnson 1984) Past experience does not support, or conflicts with, the need for union activism (Farkas et al. 2003; Johnson 1984)	The union supports and protects what members do not value or does not support or protect what members do value (Bascia 1994, 2008; Farkas et al. 2003) No role (or no strong role) for the union within members' conceptions of professional community (Bascia 1994, 2008) The union does not have an important role in teachers' daily professional lives; it only handles working conditions, salaries, and benefits (Bascia 1994, 2008; Farkas et al. 2003)

(*Continued*)

Table 8-1 Teacher union activism and nonactivism: Beliefs about teacher unions and motivational factors suggested by previous research and literature (*Continued*)

	Professional values and beliefs about professionalism (internal factors)	*Contextual and workplace factors (external factors)*	*Conceptions of professional communities (social factors)*
Questions that remained (gaps in the literature)	How, if at all, might the historical views of professionalism play a role in union activism and nonactivism today? How, if at all, have they changed? How do active and inactive union members in a single traditional union (Yonkers) define professionalism? How do different conceptions of professionalism influence teachers' decisions to be active or inactive? How, if at all, are active and inactive members' beliefs about involved citizenship similar or different?	What do members perceive to be the union's role in their school and in the district? How do members perceive their role in the union? How does workplace setting influence teachers' decisions to be active or inactive in the union? How do active and inactive members in the same workplace setting (i.e., in the same school) and across schools in the same district perceive the union's role? How, if at all, does past experience influence teachers' decisions to be active or inactive in the union? How do active and inactive members perceive and experience events in the same district, and how, if at all, do these events influence teachers' beliefs about the union and their decisions to be active or inactive in the union?	Which values are most important to active and inactive members (and why?) and how do they differ? How do the union's actions support or conflict with what members value most? How are values similar or different for teachers in a single district? How, if at all, do teachers' conceptions of their professional communities relate to their beliefs about the union or their decisions to be active or inactive in the union?

How Teacher Unions Can Build Member Capacity in the Classroom, Community, and Contract

One of the core findings that emerged from the study is that participants' perceptions of the union's *moral legitimacy* (Chaison and Bigelow 2002) influenced their beliefs about the union and their decisions to be active or inactive in the union (Popiel 2013): teachers' beliefs regarding whether the union's goals or activities held societal or professional value and enabled them to fulfill their professional goals were related to their beliefs about the union and the degree to which they were active or inactive in the union. Specifically, as discussed in greater detail in the sections that follow, while the union had sustained moral legitimacy for all active members in this study, it had no sustained moral legitimacy for most of the inactive members, and the union lacked moral legitimacy for them owing to its emphasis on job protection and its lack of social-professional supports for teachers. Although most participants believed it was important for the union to maintain protections such as tenure and seniority as a defense against unfair treatment and dismissal, 10 of the 15 inactive members said they had no direct need for the union's protection, and they questioned the union's moral legitimacy in protecting ineffective or inadequate teachers (Popiel 2013). Two-thirds of inactive members also believed that the union should do more to address issues directly related to their work with students, such as student discipline and academic preparedness and the need for additional funding for school programs. For these members, the union's moral legitimacy was weakened by its lack of attention to issues affecting teaching and learning. As one participant stated,

> I don't read much about education in the union newsletter . . . I read about grievances, I read about appointments, I read about political action . . . But I don't ever read about what the union did to improve the education or the quality of life of the children in Yonkers. That's what I want to read.

In the sections that follow, I discuss how teacher unions can develop more meaningful relationships with teachers through classroom supports and community activism and by connecting contractual protections more clearly to teachers' professional lives.

Classroom: "It's Not a Union Thing; It's a Teacher Thing"

Teacher unions can develop more meaningful connections with and among their members, if they begin in the classroom. Most teachers did not relate academic instruction or professional growth to the union. When asked what they believed to be the union's main role, in their schools and in the district, almost all interview participants identified it as "policing the contract" and protecting teachers from unfair treatment and dismissal. Most inactive members believed that they had "no need for the union" because "if you're doing what you're supposed to do, then the job security will take care of itself." When discussing academic instruction in their own classrooms, two-thirds of the participants, both active and inactive, referred to it as separate from the union. As one participant said when describing her classroom instruction, "It's not a union thing; it's a teacher thing."

Voice—"A Place at the Table"

One way teachers believed the union can support them in the classroom was by advocating policies that directly affected their work with students. More than half of the inactive members believed the union could have more value if teachers had a stronger voice in decision making—"a place at the table," "more of a say in the way the building is run"—and "discussed the real problems" in their schools and classrooms. They wanted the union to be more involved in issues directly related to their work, such as addressing student discipline and academic preparedness and improving school services for students. They wanted the union to "function collaboratively with the administration" to effect meaningful change. As one member put it,

> I would love to sit down, have a dialogue with [school leaders]. You want to make me a better teacher? . . . If you really want to do A.P. English, and you only have 12 kids who are willing to do the work, give me the 12 kids . . . You look at things like that and you say, "Why don't we ask teachers what ten priority things should be on the list?" . . . This would only happen if the union, somehow, worked with the administration. Let's sit equally. Let's talk.

Other members agreed that a voice in decision making and "real," authentic collaboration in which their voices were heard and demonstrable changes were made were key to improving instruction for students and working conditions for teachers. Specifically, almost all participants spoke about the need for teachers to have greater professional autonomy and discretion over pedagogical and curricular decision making. One participant said,

> I don't need to be chastised, "Well, you're supposed to teach fourth grade curriculum." I'm supposed to teach these children. That's what I'm supposed to be teaching . . . So what's more important now, teaching what the state is telling me to teach and teaching what the administrators are telling me to teach or teaching what the children need to learn? I mean really when it comes down to it, I should have that authority to say as a professional, "This child needs X,

> Y and Z, let me get X, Y and Z to this child." Not "I have to have these kids ready for a standardized test and if I don't blaze through this curriculum, that's it, I'm in trouble."

Twenty-two of the 30 participants mentioned student testing specifically, a lack of student preparedness, and the need for alternative programs and alternative assessments as areas in which they wanted the union to have more input. One high school guidance counselor said, "Kids come with all different issues and needs . . . [Many students] come in from other countries and yet they're expected to meet all those benchmarks within the four-year period, [which] is not always in the best interest of the student. This is one issue the union does not address."

The degree to which participants perceived the union as giving them a voice in decision making strongly influenced their decision to be active or inactive in the union. Specifically, 12 of 15 active members discussed how they perceived the union as giving them a voice in decision making, but 10 of 15 inactive members perceived themselves as having no voice in the union or perceived the union as having no voice in policy making and decision making. They expressed helplessness and frustration over what they perceived to be a lack of input regarding policies they felt were not appropriate for all students.

Visibility—"The Face of the Union"

One way participants thought the union could give teachers a stronger voice in decision making was by building member support through greater visibility of union leaders within the schools—or what several members referred to as "putting a face to the union"—and through more consistent communication with members. In fact, how participants perceived "the face of the union" strongly influenced their feelings about the union's moral legitimacy (Popiel 2013) and their decisions to be active or inactive in the union. Twelve of the 15 active members reported that positive early experiences with the union influenced their decisions to become active in the union. Twelve of 15 inactive members described how negative experiences had shaped their beliefs about the union's value in their professional lives.

Many participants, both active and inactive members, spoke about how important it was to introduce new members to the union, listen to their concerns, and create positive experiences and support systems for them. One inactive member suggested,

> Sit down with the brand new people at a luncheon. Hold a luncheon . . . to say, "Hey, we're your union. These are where your dues go to. Here are all the perks

> you have in the union and listen, if you have any problems, feel free to either go to your rep or you could actually call us." And I'll tell you if somebody had said that to me in the very beginning, things might have been a little bit different.

This participant did not think that new members really connected with the union "because the union hasn't really reached out to them and then it just kind of goes on from there" to influence their later feelings about the union. As one active member said,

> You can make or break the union by how you first experience it, so it's very important to go to brand new people and show them that you're there for them and be genuine about how you can help them, and truly help them when you need to.

This belief was supported by 24 out of 30 members whose social-professional experiences with union leaders early in their careers influenced their decisions to be active or inactive in the union.

In addition to early experiences that shaped participants' beliefs about the union, 12 of the active members said that their involvement was influenced by a single, trusted union-active colleague, often a building representative. Several other members also spoke about small personal gestures that were important to them, such as a building representative who attended a mother-in-law's wake or union leaders who offered advice, encouragement, or classroom support or materials. Both active and inactive members spoke about the need for union leaders to be "approachable," "trustworthy," "honest," and "supportive." As one member elaborated, "It all starts in the building. You have to have somebody with some kind of empathy, . . . people with character . . . [people] with great leadership skills and some kind of charisma . . . [someone] who's not afraid to stand up for teachers; someone who's in your corner."

Part of union visibility included the need for unions to communicate and publicize what they do. One active member said, "The union does a lot behind the scenes that people don't know they do." She provided specific examples:

> [The union] makes sure that the buildings are healthy and safe; making sure that learning takes place . . . They will legally represent you if you need help . . . They give out books, they make great collections. And they have fundraisers, they work for scholarships, there are a lot of things that they do and I think they need to publicize that, list everything that they do, because there is a lot.

Several of these specific union activities and services were mentioned by almost all of the 15 active members but were only mentioned by three inactive members, two of whom had been active at earlier points in their careers.

Rather, 80 percent of the inactive members believed the union did not do enough for students or the community and did not have the visibility it should have. One inactive member summarized as follows:

> You get to see them around contract time, you get to see them when there's going to possibly be a strike, you get to see them when they want you to be politically active. You do not get to see them outside of that one [building representative] when it's peace time.

Unions can reshape how their members perceive them and their role in schools, districts, and communities by developing strong, supportive leadership and utilizing existing networks, or creating new ones, to publicize their goals, policies, activities, and successes and share them with their members and the broader community. As I discuss further in the next section, some unions have begun to do this through forums that reconnect traditional union values of collaboration and collective empowerment with educational inquiry and practice.

Professional Support—"We're All in This Together"

A belief held by 13 out of the 15 active members was that their union activism represented more than protecting jobs or maintaining fair treatment. For these participants and nearly a quarter of the inactive members, union activism also represented "being there for each other" and "working together" for a common goal. As one union officer explained about why she became involved in the union, "It built some kind of community between people. We're all in this together, as teachers, here for the kids . . . I notice that has waned."

Some unions address the need to develop *professional capital* (Hargreaves and Fullan 2012) and greater collective expertise among teachers and to develop a more direct connection to members and the classroom by drawing on the union tradition of grassroots organizing and participatory self-efficacy (Markowitz 2000; Popiel 2013). Teacher unions in the United States, England, and Canada, as well as other countries, have begun to identify themselves more as professional organizations and advocates of professional growth through a variety of personal and digital means. For example, organized teacher centers in the United States sponsor and develop classes for and by teachers. Union-sponsored training and leadership programs in many countries help build professional and political expertise. Coaching, mentoring, and other nonevaluative peer partnerships connect new or struggling teachers with their more experienced colleagues. Union-led public dialogues in

Canada and other countries enable union members and other stakeholders to discuss educational trends and issues affecting public education both locally and globally. Digital forums, such as union-sponsored websites and blogs designed specifically around lesson sharing and classroom discussions, allow teachers to interact with one another and build professional relationships on a global scale (AFT 2012; ATA 2011, 2012; Popiel 2013; Weingarten 2010). These efforts create collaborative discourse and collective expertise that can empower teachers and their unions to enact change in their own practice, their schools, their districts, and their profession.

Community: "A Little More Humanistic"

Teacher unions can have a broader impact on schools and communities if they reposition themselves as advocates for students, families, and communities, as well as teachers. One participant said, "I like that the union has strength; I would like to see it be a little more humanistic." Teacher unions can reconnect with their roots as organizations whose mission is, in part, to "further the cause of social justice" (Gaffney 2007, 207) and promote social, economic, and political reform that will benefit families and communities (Gaffney 2007; Hypolito 2008; Mannah and Lewis 2008; Robertson 2008; Rousmaniere 1997, 2005; Urban 1982). One active member described this as the reason he and many of his colleagues became active 30 years ago:

> I saw the union as an agent of change. Much as I believed that unions had made a transformational contribution in moving people out of the immigrant class into a very comfortable middle class, economically, I thought they could also be an agent of change in the schools and in the community.

How can teacher unions build on this traditional social agenda in ways that members today will value and actively support?

Community Involvement—"Save the Clock Tower"

One way teacher unions can be agents of change in their communities and garner more public support is by developing partnerships with community and local, nonpartisan groups to organize regarding local community issues and needs. A labor relations specialist in New York State referred to these efforts as "save the clock tower"[3] activism, a reference to an American movie theme and analogous to the community ideal of rallying around a common cause (Christopher Corlett, personal communication). Teacher unions can develop member activism around the needs of the community. In one district, when flooding affected a local business and damaged a school building, the union organized fundraising to purchase school supplies from the store in need and donated the supplies to the school. In another district, an art teacher, working with the union, partnered with a local historical museum fundraiser by having her students create their own ornaments to decorate a Christmas tree, which was donated for its annual auction. In a small rural district, a group of teachers and school-related professionals applied their farming, educational, and culinary skills to a program that grew and used local produce for school lunches. Such efforts help unions publicize and raise awareness among members and the local community of the union's involvement as a community organization. Such efforts can also be connected to a broader social or political agenda: in another district, the union has begun to develop a campaign around "the working poor," to raise awareness of the low salaries of teaching assistants in their district and the need for broader national employment and wage reform (Christopher Corlett, personal communication).

It is important for teacher unions to develop a clear social agenda firmly rooted in education and the community, and it is crucial for the union to clearly articulate the connections between social, family, and community issues and the educational benefits for members and schools. The teachers I interviewed said they wanted the union to develop a unified political agenda connected to its education agenda. Almost all teachers in the study spoke about the importance of the union advocating for students and developing connections with families, especially parents, who, they felt, "didn't have a voice in the system."

Political Voice—"Mobilize the People"

In addition to a voice in policy making and a presence in the community, nearly all participants believed that it was important for the union to have a political voice, and nearly all participants drew a connection between the need for a political voice, or political "power and leverage," and the need for school funding to restore and improve programs for students. For two-thirds of inactive members, their decision to be inactive in the union was related to a perceived lack of political power and inability to enact change for themselves, their profession, and their students.

One member believed that the union's lack of political power was due to the fact that it did not have "a collective body" united around a single cause. Others agreed that the union had too many "conflicting agendas" or "competing interests" and needed to find common ground.

For almost all participants it was important for the union not only to keep members politically involved and informed but also to work to mobilize the community to gain additional support and funding for public schools. As one active member put it,

> We don't need to have our schools run by a mayor who may or may not want to fund us. We can speak up. We can rally. We can give out letters to sign and mail. We can mobilize the people. In the history of democracy, that's the only thing that makes change.

But it may take new ways of connecting with members to mobilize them. The challenge for teacher unions is how to enact change in the current neoliberal political climate in which unions' bargaining rights are being severely limited (Compton and Weiner 2008; Cooper 2000; Hargreaves and Fullan 2012; Rincones 2008; Robertson 2008), and to do so without eroding the rights and protections that founding members fought hard to attain and that current members want to maintain.

Contract: "The March Has Stopped"

One way teacher unions gained legitimacy (Chaison and Bigelow 2002) with their members in the past was by securing material benefits and job protections. Almost all participants, both active and inactive, believed their jobs would be less secure and that they would be more vulnerable to inequity and unfair treatment by school leaders without the union's protection. However, nearly half of the participants, both active and inactive, also agreed that there was a need for the union to change some of the ways it functioned because the needs of students, teachers, schools, and their communities have changed. As one participant summarized,

> Often, I don't think new teachers appreciate what unions did to get us to where we are but, honestly, I don't think old teachers realize that the march has stopped . . . When teachers were able to negotiate all of the things that were negotiated to make our lives easier, better—higher pay, sick benefits, everything and anything you want to talk about—we were so far behind. Unfortunately, the climate today is people don't think we're behind anymore.

Flexibility—"An Organization or an Organism"

In order to continue to act as "a voice of reality" for what teachers, students, and the community need, the union should reconnect with members to determine how those needs have changed and how they differ from one another. As one participant said, "We're either going to be an organization or organism . . . We can be an organization, which is kind of like a structure but it's dead, or we can be an organism that's living." For example, nearly half of the participants I interviewed believed that the union's dedication to traditional ideals, such as equity, has tethered it to the past and restricted its progress. Some members believed that the union did not acknowledge differences among its members and did not address important differences in the contract. Some issues they wanted the union to address were the need for flexible scheduling, more progressive student grouping, alternative uses of duty assignments, and more individualized, meaningful professional development.

Over two-thirds of active and inactive members believed that fear of losing the protections that the union has gained over the years resulted in an inability or reluctance to address larger issues of reform and change and created a focus on smaller, less significant issues. This might partly explain the lack of interest in involvement for some members. As one active member said,

> Now sometimes it seems to me we're nitpicking over tiny little nonsense business. I understand the point that you can't give too much . . . But sometimes I think it's turned into "You can't do this, but you can do that." It just seems too silly to me.

Instead, nearly half of the participants believed the union should be open to ideas that encourage flexibility and change.

History—"The Value of the Union"

In spite of many participants' desire that the union be flexible and willing to change, 25 of the 30 participants also spoke about the importance of the union's past and ways in which "the union's history is its strength." These members all spoke about the importance of educating newer teachers about the union's history, union values, and the importance of the contract—"to show new teachers where we came from and where we are now," to "explain to them why the union's there" and "the value the union has in their lives," and to help them "realize everything that has been done along the way . . . and how the union works for them." In addition to reconnecting with newer members and assessing the professional needs of all current members, teacher unions also need to argue convincingly that traditional issues, such as tenure, seniority, and other contractual protections, enable teachers to develop their talent and capacity to teach more effectively by "ensuring equity," "making sure we're treated fairly," and allowing "teachers to feel they can take risks and be themselves in the classroom."

It is also important to educate other stakeholders, such as school and district leaders, about how they can support teachers within contractual parameters. Nearly half of the participants believed that it was the union's obligation to "show the district that the contract works" when it is followed, "to express to them how students benefit from doing this a contractual way," and to emphasize how the contract benefits all members of the school community. One district leader I spoke with said, "I tell people, first and foremost, you're a teacher, you're an educator and you're here for the kids. That's why you're here and the contract is there to help you do that."

Moving Forward

In order for teacher unions to move forward and continue to engage and activate members in the future, they must maintain meaningful connections to teachers in their professional lives. Teacher union members today want the union to support and advocate policies and practices that directly affect teaching and learning. This includes offering more opportunities for collaborative decision making in their schools, communicating consistently with members to assess their needs, and supporting teachers' professional growth. Within the community, teachers want their unions to organize around issues that directly affect students and their families. Regarding the contract, members want to understand not only how the contract protects their rights but how it supports their work with students in the classroom.

The challenge for teacher unions moving forward will be to amplify the message that the union's purpose is to support their members as teachers first, in their communities, their schools, and their classrooms. Teacher unions can become more meaningful and relevant by engaging members in three fundamental areas: the classroom, the community, and the contract. To do this, unions must broaden their capacity to support teaching and learning, strengthen community involvement, and promote contractual provisions that engage members in collaborative decision making, collegial partnerships, and professional growth.

Notes

1. I define *active members* in this study as members who had served on union committees or as building representatives, attended five or more union meetings in the year prior to recruitment for participation in this study, engaged in political action, and promoted union issues in their buildings or community. I define *inactive members* in this study as members who had not served on any union committees, had not been building representatives, had attended two or fewer union meetings prior to recruitment for participation in this study, and had not

engaged in political action in the past year (Boyd et al. 2000; Chaison and Bigelow 2002; Lieberman 1997; McDonnell 1988; Moe 2006; Murphy 1990; Poole 2001; Rousmaniere 1997, 2005; Sharpe 2004; Urban 1982, 2000).

2. A more complete description of the quantitative and qualitative methods employed in this study can be obtained in the full-length doctoral dissertation (Popiel 2010).
3. Steven Spielberg (producer), Robert Zemeckis, and Bob Gale (writers/directors). *Back to the Future* (motion picture) (United States: Universal Pictures, 1985).

References

Alberta Teachers' Association. 2011. *The future of teaching in Alberta.* Edmonton: Alberta Teachers' Association.

Alberta Teachers' Association. 2012. *The new work of teaching: A case study of the worklife of Calgary public teachers.* Edmonton: Alberta Teachers' Association.

American Federation of Teachers. 2012. "AFT news: Share My Lesson offers online access to vast resources." Last modified June 19. http://www.aft.org/newspubs/news/2012/061912share.cfm.

Bascia, Nina. 1994. *Unions in teachers' professional lives: Social, intellectual and practical concerns.* New York: Teachers College Press.

Bascia, Nina. 2008. "What teachers want from their unions." In *The global assault on teaching, teachers, and their unions: Stories for resistance,* edited by Mary Compton and Lois Weiner, 95–108. New York: Palgrave Macmillan.

Boyd, William Lowe, David N. Plank, and Gary Sykes. 2000. "Teacher unions in hard times." In *Conflicting missions? Teachers unions and educational reform,* edited by Tom Loveless, 174–210. Washington, DC: Brookings Institution Press.

Buras, Kristen L., Jim Randels, Kalamu Ya Sallam, and Students at the Center. 2010. *Pedagogy, policy, and the privatized city: Stories of dispossession and defiance from New Orleans.* New York: Teachers College Press.

Chaison, Gary, and Barbara Bigelow. 2002. *Unions and legitimacy.* Ithaca, NY: Cornell University Press.

Compton, Mary, and Lois Weiner. 2008. "The global assault on teachers, teaching, and teacher unions." In *The global assault on teaching, teachers, and their unions: Stories for resistance,* edited by Mary Compton and Lois Weiner, 3–9. New York: Palgrave Macmillan.

Cooper, Bruce. 2000. "An international perspective on teachers unions." In *Conflicting missions? Teachers unions and educational reform,* edited by Tom Loveless, 240–80. Washington, DC: Brookings Institution Press.

Farber, Henry S. 2006. "Union membership in the United States: The divergence between the public and private sectors." In *Collective bargaining in education: Negotiating change in today's schools,* edited by Jane Hannaway and Andrew J. Rotherham, 27–51. Cambridge, MA: Harvard Education Press.

Farkas, Steve, Jean Johnson, and Ann Duffett. 2003. *Stand by me: What teachers really think about unions, merit pay, and other professional matters.* New York: Public Agenda.

Feistritzer, C. Emily. 2011. *Profile of teachers in the U.S. 2011*. Washington, DC: National Center for Education Information.

Gaffney, Dennis. 2007. *Teachers united: The rise of New York State united teachers*. Albany: University of New York Press.

Goldhaber, Dan. 2006. "Are teachers unions good for students?" In *Collective bargaining in education: Negotiating change in today's schools*, edited by Jane Hannaway and Andrew J. Rotherham, 141–57. Cambridge, MA: Harvard Education Press.

Hargreaves, Andy, and Michael Fullan. 2012. *Professional capital: Transforming teaching in every school*. New York: Teachers College Press.

Hypolito, Alvaro Moreira. 2008. "Educational restructuring, democratic education, and teachers." In *The global assault on teaching, teachers, and their unions: Stories for resistance*, edited by Mary Compton and Lois Weiner, 149–60. New York: Palgrave Macmillan.

Johnson, Susan Moore. 1984. *Teacher unions in schools*. Philadelphia, PA: Temple University Press.

Johnson, Susan Moore. 1987. "Can schools be reformed at the bargaining table?" *Teachers College Record* 89 (2): 269–80.

Johnson, Susan Moore. 2004. "Paralysis or possibility: What do teacher unions and collective bargaining bring?" In *Teacher unions and education policy: Retrenchment or reform?*, edited by Ronald D. Henderson, Wayne J. Urban, and Paul Wolman, 33–50. Boston: Elsevier JAI.

Johnson, Susan Moore, and Susan M. Kardos. 2000. "Reform bargaining and its promise for school improvement." In *Conflicting missions? Teachers unions and educational reform*, edited by Tom Loveless, 7–46. Washington, DC: Brookings Institution Press.

Kahlenberg, Richard D. 2006. "The history of collective bargaining among teachers." In *Collective bargaining in education: Negotiating change in today's schools*, edited by Jane Hannaway and Andrew J. Rotherham, 7–25. Cambridge, MA: Harvard Education Press.

Kerchner, Charles Taylor. 1978. "From scopes to scope: The genetic mutation of the school control issue." *Educational Administration Quarterly* 14 (1): 64–79.

Kerchner, Charles Taylor, and Krista D. Caufman. 1993. "Building the airplane while it's rolling down the runway." In *A union of professionals: Labor relations and educational reform*, edited by Charles Taylor Kerchner and Julia E. Koppich, 1–24. New York: Teachers College Press.

Kerchner, Charles Taylor, Julia E. Koppich, and Joseph G. Weeres. 1997. *United mind workers: Unions and teaching in the knowledge society*. San Francisco, CA: Jossey-Bass.

Koppich, Julia E. 2006. "The as-yet-unfulfilled promise of reform bargaining: Forging a better match between the labor relations system we have and the education system we want." In *Collective bargaining in education: Negotiating change in today's schools*, edited by Jane Hannaway and Andrew J. Rotherham, 203–47. Cambridge, MA: Harvard Education Press.

Lieberman, Myron. 2000. *The teacher unions: How they sabotage educational reform and why*. San Francisco, CA: Encounter Books.

Mannah, Shermain, and Jon Lewis. 2008. "South African teachers and social movements: Old and new." In *The global assault on teaching, teachers, and their unions: Stories for resistance*, edited by Mary Compton and Lois Weiner, 177–91. New York: Palgrave Macmillan.

McDonnell, Lorraine. 1988. *Teacher unions and educational reform*. Santa Monica, CA: RAND Corporation.

Moe, Terry M. 2000. *Teachers' unions and the prospects for better schools*. Stanford, CA: Hoover Institution.

Moe, Terry M. 2006. "Political control and the power of the agent." *Journal of Law, Economics, and Organization* 22 (1): 1–29.

Murphy, Marjorie. 1990. *Blackboard unions: The AFT and the NEA 1900–1980*. Ithaca, NY: Cornell University Press.

Murray, Christine. 2004. "Innovative local teacher unions: What have they accomplished?" In *Teacher unions and education policy: Retrenchment or reform?*, edited by Ronald D. Henderson, Wayne J. Urban, and Paul Wolman, 149–66. Boston: Elsevier JAI.

Poole, Wendy. 2001. "The teacher unions' role in 1990s educational reform: An organizational evolution perspective." *Educational Administration Quarterly* 37 (2): 173–96.

Popiel, Kara. 2010. *Protection, voice, trust and change: An exploration of active and inactive teacher union decision-making*. Unpublished PhD diss., Teachers College, Columbia University.

Popiel, Kara. 2013. "Teacher union legitimacy: Shifting the moral center for member engagement." *Journal of Educational Change* 14 (4): 465–500.

Rincones, Rodolfo. 2008. "The context of teachers' democratic movements in Mexico." In *The global assault on teaching, teachers, and their unions: Stories for resistance*, edited by Mary Compton and Lois Weiner, 217–20. New York: Palgrave Macmillan.

Robertson, Susan L. 2008. "'Remaking the world': Neoliberalism and the transformation of education and teachers' labor." In *The global assault on teaching, teachers, and their unions: Stories for resistance*, edited by Mary Compton and Lois Weiner, 11–27. New York: Palgrave Macmillan.

Rousmaniere, Kate. 1997. *City teachers: Teaching and school reform in historical perspective*. New York: Teachers College Press.

Rousmaniere, Kate. 2005. *Citizen teacher: The life and leadership of Margaret Haley*. Albany: State University of New York Press.

Sharpe, Teresa. 2004. "Union democracy and successful campaigns: The dynamics of staff authority and worker participation in an organizing union." In *Rebuilding labor: Organizing and organizers in the new union movement*, edited by Ruth Milkman and Kim Voss, 62–87. Ithaca, NY: Cornell University Press.

Spielberg, Steven (producer), Robert Zemeckis, and Bob Gale (writers/directors). 1985. *Back to the future* (motion picture). United States: Universal Pictures.

Urban, Wayne J. 1982. *Why teachers organized*. Detroit, MI: Wayne State University Press.

Urban, Wayne J. 2000. *Gender, race and the NEA*. New York: Routledge Falmer.

Weingarten, Randi. 2010. *A new path forward: Four approaches to quality teaching and better schools*. Speech delivered in Washington, DC, January 12. http://aft.org/pdfs/press/sp_weingarten011210.pdf.
Yarrow, Andrew. 2009. "State of mind." *Education Week*, October 21.

CHAPTER 9

Why and How a Teacher Union Supports Autonomous Teacher Professional Development in an Age of New Managerialism

Charlie Naylor

Contextual Factors Impacting Teachers' Professional Learning

There are five visibly current trends in the literature on teachers' professional learning, some dominant and others competing in specific jurisdictions:

- a push for greater alignment of teachers' professional learning with managerial and system goals
- system support for teachers' professional learning through government funding but with less managerial control—perhaps epitomized in Canada by the (now defunct) Alberta Initiative for School Improvement
- the creation of standards of professional learning such as those produced and promoted by Learning Forward the former National Staff Development Council (NSDC)
- dichotomous approaches to professional learning communities—some largely prescribed and others more organic and self-organizing
- the promotion of collaborative and autonomous professional learning in which teachers as professionals engage in inquiry and other self-directed approaches, which has built on the legacy of action research

Professional Learning Literature That Has Influenced the BCTF's Approach

Teachers' professional learning is currently under examination as teachers and education systems grapple with rapid changes in pedagogical approaches such as personalized learning or approaches using technology, including Universal Design for Learning.

Carrington, Deppeler, and Moss (2010, 2) emphasized the role of critical reflection in teachers' learning capacities:

> Educators are realizing that teachers (pre-service, beginning or experienced) do hold implicit theories about students, the subjects they teach and their teaching responsibilities, and that these implicit theories influence teachers' reactions to teacher education and to their teaching practice. The extent to which experienced teachers' conceptions and beliefs are consistent with their practice depends, to a degree, on the teachers' opportunities to critically reflect on their actions and consider new possibilities for teaching. Through this critical reflective process, teachers may be able to develop coherent rationales for their beliefs and classroom practice and may even become more aware of viable alternatives rather than proceeding on impulse and intuition. The continuum of teacher professional learning experiences begins in teacher education. Throughout their professional lives, teachers will continue to engage in ongoing professional development and learning.

Carrington and colleagues stressed the continuum of teachers' professional learning across their career stages and explicitly linked it to critical reflection. Webster-Wright (2009, 703) explored professional learning across a range of professions, including education, and stated,

> During the past two decades, empirical research has demonstrated that effective professional learning continues over the long term and is best situated within a community that supports learning.

Further, argues Webster-Wright (2009, 712),

> the term "professional development" (PD) is part of a discourse that focuses on the professional as deficient and in need of developing and directing rather than on a professional engaged in self-directed learning. This discourse, and the professional context of control and standardization that perpetuates it, are rarely questioned in research or commentary about PD.

Deficit model thinking is reflected in the British Columbia government's ongoing legal and contractual efforts to take greater control over teachers' professional development and reduce their autonomy. Their view of teachers as "lesser professionals" and their belief that professional learning can be controlled within the parameters of master-servant relationships run counter to a wide range of literature within but also beyond education (Naylor 2011a, 2011b).

Hargreaves (2007, 37) describes and argues for teachers controlling their own professional learning:

> Teachers [should] be the drivers, not the driven—using objective evidence to help them improve, but never undervaluing their own experiential knowledge because of it. Professional learning communities will not be places for devising quick-fix solutions to disturbing data exposed by test score results, but places where wise and critical teachers engage with each other over their accumulated (though not unquestioned) knowledge using a wide range of data (not just test scores) to devise more powerful strategies that help all children learn.

Robinson (2010, 21) connects teacher inquiry to teacher autonomy:

> [Teachers] reported more control over their teaching because inquiry helped them address, in concert with others, persistent problems of student learning in their classrooms. One teacher explained, "Inquiry is an opportunity for teacher leadership because it gives you more control over your own teaching. It gives you ownership and more autonomy in the classroom. It makes you want to do more and make your colleagues do more because you see the benefits of it all and you see how it impacts the students in a positive way."

The literature referenced here has been the focus of internal discussion within the BCTF. BCTF analyses have been shared and discussed at meetings with the 60 professional development chairs, one in every school district in the province. PD chairs sit on the local teacher union executive and support teachers' professional learning as part of their union role. They may share extracts from our analyses in newsletters or use BCTF reports in local workshops. BCTF-trained facilitators access and discuss articles during their training on supporting inquiry groups, an approach discussed later in this chapter. In this way, the union supports teachers' professional learning in our inquiry program, which is consistently linked to the literature.

Teacher Autonomy

Proponents and critics of teacher autonomy rarely engage in discussion about the concept and its components. The significant literature on teacher autonomy explored by the BCTF (e.g., Naylor 2011c) concluded that autonomy includes rights and responsibilities for individual teachers and for the collective of teachers as a profession.

Few people who write about teacher autonomy actually define it. Pitt and Phelan's (2008, 189–90) definition is one we have widely discussed with union members, and the authors have presented their work in challenging and engaging sessions with BCTF staff and members. Pitt and Phelan define autonomy in the following way:

> Autonomy refers to thinking for oneself in uncertain and complex situations in which judgment is more important than routine. For teachers, the nature of their work and its social context complicates this definition. Teaching involves placing one's autonomy at the service of the best interests of children.

For the purposes of this chapter, two key themes from our analysis of the autonomy literature will be considered:

Eagleton (2003, 332) articulates a perspective that indicates that teachers need to develop as autonomous professionals through reflection on practice with peers, recognizing a duty and a responsibility to build judgment in community rather than in isolation. He also implicitly argues against managerial control through his use of the term "fiat":

> [Professional] autonomy should not be taken to mean teachers exercising professional judgment in isolation . . . but rather that they develop their professional learning through systematic investigation, rather than by fiat.

Gabriel, Day, and Allington (2011) consider the concept of engaged autonomy, where teachers have considerable autonomy but are active and engaged in dialogue with other teachers and administrators, so that ideas can be discussed and challenged through reflective conversations. These authors stress teacher autonomy in the collective rather than as individual choice—developing judgment through reflection and dialogue. In union workshops, teachers have opportunities to discuss the nature of autonomy and their actions as autonomous professionals. In providing these spaces for discussion, we believe that discourse is more important than the assertion of autonomy as a right, as it engages teachers with concepts of judgment, complexity, and the consideration of collective rather than individual autonomy.

Burbank and Kauchuk (2003) state that autonomy, choice, and active participation are critical to effective professional development. Ingersoll (2007, 24) suggests that increased teacher control is beneficial for both students and teachers:

> Schools in which teachers have more control over key school wide and classroom decisions have fewer problems with student misbehavior, show more collegiality and cooperation among teachers and administrators, have a more committed and engaged teaching staff, and do a better job of retaining their teachers.

The link between trust, teachers engaging in collaborative professional development, and improved student outcomes has been noted in a recent paper from the *Stanford Social Innovation Review* (Leana 2011, 33):

> When the relationships among teachers in a school are characterized by high trust and frequent interaction—that is, when social capital is strong—student achievement scores improve.

Randi and Zeichner (2004, 503) argue that teachers' work as autonomous professionals is a fundamental component of teachers' professional development:

> The significance of active teacher autonomy in professional development opportunities cannot be overstated. In one study of teacher development, Sandholtz (1999) found that experiences that provide teachers with autonomy, choice, and active participation were critical to effective professional development. Further, in many "collaborative" endeavors, the framing of research questions, data collection measures, and reporting of outcomes are dictated by those outside of classrooms who are often in positions of power (Erickson and Christman 1996). Not only has teacher professional development been dictated by bureaucrats' voices within school systems, but also by those outside of schools within the higher education research community.

However, many governments have shown considerable reluctance to respect teacher autonomy, and the issue is often contentious, notably in jurisdictions with a high number and frequency of government interventions in education. Elliott (2005, 363), reflecting on action research in the United Kingdom, argued that teachers have struggled and will continue to struggle against controls that reduce autonomy and limit reflection and peer discourse:

> The space for the exercise of such [teacher] agency will not come simply as a gift from government. It will be wrought out of a political struggle by teachers and others within society to create the material conditions for a free, open and democratically constructed practical discourse to emerge as a context for professional action.

The discussion on teacher autonomy is important in the context of BC and in the context of professional learning. Such a discussion is challenging to some in the union because it adds complexity. This union exploration of autonomy emphasized responsibilities as well as rights, and on the need for developing morally acceptable judgments in community. In the complex and often fraught environment of BC public education, this exploration of autonomy by the union has offered challenges not only to new managerial proponents but also to our own thinking and learning.

The BCTF's Approach to Supporting Teachers' Professional Development

The literature on professional learning has proved to be of considerable interest and utility in the BCTF's efforts to build effective inquiry approaches. It has allowed our learning community to consider our stance in terms of *inquiry*, which is similar to what has been stated by Cochran-Smith and Lytle (2009, 121):

> Educational practice is not simply instrumental in the sense of figuring out how to get things done, but also and more importantly, it is social and political in the sense of deliberating about what to get done, why to get it done, who decides and whose interests are served. Working from and with an Inquiry stance, then, involves a continual process of making current arrangements problematic; questioning the ways knowledge and practice are constructed, evaluated, and used; and assuming that part of the work of practitioners individually and collectively is to participate in educational and social change.

Discussing and referencing the current literature helped to build credibility within the union membership and with partners in school districts and universities. The BCTF (2008) published a foundational document that provided a basis for the continued development of teacher inquiry planned and delivered by teachers for teachers. One key feature has been the partnership between local teachers' associations and the (provincial) BCTF. These partnerships have created a stronger interest among local association executives in teachers' professional learning through inquiry. All projects require school district funds to match those provided by the BCTF. This has a dual purpose: to engage union and school district management in collaboration and to send a message within and outside the educational community that the inquiry projects have both union and management support.

The BCTF sponsors approximately 12 inquiry projects across the province each year. These are cofunded by the union and by the school districts in which they occur to a total per project of $7,000. Each project proposal must be accepted and endorsed by the local teachers' association and by the school district before BCTF funding is provided. The BCTF trains and provides facilitation, using a cadre of 18 provincial facilitators. Facilitators are allocated to each inquiry project approved by the BCTF. They work with an inquiry group, meeting with them five or six times a year. Facilitators' training includes refining teachers' inquiry questions; the use of protocols; when to use individual, small-group, and whole-group exercises and discussions; supporting data gathering and analysis; and helping teachers report their progress. Reporting progress is a requirement and provides a measure of accountability, but participants are encouraged to use ways of reporting that work for them, so paper reports, posters, PowerPoint presentations, and videos are among the reporting approaches used. In some cases, presentations are made and union presidents/executives, the district superintendent and other senior staff, trustees, and other interested educators are invited to attend and to engage in discussions of the learning.

Facilitation costs (teacher release time, travel, and accommodation) are fully paid by the BCTF and are in addition to the $7,000 provided to groups. Recent projects included building collaboration in professional learning communities; exploring ways of increasing student engagement; self-regulation; and inquiry learning for students.

As we progress with training facilitators and participate in inquiry groups across the province, we reflect on the components of inquiry that have become of particular significance for us. Three components that we believe are important to our better understanding of inquiry are explored and discussed below.

"Going Deeper" in Professional Conversations

A primary goal of the union's inquiry approach is to encourage in-depth reflection and discussion of teacher practice. In "going deeper," participants ethically and respectfully (but also critically) engage in discourse about their own practice and the practice of other participants. Such reflection and critical thinking are possible with the amount of time allocated to inquiry meetings (three-hour meetings generally occur five or six times during the school year) and by building skills to extend professional conversations so that they become richer and more focused than an exchange of pleasantries or a simple sharing of teaching strategies.

Much has been written about differences between conversation and dialogue, mostly differentiating the more mundane and uncritical discussions as conversation and more meaningful exchanges as dialogue. Burbules (1993) has written that dialogue is "at heart a kind of social relation that engages its participants," entailing certain virtues and emotions including trust, respect, appreciation, affection, and hope—values that we want to encourage in inquiry groups. These values, or states of mind, impact professional discourse within inquiry groups and become part of the union's thinking about how to take conversations deeper. We also utilize and build on skills and techniques that promote more in-depth discussion.

Within our inquiry groups, we have learned how conversation can extend thinking and about how probing questions might enable deeper understanding by, as one participant called it, "taking the conversation to a different level." While teachers in the groups rarely engage in discussion about the nature of dialogue, they have commented on the fact that the discussions within inquiry groups are often significantly different from other conversations they have in schools.

Facilitators are encouraged to reflect on their experiences with inquiry groups during their twice-yearly meeting in Vancouver. One facilitator stated,

> In conversation with my colleagues, and with the other facilitators, knowledge deepens. The opportunity to have shared conversations is so rich.

What makes a conversation rich? Participants felt that conversations were rich when they extended their thinking and occurred over time, when they were geared not to immediate action but to generating deeper understanding, perhaps having explored different ideas and in some cases even going down a few dead-end roads. Both the trained facilitators and inquiry group participants have stated that specific techniques and protocols utilized in inquiry enabled them to "go deeper" than had been their experience in more casual discussions about teaching and learning.

We have also progressed with an approach that we term "cognitive reflection." This occurs when, within a group, a person (either the facilitator or a participant) uses a strategy such as an extending series of questions. We often utilize what we term a "fish bowl" technique. This entails the demonstration of a protocol where examples of specific facilitation techniques are demonstrated by two or three experienced facilitators in the center of a room, with the rest of the group surrounding those demonstrating the technique to observe it. One such example is a protocol for professional conversation, where three people adopt three different roles. The purpose is for each person to take a turn articulating their inquiry question and explaining why the question is important to them. One describes his or her inquiry focus and rationale. The second utilizes active listening skills and responds to the first speaker by reflecting, synthesizing, and extending the comments made by the first speaker. By asking these questions of clarification and reflecting on some ideas, the first speaker gets a second perspective on the inquiry question. The third observes, manages the time allocated to the exercise, and adds any reflections to those offered by the second speaker. This exercise typically takes ten minutes per group, so when roles are changed, 30 minutes are allocated to allow each facilitator an opportunity to engage in each role.

During such an exercise, the group leader for the facilitation training might pause the conversation and ask the whole group to reflect on what happened, identifying a probing question or synthesizing the context. Identifying the technique as it occurs is the moment of cognitive reflection. The group identifies and reflects on the extending questions (or a perceptive comment, a constructive challenge, etc.) and considers their utility in terms of the subsequent discussion and their possible utilization when they facilitate teacher inquiry groups. Participants might be asked to consider questions such as the following: Could you have done this? When might you use the technique? How might you vary it to fit within your own style of facilitation? This allows participants to recognize and build on skills to be used in extending thinking and discourse by recognizing the moments when they happen. Cognitive reflection identifies the specific skill, makes it overt, and encourages facilitators to consider whether and how the skill might be used with groups.

We are building on the collaborative conversation model by the use of protocols to support inquiry discussions. These have included a range of techniques promoted by Lipton and Wellman (2003). Nelson and colleagues (2010, 177) have considered the use of protocols and have suggested that they may have positive uses and potentially negative consequences:

> A shift from congenial to collegial conversations can also be supported by using protocols that provide processes for eliciting ideas and feedback from all group members . . . Also, teachers frequently tell us that these formal protocols feel artificial and awkward, as if they were trying to speak in a newly studied language.

"Going deeper" in richer conversations requires explicit strategies and the skill of facilitators in applying those strategies. Techniques such as questioning, probing, extending, and connecting conversations and themes allow different understandings to emerge and new thinking about practice to evolve, both for the individual and for the collective. Our research indicates that the individual's focus on a specific inquiry question is enhanced through conversation, but we are also finding that the group as a collective benefits from shared thinking about the refining of questions and the context impacting the individual's inquiry focus.

Effective, Supportive Facilitation

Facilitators offer a process while participants control the content; manage time and focus; ensure generally equitable participation; and extend and deepen the learning through supportive processes, enabling conversations, and challenging questions. The role of the facilitator within the inquiry groups is seen as both logistical (time management, equal participation) and ensuring that the overall process works in a way that engages and extends the thinking of participants within a supportive and collaborative group. It's a mix of trying to build the group's sense of safety and encouraging participants to take risks. The facilitator ensures safety for participants by adhering to a series of processes that are sufficiently explicit yet also flexible enough to meet a range of participant needs. The facilitator also encourages but manages risk by encouraging participants to explore areas of practice where they may have concerns, thereby moving to some extent outside the individual comfort zone but within the safety of the group. Developing a safe environment can be managed by engaging participants in considering the group environment and their roles and actions within the group.

One example of how we create safe environments is a discussion early in the duration of an inquiry group about individual learning needs, focusing on these questions: What do you need in order to learn? What are you willing to contribute to others' learning? How do we want to be together as a group?

These questions deal with the development of norms of behavior, where group participants first brainstorm then decide through consensus on which norms will govern their participation and discussion. These might include the following norms, which were developed in one inquiry group:

- Offer a positive approach.
- Be a part of the structure that supports or facilitates sharing in between the sessions.
- Be honest: open up to speak about my practice and what does or does not work.
- Share experience—failures and successes and how failures turned into success.
- Avoid dominating conversations.
- Provide affirmation and validation for one another.
- Show inspiration: offer ideas and get people fired up in their passion.
- Resource one another—depend on others and use one another as resources.
- Find one another's skill sets and share them in order to work as a team.
- Share one another's strengths/weaknesses, goals, and passions.

By discussing and agreeing on norms, the group builds a space for communication by articulating what each person needs, what she or he might contribute, and how she or he wants to act as part of a group. Because these norms are explicit and documented, they can be referred to at any time in which groups are together, and they become a focus for further reflection and discussion.

Early in the inquiry process, facilitators use processes to narrow participants' focus so that they can explore an area of their work by forming an explicit inquiry question. We have found the formation of a question crucial to starting an inquiry. Participants are encouraged to limit the scope of their inquiry to focus on a question that is within their capacity to address, focuses on their practice rather than the practice of others, but is also sufficiently open-ended to allow for exploration and discourse. In the early exploratory phase, the probes, extensions, and challenges build a frame within which individual reflection, data collection, and discussion with others can occur. At some stage the focus narrows and some form of action—a change in practice, or the articulation of a new understanding—occurs. One facilitator likened the process of widening the focus to "peeling the onion"—layers uncovered and opened up using effective facilitation.

Partnerships with School Districts and Universities

The inquiry projects have acted as a catalyst in building professional learning, fostering debate about professional development within the union and between union and management in school districts. From our perspective as a teacher union, inquiry is an approach to self-directed professional development, thereby opening up the approach for consideration by teachers and school district staff and engaging union members in autonomous learning (where they choose the focus of their inquiry) while also creating and extending partnerships with school districts. Reactions among school district management have been positive and supportive. Such responses bode well for an emerging possibility: many districts' management may not wish to control teachers' professional learning, but they want to see it happening. When viewing our projects, they have seen teachers engaged, excited, and linking their learning to the needs and learning of their students, and they appear satisfied and do not pressure teachers into other forms of management-directed professional learning. At the outset of a local/district inquiry project, one district administrator commented, "This is an exciting initiative which fits well with the district focus on collaboration and our strong history regarding teacher involvement in action research."

In most of the districts where inquiry groups have occurred, union staff engaged in both formal and informal discussions about the establishment, operations, and reflections of the inquiry group with superintendents or senior district staff. During a presentation by inquiry group participants to district staff and trustees, one superintendent stated, "Personally, I believe that this is the best kind of PD there could be, so we will do the best we can to find whatever funds we can find . . . Let's make it happen."

Local union leaders stated that this project gave them a professional development leadership opportunity with their members, as well as the school district's management and board. It allowed them to initiate a union/board professional learning partnership, with shared resources, inclusive group participation, and a common interest in topics of mutual concern to the district and teachers.

Distributed leadership has also occurred within the inquiry projects as facilitators become champions of inquiry in their local teacher unions and school districts, new facilitators gain the confidence to lead, and some participants offer leadership skills within group processes. All of these leadership skills benefit both union and school district management, especially where inquiry facilitators are active in both unions and school district communities.

Dissemination Approaches

The learning approach developed by the BCTF has been the focus of reports on the BCTF website, as well as being presented at national and international conferences, including the conferences of the American Educational Research Association and the Canadian Society for Studies in Education. Whenever possible, papers are cowritten and copresented by teachers and BCTF research staff members (e.g., Naylor, Fry, and Filleul 2012). By articulating its stance through web-based publications and conference presentations, the union thus reaches out and contributes to the educational discourse within and beyond British Columbia. Our research and information about our approaches to professional learning are publicly accessible through the BCTF website, and are thus open to consideration and critique by union members and others in the community. In addition, BCTF facilitators have written for journals (e.g., Filleul 2009), thereby moving beyond the spaces of inquiry within the union so as to contribute to a wider understanding.

Conclusion

The BCTF is well known as a vocal partner in any endeavor. But in its inquiry approach it has offered what could perhaps be termed quiet leadership:

promoting, funding, and staffing inquiry in ways that enable both local and provincial initiatives to occur. Its approach to working with districts has been overt and unequivocal; professional learning can be a partnership between union and school district management, with benefits for both and for teachers who participate. Good professional learning can coexist with teacher autonomy. The partnerships have been based on the principles of inquiry stated in the *Teacher Inquiry* report (BCTF 2008), have been fully facilitated at BCTF expense, and require only a matching grant from school districts to provide for some release time and meeting expenses.

In many countries, teacher unions are considered reactive rather than proactive organizations (Naylor 2002). Their engagement in bargaining entails building and defending positions to improve teachers' pay and working conditions, as well as students' learning conditions. Inquiry offers a different dynamic in that teachers make their own practice problematic and open to scrutiny in a community of peers. This requires a mind-set different from the positional certainty and advocacy reflected in bargaining. In inquiry meetings, we understand that practice is often problematic and that we all have uncertainties about our work. It is by exploring and better understanding those uncertainties in discourse with peers and through data collection and analysis that we aim to improve our practice. Thus, inquiry, with its reflection and uncertainties, appears almost directly opposed to the clear positions and stances taken by union bargaining teams.

Engaging in inquiry has moved one area of teacher union work from reactive to proactive by constructing teacher inquiry approaches, training cadres of facilitators, and building partnerships with school districts and universities. The approach allows teacher unions to engage differently both with their own membership and with a wider educational community. By building partnerships and collaborations, the union moves itself into a more "public space" (Coulter 2002) in which its ideas contribute to discourse and are open to challenge, which moves teacher unions out of isolation and into proactive engagement with broader communities. The better we can understand and articulate such shifts, the more prepared we are to engage as a union in a wider community of learners. We are better prepared because we can state and demonstrate our intent to create rather than just critique, and because we are overtly looking for, creating, and extending collaborations with school districts and universities. By moving in these directions, the BCTF can offer attractive professional learning opportunities for teachers and counter what we consider to be the negative aspects of new managerialism. We can also create and extend collaborations so that the union can be seen as a viable partner within the BC education system rather than as an obstacle to be overcome.

References

British Columbia Teachers' Federation. 2008. *Teacher inquiry in the BCTF: A focus for supporting teachers' professional development.* Vancouver: British Columbia Teachers' Federation.

Carrington, Suzanne, Joanne Deppeler, and Julianne Moss. 2010. "Cultivating teachers' beliefs, knowledge and skills for leading change in schools." *Australian Journal of Teacher Education* 35 (1): 1–13.

Cochran-Smith, Marilyn, and Susan Lytle. 2009. "Teacher research as stance." In *The Sage Handbook of Educational Research*, edited by Susan Noffke and Bridget Somekh, 39–49. Thousand Oaks, CA: Sage Publications.

Coulter, David. 2002. "Creating common and uncommon worlds: Using discourse ethics to decide public and private in classrooms." *Journal of Curriculum Studies* 34 (1): 25–42.

Dana, Nancy Fichtman, and Diane Hoppey. 2009. *The reflective educator's guide to classroom research: Learning to teach and teaching to learn through practitioner inquiry*. Thousand Oaks, CA: Corwin Press.

Eagleton, Terry. 2003. *After theory*. London: Allen Lane.

Easton, Lois Brown (ed.). 2008. *Powerful designs for professional learning*. Oxford, OH: National Staff Development Council.

Ingersoll, Richard. 2007. "Short on power, long on responsibility." *Educational Leadership* 65 (1): 20–25.

Leana, Carrie. 2011. "The missing link in school reform." *Stanford Social Innovation Review* 22(1): 1.

Lipton, Laura, and Bruce Wellman. 2003. *Mentoring matters: A practical guide to learning-focused relationships*, 2nd ed. Sherman, CT: MiraVia.

Naylor, Charlie. 2002. *Reconciling teacher unionism's disparate identities: A view from the field.* Vancouver: British Columbia Teachers' Federation.

Naylor, Charlie. 2011a. *The rights and responsibilities of teacher professional autonomy: A BCTF discussion paper*. Vancouver: British Columbia Teachers' Federation.

Naylor, Charlie. 2011b. *Professional development/professional growth and engagement: What's wrong with the BCPSEA picture?* Vancouver: British Columbia Teachers' Federation.

Naylor, Charlie. 2011c. *The rights and responsibilities of teacher professional autonomy: A BCTF discussion paper*. Vancouver: British Columbia Teachers' Federation.

Naylor, Charlie, Theresa Fry, and Mary Filleul. 2012. "The catalytic and collaborative role of a Canadian teacher union." Paper presented at the American Educational Research Association, Vancouver, British Columbia, April.

Pitt, Alice, and Anne Phelan. 2008. "Paradoxes of autonomy in professional life." *Changing English* 15 (2): 189–97.

Randi, Judi, and Kenneth Zeichner. 2004. "New visions of teacher professional development." In *Developing the teacher workforce: 103rd yearbook of the National Society for the Study of Education*, part 1, edited by Mark Smylie and Debra Miretzky. Chicago: University of Chicago Press.

Robinson, Marian. 2010. "School perspectives on collaborative inquiry." Paper presented at the Consortium for Policy Research in Education, Teachers College, Columbia University, New York, November.

Webster-Wright, Ann. 2009. "Reframing professional development through understanding authentic professional learning." *Review of Educational Research* 79 (2): 702–39.

CHAPTER 10

Crossing Boundaries to Support Strategic Foresight

Jean-Claude Couture

The Strategic Challenge of Preferred Futures

The Alberta Teachers' Association (ATA) is a professional organization that serves over sixty thousand members including those who hold life, student, associate and substitute, and part-time and full-time active status as teachers. Importantly, all teaching certificate holders (including principals) who are employed in a publicly funded school in Alberta are required to hold membership in the ATA.

The current reputation of the province of Alberta, Canada, as a high-performing education jurisdiction and the role of the ATA in supporting this accomplishment form a well-documented story that over many decades has been shaped by key defining moments.[1] Three themes define the parallel growth of the capacity of Alberta's K–12 system and the enhanced status of the ATA: basic guarantees regarding the welfare of teachers; ongoing enhancements of their professional status; and the commitment of the association to engage the public about the importance of a vibrant public education system. The enactment of the progressive Teaching Profession Act in 1935, which accorded professional status to teaching and made membership in the association automatic for teachers and principals employed by public and Catholic school boards, was just the beginning of a long list of accomplishments.

Thanks to strategic foresight work undertaken in the last decade, a fundamental shift has taken place in what the ATA leadership considers to be inside or outside the organization's core work. In this regard, the association's Preferred Futures document, which lays the foundation for its Strategic Plan, stands "as a promise the organization is making to itself and the membership and also as an invitation to Albertans to join the ATA in co-creating the next Alberta."[2]

According to the Preferred Futures document, the Alberta of 2030 will find itself living a new story written by Albertans, rather than by outside forces. Alberta has moved beyond the scarred prosperity of its boom-and-bust economy. The volatile decades of the initial shale and oil sands development have given way to steady progress in greening the province's energy-driven economy. Most important, recognizing what the world needs from them, Albertans have turned to meeting their fundamental design challenge for the future: sustained prosperity in a culture of learning and innovation.

The Preferred Futures document goes on to identify commitments that arise from four strategic directions that should guide the work of the ATA in the years ahead. But while this document is aspirational and a declaration against fatalism, the day-to-day realities of operating a teacher organization often draw attention and resources away from the long-term strategic goal: How might we describe the complex leadership challenges for the association in mediating the immediate demands of members and expectations for its resources while attempting to be mindful of the long-term opportunities and critical influences on any teacher organization? Consider figure 10-1 as a thought space that captures some of the diverse functions and influences that characterize the ATA's work. As this graphic organizer indicates, the range of influences on a teacher organization can be positioned along a time continuum over the short to long term, moving from the left to the right on the horizontal axis. For a teacher organization like the ATA, the time frame from short term to long term might include more immediate events on the left-hand side (e.g., immediate impacts on teachers' conditions of practice, "shock-jock" radio coverage on teachers embroiled in discipline cases) to longer-term trends impacting education policy (e.g., neoliberal fiscal policies, lobbying efforts by corporations to privatize education).

The vertical axis distinguishes internal factors within the organizational boundary of the ATA in the bottom half (e.g., dramatic declines in government revenues, changes in ministerial appointments) from external influences and environmental impacts in the top half (e.g., changing demographics of the membership, growing economic disparity).

The strategic foresight work of the association includes ongoing consideration of the interplay among all four quadrants. For the ATA, like any other teacher organization, short-term developments driven by internal influences that reside in the bottom left-hand quadrant are an important and necessary preoccupation. The conventional wisdom of prioritizing teacher welfare issues and the immediate needs of teachers serves to sustain member affinity

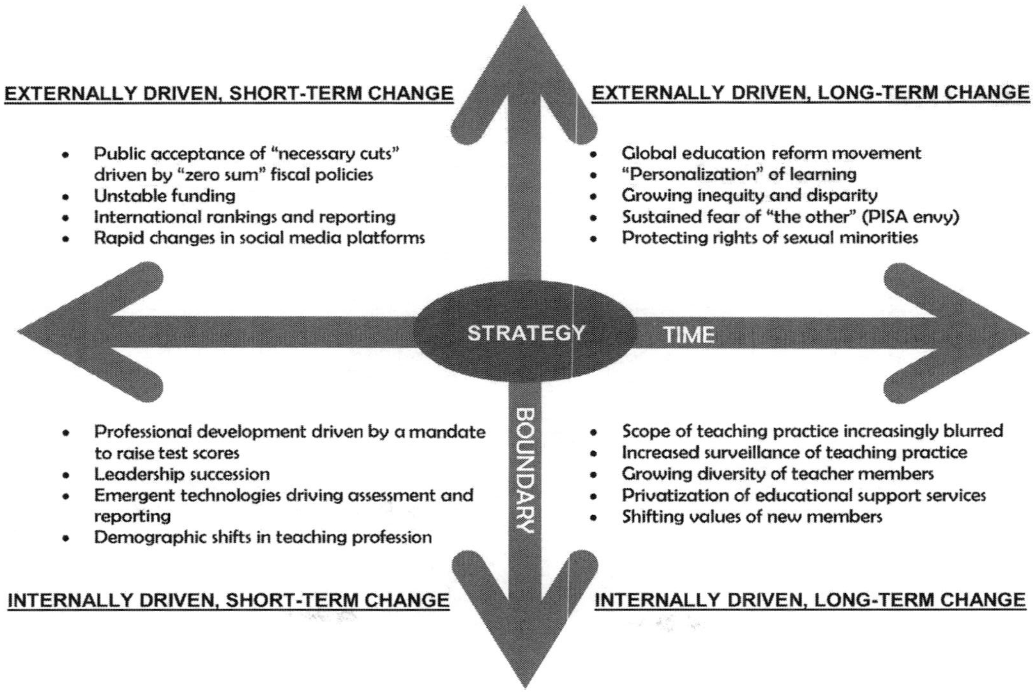

EXTERNALLY DRIVEN, SHORT-TERM CHANGE

- Public acceptance of "necessary cuts" driven by "zero sum" fiscal policies
- Unstable funding
- International rankings and reporting
- Rapid changes in social media platforms

EXTERNALLY DRIVEN, LONG-TERM CHANGE

- Global education reform movement
- "Personalization" of learning
- Growing inequity and disparity
- Sustained fear of "the other" (PISA envy)
- Protecting rights of sexual minorities

STRATEGY

TIME

BOUNDARY

INTERNALLY DRIVEN, SHORT-TERM CHANGE

- Professional development driven by a mandate to raise test scores
- Leadership succession
- Emergent technologies driving assessment and reporting
- Demographic shifts in teaching profession

INTERNALLY DRIVEN, LONG-TERM CHANGE

- Scope of teaching practice increasingly blurred
- Increased surveillance of teaching practice
- Growing diversity of teacher members
- Privatization of educational support services
- Shifting values of new members

Figure 10-1 Thought space characterizing the work of the Alberta Teachers' Association

with the organization (Naylor 1997; Rodrigue 2000). The longer-term strategic question is whether teachers' organizations can ever break out of the cycle of creating a better version of yesterday when they attempt to recalibrate resources or change the focus of their operational priorities.

Longer-term internally driven priorities illustrated in the bottom right-hand quadrant currently include advocating greater autonomy related to professional development and the impact of the growing use of digital reporting tools that are increasing teachers' workload.[3] Other influences such as the changing demographics of the teaching population offer both short- and long-term challenges to the association, as we see almost half of the membership turnover driven by retirements and population growth in a ten-year period.

Externally driven short-term activities identified in the top left-hand quadrant include responding to inadequate government or responding to media reports concerning rankings on international tests such as the Program for International Student Assessment (PISA).

In the top right corner lies the truly strategic work of teachers' organizations. This is a zone outside the organization's boundary where action is focused on efforts to reshape the critical influences that impact the education sector and the organization. Robust strategic foresight involves much more than adapting to the impacts of long-term external influences—teachers' organizations in the top right quadrant create environmental change to drive innovation that makes an enduring impact on students' learning conditions and teachers' conditions of practice. Other examples of this work would include the successes of the ATA in advancing the rights of sexual minorities in Alberta school communities, including changes in the Professional Code of Conduct.[4]

The complex array of often-conflicting priorities captured in figure 10-1 reveals the paradoxical nature of Alberta teachers' status as "professional employees"—a predicament typical of teachers across North America. Despite this paradox, as Dennis Shirley and Andy Hargreaves (2012) argue, there is a strategic opportunity for teachers' organizations to become more connected to the core work of their profession—teaching and learning. In doing so, they help to position themselves as authoritative voices on public policy matters. Moving beyond the conventional narrative of teachers' organizations opposing testing programs, they invite teacher leadership that offers alternatives to these programs. Further citing the ATA as a powerful example of a progressive teacher organization, Shirley and Hargreaves point out that over 50 percent of the revenues of the Alberta Teachers' Association are allocated to professional development. This contrasts with a figure of under 5 percent in most US teachers' associations.

International Partnerships as a Catalyst for Leadership in Innovation

Managing priorities in the ATA's context of short- and long-term needs both inside and outside its organizational boundaries involves strategic foresight and action. It is in this context that the association initiated a strategic international partnership with Finland in 2011. This effort to cross traditional organizational boundaries was motivated by the association's attempts to develop a comprehensive road map for educational reform that led to a 12-point plan: *A Great School for All—Transforming Education in Alberta Schools* (ATA 2012). Key to this document was a theory of educational change that focused on building the capacity of networks of schools committed to educational development. In the fall of 2010, the association, in collaboration with the Finnish Board of Education, the Center for International Mobility, and Alberta Education, initiated the Finland-Alberta (FINAL) international partnership, with the following goal: "Education partners in Finland and Alberta advance international educational and policy development through a shared commitment to provide a great school for all students." The partnership was officially launched with representatives from high schools involved, and others, in the international symposium Educational Futures: International Perspectives on Innovation from the Inside Out (FINAL), and a follow-up symposium focused on curriculum redesign, with Finnish ministry officials as lead speakers.

From its inception, FINAL was driven by the principle that educational improvement is best enabled by systems that support local innovation. From the perspective of the international team of researchers who helped to establish the partnership, Finland is an exemplar of this approach because the locus of control in Finland is at the school-community level. Finland's highly decentralized governance system with is relatively small education ministry (about 150 individuals) stands in contrast to Alberta's education ministry staff of 640.

As a counterweight to the current reliance on neoliberal system reforms driven by the global education reform movement (GERM), FINAL has demonstrated how international partnerships can be a way to sustain local innovation and creativity at the school level while disseminating and scaling innovation throughout the system. This is a key conclusion of the external research team that has evaluated the progress of the partnership (Shirley and Lam 2012).

GERM, a political-cultural meme, distracts policy makers from considering the complex intersection of social, economic, and political forces that inhibit the capacity of schools to achieve the broader goals of social justice and equity. Lateral networks of schools working together to counter GERM

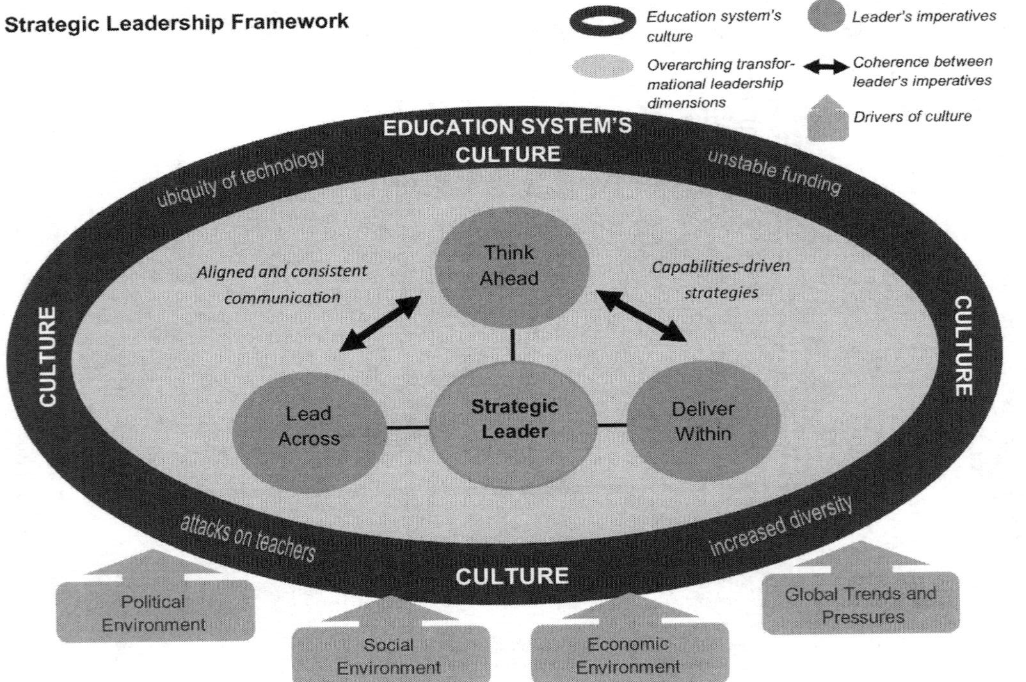

Figure 10-2 Strategic Leadership Framework

is best understood by viewing school development as part of the internationalization of educational development, achieved through three bold strategies formally endorsed at the FINAL summit held in Helsinki in 2012:

1. Thinking ahead—leaders (both at the local and system level) being boldly committed to the values of equity, community, and responsibility while being visionary and forward thinking in aspiring to create a great school for all students
2. Delivering within—sustained support for local innovation while avoiding "the perniciousness of the present" (Hargreaves 2009) and the privileging of inappropriate technology as a driver of school reform
3. Leading across—principals, teachers, and students reaching across school and other jurisdictional and political boundaries to learn from one another

These three leadership dimensions, developed as part of the Strategic Leadership Framework presented in figure 10-2, were developed in collaboration with Pasi Sahlberg, executive director of one of our partner organizations, the Center for International Mobility, which promotes crossing institutional and system boundaries in order to support the "internationalization of education" (Sahlberg 2011).

Thinking Ahead, Reaching Across, and Delivering Within

Enacted together, these three leadership dimensions form the ongoing design frame for the FINAL partnership: to sustain the work of leadership in high-performing schools across the globe. For the five Alberta high schools and seven Finnish high schools involved in the FINAL project, one key requirement is building a culture of trust (illustrated in the outer circle) to sustain principal, teacher, and student leadership in the daily work of risk taking and innovation while remaining focused on the need to nurture human relationships.

As indicated in the bottom of figure 10-2, the Strategic Leadership Framework recognizes the critical influence of political, social, economic, and global trends that shape the culture of the education system. Alberta's high school culture is characterized by the push for ubiquitous technology in schools, attacks on teachers from some right-wing media outlets, and school rankings and league tables—all amid growing classroom diversity and complexity. Time and again, the Finnish educators and students were struck by the ways the Alberta government's testing programs garnered so much attention, including the 50 percent weighting of grade 12 students' final marks. The cultural differences between the FINAL partners' education systems became apparent as the Finns questioned why the Alberta media appeared to pay significantly more attention to the PISA rankings than their media back home. One Finnish principal recalled an often-told joke in a media interview: "Sure we are close to the top in PISA rankings but our only concern is not to be number 1 in the world—our goal is just to beat Sweden both in PISA and ice hockey." Humor aside, participants on both sides of the FINAL partnership recognized what Yong Zhao (2012) has characterized as the global rise of "PISA envy"[5] and the irony in the fact that one of the reasons Alberta and Finland forged their partnership was their high international rankings.

These activities of delivering within and leading across involved school reform from the inside out by linking students, teachers, and principals as agents of change. Some examples include student-produced videos profiling the FINAL partnership; school improvement projects shared by principals; videoconferencing to discuss and debate global issues; documenting comparative local community histories; exploring the local impacts of globalization;[6] and creating more inclusive learning environments by providing free lunches in schools and graduate studies on leadership in inclusion. Teachers participating in the FINAL Art Collaboration regularly exchange ideas related to their teaching practice. They post these conversations on their blog and chat site. Both teachers and students are able to see all these posts and participate in the dialogue.[7]

From 2012 to 2014, principals and the organizational leaders involved in the partnership have been able to draw on their international experiences to reconceptualize curriculum design, assessment practices, and fundamental assumptions such as the need for grades in high school. Finnish and Alberta colleagues focused on "big picture" policy issues aimed at bringing about structural reforms and strategic shifts in their work. For example, the Finnish education system (in contrast to Alberta's current emphasis on choice and competition) "has been built upon values grounded in equity, equitable distribution of resources rather than competition and choice" (Sahlberg 2011, 96). For Alberta school administrators, the focus on "excellence through equity" that drives Finnish education has been a powerful reminder that foundational to educational success is systematic attention to out-of-school factors. In Canada, for example, according to recent PISA data, about 42 percent of the variation seen in student test scores is related to outside-the-classroom factors.[8]

As many of the Alberta students, teachers, and principals continued to reflect on their Finnish school visits, they were continually struck by the taken-for-granted assumption by the Finns that education is not possible unless students are well fed and ready to learn. In addition, the Alberta students were struck by the early learning programs that the Finnish high school students recalled from their younger years. The comprehensive supports aimed at mitigating the impacts of family and community circumstances in Finland stand in contrast to resource-rich Alberta, where school breakfast and lunch programs remain an afterthought of government and where only a patchwork of supports for early childhood exists. While some progress is being made in this area, it is worth noting that Alberta ranked second to last on the most recent national comparison of early education services across Canada.[9]

Perhaps one of the most significant successes of the FINAL partnership has been the development of student leadership. Reaching across school and international boundaries to learn strategies to create great schools for all became a focus of student projects and reflection. Consider the journal entry from a grade 12 Alberta student:

> When I travelled to Finland in October of 2013, I went under the impression that our public education was nearly flawless. I had all the options I could have dreamt of, my teachers were passionate about their material, and I had a nicely designed school. However, after spending a week in Kitee, I learned that maybe I was slightly naive. This school, a school not much different than ours, was able to offer everything and more to its students. They were fed healthy lunches, had options classes that I didn't even know were possible. This raised another question for me. If Finland is able to do this, and still have a sound economy and stable country overall, why don't we have these things in Alberta?

As part of a team of students in a small rural Alberta school that examined the ways students were unintentionally excluded in the day-to-day life of her school, this student developed a broader perspective as she met with her counterparts in Finland during the year:

> No matter what happens in the future, no matter who enters the seat, no matter who spends countless hours pounding the importance of Alberta's economic development into us, I hold onto the hope that every student can experience the same kind of growth in awareness that I was able to.

Beyond Educational Tourism

The FINAL partnership has garnered international attention and has been profiled at a number of international conferences and in publications as well as in community newspapers and social media in both countries.[10] In addition, in his interim report on the FINAL partnership, Dennis Shirley has documented how the FINAL partnership can be a catalyst and source of sustainability for advancing the association's road map for school improvement outlined in *Creating a Great School for All—Transforming Education in Alberta Schools* (ATA 2012).

As Shirley concludes,

> Ideally, our lives are rich both horizontally and vertically, when we cross the self-imposed artificial barriers we ourselves have created: our own school walls, system boundaries and jurisdiction bureaucracies. We benefit the most when we can harmonize ways of looking without and looking within. In that way we can transmit to our students our own excitement with the unending project of education, whatever form it may take in the ever mysterious and unpredictable pathways of our lives.

Based on the work of the FINAL partnership in 2014, both Alberta and Finland will focus on building capacity at the school level and developing powerful networks of teachers and policy makers who can learn from one another. A particular emphasis will continue to be on strategies that focus on equity as a path to excellence.

The FINAL partnership has also reinforced the view that Alberta needs to develop a coherent policy framework, something that it can learn about by studying Finland's Development Plan for Education and Research 2007–12. Although developed by the national government, this strategy for supporting innovation in all sectors is tied to initiatives at the community level. In the past year, the association has worked with partners in Singapore to enhance its own strategic foresight work, and it hopes to share its strategic directions work in the years ahead.

The FINAL partnership has informed the ATA's strategic foresight work outlined in its Strategic Plan (ATA 2013c). As outlined in the introduction, the association's Preferred Futures document articulates a vision for the organization and Alberta for the year 2030 that invites the organization to see boundary crossing as a core part of its operations. This resonates with the three transformational leadership dimensions that shaped the FINAL partnership and will inform prospective partnerships that the association is currently exploring: (1) thinking ahead (being courageous and forward thinking in leading educational change and development); (2) delivering within (committing to the long-term goals of improving teaching and learning while avoiding the distractions of "doing business as usual" and continually asking, "Why do we do things this way?"); and (3) leading across (crossing system, institutional, and geographical boundaries to lead in learning from other forward-thinking individuals and organizations).

Hargreaves and Shirley (2012) argue that a society's vision for the future should be created by citizens and community members who are actively engaged and by leaders who can tap into and elevate public spiritedness. The ATA aspires to be a leader in this conversation. The association posed the following existential questions to Albertans in a series of public engagement events over the past few years called Learning Our Way to the Next Alberta:

What is the Alberta that the world needs to see?

What kind of Albertans do we need to become to get us there?

How will leadership in learning help us become our best selves?

A key challenge for the ATA and a continued aspiration for the future is for both the membership and leadership to turn these questions on themselves by asking the following provocative question: Given the future that Albertans aspire to, what will be the role of public education, teachers, and their organizations in helping to cocreate that future?

Given the day-to-day pressures placed on teacher organization leaders, it is understandable that the challenges ahead seem daunting, but the association will remain committed to strategic foresight and action informed by the internationalization of education reform as pursued in the FINAL partnership. The leadership developed by the students, teachers, and principals in the 12 schools involved to date speaks to the power of vision, courage, and persistence. As memorably noted by the English historian and politician Edward Gibbon, "The winds and waves are always on the side of the ablest navigators."[11]

Notes

1. See, for example, "Lead the Change—Q&A with J-C Couture," AERA Educational Change Special Interest Group issue, no. 22, November 2012. Key to the success of these policies and supports is that since its inception, the ATA has been a unitary organization with school administrators as fully integrated members of the organization. Even to this day many policy makers fail to recognize the pivotal cultural driver that exists for Alberta school leaders: they remain primus inter pares, or first among equals, and are teachers first.
2. Special thanks here to Wilson Winnitoy who not only coined this phrase but has been a critical factor in informing the strategic planning work of the association. The association's Strategic Planning Group sits as an arm's-length advisory body to the organization's Provincial Council and includes elected representatives, staff, and field members.
3. The average teacher in Alberta works 56 hours a week, the equivalent of almost two days a week of unpaid time. Thirty-two percent of Alberta teachers report that they have little control over their work lives, and 72 percent report high

levels of conflict between their working life and their personal time. In a comprehensive province-wide study, the Alberta Teachers' Association and the Alberta Assessment Consortium (study available upon request) found that more than 15 digital reporting platforms were in use in the province, most of them frustrating to work with and not particularly effective. More than half of the study participants reported that their workload had increased by an average of 15 hours per term. Most participants (78.2 percent) indicated that they had not been consulted regarding choosing and implementing the reporting tool.

4. In 2000, the association established the provincial Diversity, Equity, and Human Rights (DEHR) committee, and ever since, the DEHR committee has been an active committee that advises the association on initiatives related to the goal of promoting diversity, equity, and human rights. In addition, the association's collaboration with the Canadian Teachers' Federation (CTF) in national and international human development programs and advocacy remains an ongoing priority. This work with CTF includes efforts to oppose public-private partnerships (P3s), the creep of institutional assessment, and the excessive influence of the Organization for Economic Cooperation and Development, the International Monetary Fund, and the World Bank on education and human development issues.
5. For a current analysis of the impact of PISA and the possibility that the global high performer Shanghai is considering withdrawing from the testing program, see http://zhaolearning.com/2010/12/10/a-true-wake-up-call-for-arne-duncan-the-real-reason-behind-chinese-students-top-pisa-performance/.
6. See Changing Landscapes 2012, https://vimeo.com/38657681, and FINAL Network, https://vimeo.com/41102958.
7. http://finalart.ning.com/photo/moonlight-william-shakespear?context=latest.
8. David Berliner has undertaken extensive review of the latest PISA data from Canada and has written and lectured extensively on this topic. See, for example, David Berliner, Gene Glass, and associates, *50 Myths and Lies That Threaten America's Public Schools—The Real Crisis in Education* (New York: Teachers College Press, 2014).
9. Margaret McCain, Fred Mustard, and Katherine McCuaig, *Early Years Study 3: Making Decisions, Taking Action* (Toronto: Margaret and Wallace McCain Family Foundation, 2011). Alberta is at the bottom of the 25 economically advanced jurisdictions with respect to children's readiness to learn by age six. The independent report ranked provinces on 15 benchmarks associated with the delivery of high-quality early childhood programs. The benchmarks were organized into five categories: governance, funding, access, learning environment, and accountability. Alberta scored 3 out of a possible 15 points. Quebec, which received 10 points, was the most highly rated province.
10. See, for example, "Finland and Alberta Join Forces to Keep Their Schools on Top of Their Game," *Canadian Embassy News*, February 13, 2013. http://www.finlandalberta.fi/wordpress/wp-content/uploads/2013/02/enbassy-news.pdf.
11. http://www.values.com/inspirational-quotes/6937-The-Wind-And-The-Waves-Are-.

References

Alberta Education. 2010. *Inspiring education: A dialogue with Albertans—Steering committee report to the honourable Dave Hancock, minister of education*. Edmonton, AB: Alberta Education.

Alberta Teachers' Association. 2012. *A great school for all—Transforming education in Alberta*. Edmonton, AB: Barnett House.

Alberta Teachers' Association. 2013a. *Changing landscapes—Alberta 2015–2035*. Edmonton, AB: Barnet House.

Alberta Teachers' Association. 2013b. *Member opinion survey*. Edmonton, AB: Barnett House.

Alberta Teachers' Association. 2013c. *Strategic plan*. Edmonton, AB: Barnett House.

Berliner, David, Gene Glass, and associates. 2014. *50 myths and lies that threaten America's public schools—The real crisis in education*. New York: Teachers College Press.

Booz and Co. 2012. "Transformational leadership in education: Three imperatives for lasting change." Research paper presented at the Transforming Education Summit, Abu Dhabi, United Arab Emirates, May.

Center for Strategic Futures. 2013. *Causal layered analysis project: An inter-agency project to explore the socio-economic aspirations of Singaporeans*. Retrieved from http://www.soif.org.uk/wp-content/uploads/2013/09/Causal-Layered-Analysis-Project-Report-final.pdf.

Couture, J.-C., and Stephen Murgatroyd. 2012. *Rethinking school leadership—Creating great schools for all students*. Edmonton, AB: Future Think Press.

Couture, J.-C., and Stephen Murgatroyd. 2013. *Rethinking equity—Creating a great school for all*. Edmonton, AB: Future Think Press.

Gregg, Allen. 2012. "1984 in 2012—The assault on reason." Last modified September 5. http://allangregg.com/1984-in-2012---the-assault-on-reason/.

Hargreaves, Andy. 2009. "Real learning first through the fourth way: An invitational symposium." Public lecture given in Calgary, Alberta, April 28, 2009.

Hargreaves, Andy, and Dennis Shirley. 2012. *The global fourth way—Architectures of educational excellence*. Thousand Oaks, CA: Corwin.

Hoteit, Leila, Chadi N. Moujaes, Jussi Hiltunen, and Pasi Sahlberg. 2012. "Transformational leadership in education: Three imperatives for lasting change." Paper presented at the Transforming Education Summit, Abu Dhabi, United Arab Emirates, May.

Hudson, Carol-Anne. 2012. *Poverty costs 2.0: Investing in Albertans*. Calgary, AB: Vibrant Communities Calgary and Action to End Poverty in Alberta.

Murgatroyd, Stephen. 2010. "'Wicked problems' and the work of the school." *European Journal of Education* 45 (2): 259–79.

Naylor, Charlie. 1997. "Developing pro-active research roles for teacher unions." Paper presented at the annual meeting of the American Educational Research Association, Chicago, March.

Rodrigue, A. 2000. "Teacher unionism: Building relevancy for the next decade." *Education Canada* 40 (1): 21–27.

Rorty, Richard. 1989. *Contingency, irony and solidarity*. New York: Cambridge University Press.

Shirley, Dennis, and Karen Lam. 2012. "Fourth way FINAL: The power of the internationalization of networks of school leaders." *In rethinking school leadership—Creating great schools for all students*, edited by J.-C. Couture and Stephen Murgatroyd, 112–41. Edmonton, AB: Future Think Press.

CHAPTER 11

Education Reform in England and the Emergence of Social Movement Unionism: The National Union of Teachers in England

Howard Stevenson and Justine Mercer

Introduction

For many years, education policy in England has been at the forefront of what has become known as the global education reform movement (Sahlberg 2010). England has appeared in the vanguard in terms of neoliberal reform and restructuring of public education. English education policy has had profound effects on relations with teachers as an occupational group, and on teachers organized in their unions in particular.

Relationships between teacher unions and the state have provided a key focus for reform in England, because teacher unions are presented as an obstacle to many of the key reforms, such as vastly increased private sector involvement in public education (Guardian 2010). However, organized teachers are more directly a target of the reforms for other reasons. First is that teachers' pay is a significant cost to government, and a neoliberal commitment to "small government" dictates a constant need to contain payroll costs. Second, and perhaps more importantly, teachers are a strategically important group of workers who perform a critical ideological function. If the education system is to be subordinated further to meeting the needs of capital, it is essential that there be greater control over the curriculum, and hence over teachers' work. In England, this control is being achieved through a combination of market forces and state-driven managerialism (Stevenson and Woods

2013). Attacking the power and influence of teacher unions, as the collective representation of the teaching profession, is therefore both a policy end in itself and a means to an end.

The scale of the attacks on organized teachers is considerable but should be seen as part of a longer-term project. Over time, centralized national collective bargaining has been replaced by fragmentation, including individualized pay and increasing contract flexibility. Traditional union structures and ways of organizing now seem out of kilter with this new landscape. In this chapter, we focus on how one teacher union in England, the National Union of Teachers (NUT), is responding to these changes. English teacher unionism is characterized by a complex multiunionism (Stevenson and Bascia 2013) in which at least six different unions compete for members among different, but often overlapping, sectors of the school workforce. Our justification for focusing on the NUT is twofold: it is the largest classroom teacher union in England, and it arguably has made the most radical strategic choices in response to the major changes in English education policy.

In this chapter we set out the background to the changes in English education policy and demonstrate how these have shaped teacher unionism over a period of more than two decades, with a particular focus on developments since 2010, when the restructuring of schools accelerated and deepened. This has been accompanied by a more explicit antiunionism at the government level (Gove 2013). By drawing on data collected from three different localities and exploring national developments in the NUT, we highlight how education policy has radically altered the industrial relations landscape within which teacher unions function. This chapter focuses on the response of the NUT locally and nationally and identifies a shift toward a more decentered, activist-based unionism that has its roots in an organizing tradition (Heery et al. 1999) combined with social movement unionism (Waterman 1993). However, the data highlight the very difficult circumstances the NUT faces, the uneven nature of its response, and the considerable challenges of cohering local activism into a national strategy.

Education Reform in England: Understanding the Context

During the last 25 years, school sector education policy in England has seen the most comprehensive market-driven reforms of almost anywhere in the world. For much of the twentieth century, England's school system was best described as a "national system, locally administered" (Gillard 2011). The powers of central government were extremely limited, with virtually no influence over curriculum issues; local governments' responsibilities were substantial—they had authority over the building of schools and were the employers of teachers. Relationships between the central state, the local government, and the teaching profession were considered a partnership, with individual teachers enjoying considerable control over curriculum and pedagogical issues, while collectively teacher unions were able to negotiate pay rates across the system through a process of national collective bargaining. Lawn (1996) describes the teaching profession as having a form of licensed autonomy.

During the last 25 to 30 years, this system has now been largely transformed. Identifying any single point in time when such a process "began" is inevitably difficult and feels arbitrary, but there can be no doubt that the 1988 Education Reform Act represents the decisive point when system transformation began in earnest, and when England's public education system was set on an entirely different trajectory (Stevenson 2011). This legislation introduced many linked changes, the intention of which was to "rebalance" the school system in a way that marginalized the contribution of local government and the teacher unions and instead privileged a "consumer-driven" market model combined with substantial amounts of central government control (Tomlinson 2006).

The period since 1988 has seen this restructuring of state education unfold in complex and sometimes contradictory ways, but for all the messiness in national policy among different political parties and among individual government ministers, it has been possible to discern a clear trend toward the fragmentation of the school system and the increasing role of private providers (Ball 2008). This became particularly apparent following the election of a Conservative Party and Liberal Democrat coalition government in 2010, but as Ball's work (2007) demonstrates, the development of private sector influence in the English "state" system was already well established under the previous Labor administration.

Since 2010, the decisive action of the coalition government has been to pursue an aggressive policy of "academization" whereby the goal is for all schools to be removed from local authority and established as state-funded independent schools (Department for Education 2010). The previous Labor government had paved the way for such a policy by establishing academy schools as its strategy for tackling "underperformance" in urban areas. Under Labor, academy schools were free to depart from the national curriculum and were also able to adopt their own pay and conditions for employees. Additionally, Labor's academy school policy sought to attract significant sums of private sector funding to complement public provision (Chitty 2013).

The shift in gears, presaged by the election of the coalition government in 2010, was to transform academization from a policy focused on a minority of

Table 11-1 Academy conversion rates nationally and across case study local authorities

	Primary		*Secondary*	
	Academy	*Maintained*	*Academy*	*Maintained*
National	13%	87%	63%	37%
Local authority 1	36%	64%	83%	17%
Local authority 2	10%	90%	88%	12%
Local authority 3	38%	62%	82%	18%

"turnaround schools" to one intended to be the default model of the English state system. Although in most cases the decision to convert to an academy school was taken at the individual school level, in many cases where schools were deemed to be "failing" conversion to academy status was ordered by the government (sometimes in the face of considerable community opposition; see Yarker 2009).

The consequence of this policy development was the transformation of the English school system. From a handful of academy schools in 2010, the situation within a single term of office was that substantially more than half of all secondary schools had become academies (see table 11-1). However, the figure for primary schools was much lower, with the vast majority (over 80 percent) opting to continue as local authority–maintained schools. Many academy schools were "stand-alone" conversions; however, a clear policy direction was for groups of schools to form "multiacademy trusts." A related feature has been the emergence of so-called "academy chains" managing several academy schools. Some of these chains were new, while others were already established providers of educational services. In some cases, chains had strong connections to organizations doing similar work elsewhere, most obviously the charter school movement in the United States (Ball 2012).

The New Educational Landscape: Implications for Teacher Unions

The changes outlined above represent a fundamental reshaping of school sector labor relations in England, although, as indicated, recent changes build on many years of more incremental change. The difference after 2010 was that the pace of change accelerated and the scale of change became much more visible.

Until the mid-1980s, teacher unions enjoyed considerable influence in a world where national collective bargaining was dominant, and teacher union influence at the local authority level was also considerable. Union organization tended to mirror this centralized structure in which national and local authority level negotiations established the framework in which teachers performed their work in schools. School-level union organization was minimal as key bargaining and decision-making structures operated at higher levels in the system. Put simply, teacher unions organized at the points where decisions were made (Stevenson 2003).

This changed in 1987 when national collective bargaining rights were unilaterally abolished (following extended industrial action by teachers between 1984 and 1986); a year later, the introduction of site-based management (known as local management of schools) was intended to weaken union influence at the local authority level. In reality, the appearance of change was often greater than the substance. National collective bargaining was abolished, but the model that replaced it (an independent pay review body) maintained national pay scales. At the same time, local authority structures were often retained as school leaders, union activists, and local authority officers largely reestablished the bargaining structures that had existed before 1988 (Carter et al. 2010). Indeed, for a spell between 2003 and 2010, a national relationship between central government and school sector unions was reestablished, officially referred to as the social partnership, in which formal agreements relating to teachers' contracts were negotiated (Carter, Stevenson, and Passy 2010). However, the precise nature of the negotiations, and the scope for genuine bargaining, was contentious within the teacher union movement, and not all teacher unions participated (see Stevenson 2012).

All of this changed rapidly in 2010. As soon as it was elected, the coalition government abandoned the national social partnership, while the drive toward academization posed an immediate threat to teacher union organization at the local authority level. What became apparent was that the commitment to fragmentation, marketization, and privatization that had been set in motion in the late 1980s, but which had developed relatively slowly since then, was now emerging in a much more explicit form. This was perhaps best illustrated in 2013, when the government dismantled national pay scales for teachers and effectively introduced institution-based pay bargaining into all of England's twenty-four thousand state schools, whether academies or local authority maintained (Department for Education 2013).

It is clear, therefore, that England's school system has been substantially reconfigured. The problem facing all of the teacher unions in England is that their structures and modes of working largely reflect a labor relations environment that no longer exists. For many years, teacher unions fought for national collective bargaining, and once this was achieved, they consolidated their own structures in ways that reflected a highly centralized model of negotiating. However, that centralized framework has been progressively dismantled. Teacher unions therefore need to find different ways of organizing that reflect a sharply fractured and highly decentralized school system, in which the school, or the academy chain, is increasingly the principal bargaining unit.

Education Reform and Teacher Union Responses

The labor relations framework that existed for many years in England is now barely recognizable, and teacher unions must adapt to the new landscape. However, identifying what the strategic options for unions are, let alone the extent to which they may be adopted by unions, is not straightforward. Our approach here is to draw on a framework developed by Carter et al. (2010) in an earlier study of English labor relations and identify three possible responses to reform—rapprochement, resistance, and renewal. We use this framework as a useful starting point for analysis, while recognizing that it was developed in the context of a very particular set of circumstances. Since 2010, those circumstances are much changed.

In the framework presented by Carter et al. (2010), rapprochement can be considered to be a pragmatic "coming to terms" with the direction of neoliberal restructuring and an attempt within those parameters to develop arrangements for consultation and negotiation that maximize the benefits for union members. This approach does not necessarily accept the logic of policy reform, but it does, pragmatically, go with the grain of policy when seeking to further the interests of members.

Carter et al.'s second approach was identified as "resistance," whereby teacher unions seek to challenge the trajectory of policy and indeed explicitly reject its neoliberal dimensions. This challenge to policy is active in form and involves efforts to mobilize members collectively, often through industrial action (for example, strikes and working to rule), as a means of directly confronting the reform process. However, while the strategy may be radical in its intent (the challenging of neoliberal restructuring), it remains more conservative in its form. There is a strong emphasis on member mobilization and "action," but the union's organizational form remains largely centralized. Such an approach was identified by Carter et al. in the 2010 study and was closely associated with the approach of the NUT during that time (as the main union that remained outside of the social partnership). While the approach had some successes, it also suffered from two weaknesses. There was little understanding of how, or under what specific circumstances, members might take such action, and the approach remained dependent on a small number of "hero-activists" undertaking disproportionate amounts of union work. The frailties of this model are exposed by the data presented later in this chapter.

The third approach presented by Carter et al. draws on the "union renewal" thesis (Fairbrother 1996, 2000). While the union renewal thesis rejects neoliberal reform and is committed to challenging it through mobilizing collective action, it goes further by recognizing the need for unions to adapt their own form and organization to align with changed circumstances. There is recognition that decentralized decision making (even when highly centralized elements of authority remain) requires unions to adapt their structures in ways that mirror this. Fairbrother's analysis recognizes that there is some element of threat from these developments (with employee isolation undermining traditional solidarities), but he also argued that the emergence of new bargaining issues in the workplace represented an opportunity to draw union members into engagement with the union. Renewal would follow when increased rank-and-file participation rejuvenated what could sometimes be moribund and bureaucratic union structures. The extent to which this might happen would depend in large part on the extent to which the union restructured in order to encourage this rank-and-file participation.

The three-approach model presented by Carter et al. provides a useful starting point for discussing teacher union responses to neoliberal reform, but it is important to recognize that these approaches were developed during a very specific period of English education policy, when the system remained quite centralized and when state-teacher relations were defined by a social partnership between employers and unions. The purpose of this chapter is to explore developments in school sector industrial relations in a new phase, since aggressive fragmentation, marketization, and privatization have been introduced.

Data Collection and Analysis

This chapter brings together work from two separate research projects focusing on different aspects of teacher union activity in two areas of the English Midlands. The first study focused on the changing nature of labor relations in academized environments in a single local authority area, and the second study concentrated across two local authorities, explored the ways in which union and community organizers sought to form alliances to resist the academization of local authority schools. The study therefore covers events across three local authority areas, identified in this study as LA 1, LA 2, and LA 3. Neither study focused specifically on the NUT, although for the purposes of this chapter, we have focused on the data that relates most obviously to the activities of the NUT.

Most of the data were collected through interviews with key participants, and between the two studies a total of 32 people were interviewed: union officers, school principals, school union representatives, a local authority officer, and community activists. In addition, one of the authors participated as a member of two community-based groups in LAs 2 and 3, one established to oppose academization and the other to promote public education issues generally.

Such an insider role inevitably creates complexity in research, with all the obvious dangers of bias and a lack of objectivity. We recognize these problems and seek to be transparent about them. By being open about our positions (as two authors, we clearly hold individual views and robust discussions about the project, which provide further checks and balances) and by being rigorous in our data analysis, we hope readers can make informed judgments about the credibility of our arguments and the claims we make.

School Restructuring: *"It's a Revolution . . ."*

The quote that heads this section was provided by a senior local authority officer as he described the pace and scale of changes taking place across the local authority in which he worked (LA 1), and in particular the extent to which schools in his area were converting to academies. In 2014, nationally, 18 percent of all schools had become academies, although lower figures for the conversion of primary (and therefore smaller) schools skew these results.

Various Sources

One practical consequence of this level of academization is that money that was provided to local authorities from central government is now directed immediately to academy schools. In the cases that follow, we set out how these changes in the role of local authorities began to impact on the relationship between the local authority and the teacher unions, in particular in relation to facilities agreements (the employer provided support for unions to perform their industrial relations function) and also the role and status of formal negotiating and consultative committees.

Within the three different local authorities, the impact of these changes was at its sharpest in LA 1, where the local authority actively sought to encourage all its schools to become academies: that is, it intentionally sought to divest itself of any active involvement in the running of schools. In this case, the local authority presented itself as a "market shaper," whose role was to ensure an adequate supply of good-quality schooling within its borders. Where supply might be inadequate, the role of the local authority was to encourage other providers to enter the market. The authority took the view that it should no longer be a provider of services to schools, and it did not see itself as having an employer responsibility. The senior officer we interviewed described the LA as "increasingly and unambiguously on the side of the school user." The clear implication here is that the LA is not on "the side" of providers, whether defined as schools or the people who work in them.

The inevitable consequence of this thinking was that the local authority sought to withdraw from its employer role and in particular its industrial relations function. At a practical level, this was an economic argument. If the LA no longer received grant funding from central government for schools that were now academies, why should it continue to provide an industrial relations infrastructure that was historically based on all schools being part of the local authority? However, arguably more importantly, at an ideological level there was an increasing dissonance between the LA's role as a "market shaper" (on the side of the user) and that of having an industrial relations stance (and working with providers). Given these developments, it became inevitable that the LA's support for union engagement would diminish. In LA 1 this occurred dramatically in 2012 when the authority announced it would cease to provide support for its negotiating and consultative committees—these structures would be dismantled—while it also indicated it would withdraw from any facilities time arrangements. For the NUT association secretary, this was a period of extreme turbulence. In a short space of time, he moved from dealing with one employer (the local authority) and having 100 percent release time to support this, to having no release time and having to deal with nearly 150 separate employers (the local authority plus all the academy schools in the area).

Within the two other local authorities covered in this study, the situation proved to be less dramatic, although the overall picture is one of year-to-year decisions and longer-term precariousness. Both local authorities 2 and 3 have been able to retain their facilities time for union officers, but with difficulty and, particularly in LA 2, with a strong feeling that the situation would be difficult to maintain in the longer term. In LA 2, all schools (LA maintained, stand-alone academies, and "chain academies") were invited to contribute to a central fund managed by the local authority that would provide facilities time. There have been good levels of "buy back," but a significant number of schools do not contribute. This potentially creates divisions, as schools that have decided to contribute are concerned that they may be subsidizing a service to other schools that choose not to contribute. In other cases, and most commonly in academy chains, there are emerging signs of a "go it alone" approach. For example, one large chain with schools across the Midlands and northern England (and some schools in LA 2) was prepared to fund facilities time for its own schools as long as the union representative was an employee of the chain. In this case, the nominated NUT representative works in a school a considerable distance from LA 2. Within LA 2, therefore, it was possible to discern a very diverse picture with a wide range of different arrangements. What was also identified by the local union secretary was the emergence of a more overt antiunionism in schools—"we know of schools where teachers are actively discouraged from engaging with the union."

In LA 3, the local unions were successful in establishing a "service level agreement" (similar to the arrangement in LA 2) by which academy schools contribute to a fund managed by the local authority, and this continues to support facilities time for union officers at levels similar to those existing prior to 2010. However, more officer time is now devoted to school-based bargaining and casework, and less time is devoted to local authority level negotiation. Some school-based work is undertaken by school-based union representatives, but the association secretary in LA 3 recognized that this is done well in relatively few schools. School representatives often lack the skills, knowledge, time, and hence confidence to undertake this work effectively.

In both LAs 2 and 3, local authority level bargaining structures (negotiating and consultative committees) still existed, but as with LA 1 they were now much diminished in their role. In an academized environment, the influence of these committees was necessarily reduced (as their outcomes apply only to LA maintained schools), but at a practical level, union officers conceded that their local authorities no longer had the resources to service such committees. The branch secretary for LA 3 commented, "I used to be at County Hall for meetings every couple of weeks—but not now. Quite often meetings are cancelled because we are told there is no business. There is nobody available at the LA to do the work."

What is clear from this analysis of the experience is that an industrial relations infrastructure that had withstood the intended consequences of the 1988 reforms is now being dismantled. This appears more dramatically in some instances, but there are a number of common features across all three local authorities reported here, whereby industrial relations structures are looking increasingly diverse, the role of formal local authority structures is diminishing, and power is transferring to schools, even when those schools are local authority maintained. Traditional industrial relations structures, based on union officers conducting formal negotiations with local authority personnel, are increasingly irrelevant to teachers in English state schools.

The NUT's Response: Challenging the Revolution from Above

As has been argued, historically the NUT's priorities have been the maintenance of a local authority–based school system, and ultimately a return to national collective bargaining. As long as these goals seemed like possibilities, it made sense to retain union structures and ways of organizing that reflected these objectives. However, after 2010 it became palpably clear that traditional ways of doing things were no longer effective. A revolution from above was taking place, and the landscape was being changed, perhaps irrevocably.

Although this comment was understandable, arguably it was not technically accurate. In light of the changing policy context, all the major classroom teacher unions undertook reviews of their work and began to reassess the union's traditional aims and strategies. For the NUT, this involved the formation of a high level working party of national officials and executive committee members tasked with reviewing fundamental aspects of union structure and organization in light of, in particular, the growth of the academy sector. What was clear was that the union's dependence on a core activist base, working in the local authority, was no longer tenable. The frailties of a system based on a combination of hero-activists and employer support (in the form of facilities agreements) were being exposed. The working party itself was formed from a membership that reflected all the major factions in the union, with the aim of securing cross-union consensus around possible organizational reforms. In a union that has historically been characterized by high levels of factional activity (Seifert 1984) and within-union conflict, the establishment of a group of this type marked a significant development and highlights a recognition of the need to transcend traditional sectarian divides.

What has since emerged is a longer-term strategy for the union that seeks to draw on, and integrate, two complementary developments in contemporary trade unionism. First is an explicit shift toward an organizing culture that draws on organizing practices, and associated research, that has emerged in recent decades in the United States. Second is a developing form of social movement unionism in which the union has sought to connect its industrial and political campaigns to a broader base of parental and community support (Weiner 2012). This latter approach draws on the experience of the Chicago Teachers Union (Horn 2014), with which the NUT has had increasing contact.

Evidence of the union's commitment to an organizing strategy had already begun to emerge prior to the election of the coalition government in 2010. In August 2009, the union appointed a Head of Organizing at a senior level, and by 2011 the union had a team of 11 organizers working in regions across the country. The job of a local organizer was a new role in the union, as previously full-time union officials in these regions focused on supporting branches with their negotiations while also undertaking considerable amounts of casework (mostly representing individual members). In contrast, the role of union organizers was to work with local branches to build local union capacity. Their focus therefore was principally on membership recruitment and also recruiting and supporting school-based union representatives—that is, teachers in schools who are the named union officers for their institutions. This highlights a shift in focus to the increasingly important level of the school. In 2013, the union appointed 20 organizers, many on fixed-term contracts, but by 2014 this team had grown to 32 organizers, overwhelmingly in permanent positions.

This expansion in the union's organizing activities has been costly, and not without controversy. Such support was largely directed to areas that had been most affected by cuts in facilities time, and so LA 1 was a major beneficiary of organizer support. In LA 1, where all facilities time had been removed, the attachment of a full-time organizer was reported as important and effective in rebuilding the branch, most notably in terms of recruiting school representatives. LAs 2 and 3 received less support, as they had been relatively more successful in sustaining their facilities arrangements. Nationally, the union has been able to report an increase in school representative density from 27 percent in 2009 (when organizers were first deployed) to 40 percent in 2014 (this figure rises to 64 percent when school groups with four members or fewer are discounted). It is very likely that the introduction of local organizers is an important factor in explaining the increase in rep density, but it is also important to recognize the link between organizing as a purely bureaucratic activity and the need to build organizing activity around the concerns and grievances of members. The danger is that without this link, any increase in member engagement would be largely ephemeral.

The importance of the symbiotic relationship between the development of the union's activist base and the union's ability to mobilize members around core concerns was best illustrated in LA 3, when the local authority announced plans to introduce a five-term year. This happened during 2011 and 2012, and the NUT immediately sought to mobilize its membership in opposition to the proposed changes. The union tried initially to work with other teacher unions, but as strike action became likely, support from other unions was not forthcoming. The NUT locally realized it would have to work exceptionally hard to mobilize members, who had only recently been on strike in relation to pension cuts. Considerable effort was put into building the base by deploying classic organizing strategies. As one account of the dispute highlighted,

> In the short space of time leading up to the first strike a significant amount of "capacity building" took place. This meant ensuring that not only local officers of the union but school reps and members in schools took on organising roles. (Wheatley, Artis, and Unterrainer 2013)

One obvious manifestation of this "capacity building" was that the union's school rep density increased from 31 percent to 72 percent between March and November of 2012.

The campaign itself involved several days of strike action accompanied by a range of campaigning tactics. It was ultimately successful, with the local authority withdrawing its original plans, although central to this success was the alliance that the union managed to forge with parents. This was made easier by the formation of a parents' group, called PA5TY—Parents Against the 5-Term Year. The group's title allowed a play on words in relation to a savory meat dish encased in pastry called a pasty. This was not important except that it allowed the group to achieve publicity by arranging deliveries of pasties to school gates and even a council meeting. It represented a type of stunt politics advocated in Saul Alinsky's (1971) seminal handbook for community organizers and proved highly effective in attracting media interest. It also demonstrated how a union-parent alliance was able to combine traditional industrial tactics (striking) with new and novel methods of engagement. This was highly effective in this dispute, although it is important to note that elsewhere in the study, there was evidence of considerable difficulties encountered when trying to build union-parent alliances, for example in relation to resisting academization (Stevenson and Gilliland 2014). Such alliances are powerful, but they appear to be contextually specific and cannot be assumed or taken for granted.

At a local level, the union's campaign against the five-term year was both successful in terms of its campaigning objective but also more widely successful in terms of engaging members and building the union branch (Unterrainer 2014).

This example represents a case at the local authority level of the strategy that the union has increasingly adopted nationally. In 2011, the NUT had been at the forefront of a public sector-wide campaign opposed to austerity-imposed pension cuts, although the alliance of public sector unions that was formed could not be sustained, and the dispute ended in frustration. Failure to adequately resolve the NUT's concerns about pensions, combined with grievances across a range of other issues, resulted in a new campaign of industrial action in 2013. Serious efforts were made to forge an alliance with other teacher unions, but although agreement was struck with one of the large classroom unions, it was not possible to maintain unity for very long. Although alliances with other teacher unions proved problematic, what emerged was a determined effort by the union to build community links and to engage with parents. The campaign developed under the banner of "stand up for education," and this slogan was used as a focal point for a range of community-focused organizing. This included organizing public meetings, extensive use of social media, and also regular street stalls organized by union members.

The action described above took place alongside a rolling campaign of strikes at both regional and national levels. The strategy is elaborated most clearly in an article cowritten by the union's deputy general secretary Kevin Courtney with executive committee member Gawain Little. The article explicitly locates the union's "stand up for education" campaign in a Gramscian analysis that aims to develop broad alliances across civil society. It presents this model of social movement unionism as a vehicle for articulating a counterhegemonic narrative capable of challenging the dominant discourse of "standards" and market-driven change. Moreover, there is a clear shift in the union's narrative that goes beyond making the general case for education as a public good, publicly provided, and that increasingly frames the union's objectives as opposing neoliberal reform in its broadest sense. The language used in union campaigning often couches this analysis in terms of opposition to GERM (the global education reform movement), although in some instances there are explicit references to neoliberalism as part of a more overtly political critique of the education reform movement.

This commitment by the NUT represents a bold shift in direction as the union comes to terms with considerably changed conditions. The prize is a genuine renewal of the union, in much the way argued by Fairbrother. That is, the union goes beyond a "resistance" approach to neoliberal restructuring and fundamentally reforms its structures in ways that align with the changed environment in which it functions. The union's emphasis on organizing in the workplace opens up the possibility of connecting with members in ways that draw them more readily into union activism. The union potentially becomes a vibrant grassroots-driven organization with high levels of member participation and engagement. Moreover, the clear commitment to engaging with parents represents an opportunity to connect teachers' immediate concerns with a wider set of issues about the future direction of public education. There is an emergent social movement unionism that seeks to link industrial and professional issues, adopting both industrial and political strategies. Underpinning all of this is a commitment to working within and beyond the union by developing alliances with parent and community organizations. The coming together of this approach is perhaps best represented in the union's campaign launched prior to the 2015 general election in which it set out a strategy for change based on mobilizing members to campaign with parents, combined with a commitment to industrial action.

However, such a shift in direction brings with it a number of attendant dangers and risks, and it is important to identify these if problems are to be avoided.

First is the need to avoid underestimating the scale or the difficulty of the task involved. England's school sector industrial relations prior to 1988, and for some time after that, functioned as a stable, and in large measure, sustainable model. The state was broadly supportive of, or pragmatically accepted, union participation in decision-making processes, and structures were established to support this. Formal negotiating committees provided the opportunity to assert a level of influence, while union officers supported by facilities time offered an "efficient" way to help manage conflict in the workplace. This was a system that could function on relatively low levels of activism, with a small number of union officers servicing a largely passive membership. The NUT's shift to an organizing culture is no longer predicated on passivity, but rather it raises expectations of union activism and engagement. This is the essence of renewal and might be seen as fundamental to what Sachs (2003) has referred to as an "activist profession." However, this must be achieved in a context where teacher workloads are increasing, the pressures to meet performance targets are intensifying, and performance-related pay, for example, introduces a level of managerial authority that can make union activism difficult. The paradox the union faces is that all these developments have the potential to both radicalize teachers while at the same time making resistance more difficult. None of this obviates the strategy, but it is important to recognize the scale of the challenge.

The problems are compounded by the fragmented multiunionism that has bedeviled English teacher unionism for decades. More recently, there have been encouraging signs that two of the large classroom teacher unions, including the NUT, are considering at least closer cooperation and possibly merging into a new, united union. Such an initiative seems essential if organized teachers are to overcome the divisions that are already embedded in a highly fractured school system, and which militate against developing collective identities and building effective solidarity. The activity described in this chapter has often been undertaken by the NUT alone, and the union can point to growing membership and some important victories as signs of its success. However, it would be complacent to suggest that this is evidence that the NUT does not need the support of other teacher unions; yet, as several examples from these studies demonstrate, securing unity in practice, and in particular when practice involves industrial action, is difficult.

The final danger we would identify is that of a retreat into a limited economism in which union activism focuses almost exclusively on workplace pay and conditions issues. This is not because the union is no longer concerned with professional issues and questions of policy. Indeed, a commitment to a social movement union requires a focus on issues that transcend the sectional concerns of teachers. However, the danger is that in a much more fragmented system, driven by a localized activism, it may become correspondingly more difficult to develop and articulate discourses about professional issues and to organize and mobilize around such issues. The danger is that the union is pulled into organizing around issues of most pressing concern—which are likely to be local and focused on so-called industrial issues. While this may offer short-term dividends, it is unlikely to create the conditions where the union is able to challenge neoliberal restructuring at a more ideological level. The challenge is to connect local activism (which may be quite fragmented in nature) with a much more overarching vision of what an alternative education service might look like.

Conclusion

The English school system has been transformed. This has taken place over many years, but the pace and scale of change have increased dramatically in recent years. Throughout the years when change was substantial, but still incremental, it was possible for the NUT to focus on a strategy of resistance. Challenging the direction of policy travel, and hoping at some point to reverse the trajectory, was always a possibility, albeit a distant one. This approach is no longer tenable, as the system has fragmented so much and teacher unions have been deliberately challenged in their traditional bases of power—whether that be national collective bargaining or negotiating committees in local authorities.

This chapter highlights how the NUT in England is adapting to these new circumstances. Having made limited organizational changes in the two decades following the 1988 act, the union has clearly begun to reorient both organizationally and politically. The union has made a clear shift toward an organizing culture in which there is no longer a dependence on a small number of superexperienced lay officers, supported by employer-provided facilities agreements. Rather, there is a commitment to "broadening the base" of activism, and often in ways that do not rely on employer-provided support. There is also a clear commitment to developing a form of social movement unionism that seeks to develop broad alliances between organized teachers, parents, and their communities.

Initial indications are that this reengineering of the union is having some success. Its "stand up for education" campaign achieved widespread recognition and can claim to have played a decisive role in toppling a particularly despised education minister. Meanwhile, the union's membership has been growing, and key local indicators, such as the percentage of schools with a school-based union representative, are also on the increase. However, there are many difficulties facing the union, and the longer-term success of the union's strategy remains uncertain. The three case studies highlighted in this chapter illustrate the scale of the problems. While there are clearly successes, the picture remains uneven, and the challenge will continue to develop traditional notions of trade union unity and solidarity, but in a context where the experience of teachers is increasingly diverse.

References

Alinsky, Saul. 1971. *Rules for radicals*. New York: Vintage.

Ball, Stephen. 2007. *Education plc: Understanding private sector participation in public sector education*. London: Routledge.

Ball, Stephen. 2008. *The education debate: Policy and politics in the 21st Century*. Bristol, UK: Education Policy Bristol: Policy Press.

Ball, Stephen. 2012. *Global Education Inc.: New policy networks and the neoliberal imaginary*. London: Routledge.

Blower, Christine. 2014a. "Empowering lay structures." *Morning Star*, April 19.

Blower, Christine. 2014b. "The NUT is rising to the academy challenge." *Morning Star*, April 21.

Blower, Christine. 2014c. "Putting the union at the heart of our communities." *Morning Star*, April 22.

Carter, Bob, Howard Stevenson, and Rowena Passy. 2010. *Industrial relations in education: Transforming the school workforce*. London, Routledge.

Chitty, Clyde. 2013. *New Labour and secondary education, 1994–2010*. London: Palgrave Macmillan.

Courtney, Kevin, and Gawain Little. 2014. "Standing up for education: Building a national campaign." *FORUM* 56 (2): 299–317.

Department for Education. 2010. "The importance of teaching: Schools white paper." Accessed December 20, 2012. http://www.education.gov.uk/schools/toolsandinitiatives/schoolswhitepaper/b0068570/the-importance-of-teaching.

Department for Education. 2013. "School teachers' pay and conditions document 2013 and guidance on school teachers' pay and conditions." Accessed September 1, 2013. http://media.education.gov.uk/assets/files/pdf/s/130806%202013%20stpcd%20master%20final.pdf.

Fairbrother, Peter. 1996. "Workplace trade unionism in the state sector." In *The new workplace and trade unions*, edited by Peter Ackers, Chris Smith, and Paul Smith, 110–49. London: Routledge.

Fairbrother, Peter. 2000. "British trade unions facing the future." *Capital and Class* 24 (2): 11–42.

Gillard, Derek. 2011. "Education in England: A brief history." Last modified January 2011. http://www.educationengland.org.uk/history.

Gove, Michael. 2013. Speech to teachers and head teachers at the National College of Teaching and Leadership. Last modified April 25, 2013. https://www.gov.uk/government/speeches/michael-gove-speech-to-teachers-and-headteachers-at-the-national-college-for-teaching-and-leadership.

Hannaway, Jane. 2006. *Collective bargaining in education: Negotiating change in today's schools*, edited by Andrew Rotherham. Cambridge, MA: Harvard Education Press.

Heery, Edmund, Rick Delbridge, and Melanie Simms. 1999. *Organise or fossilise? The revival of union organising*. London: Palgrave Macmillan.

Horn, Bian. 2014. "Moments or a movement? Teacher resistance to neoliberal education reform." *FORUM* 56 (2): 277–86.

Kerchner, Charles Taylor, and Douglas Mitchell. 1988. *The changing idea of a teachers' union*. London: Falmer Press.

Klingel, Sally. 2003. *Interest-based bargaining in education*. Washington, DC: National Education Association.

Koppich, Julia. 2006. "The as-yet-unfulfilled promise of reform bargaining." In *Collective bargaining in education: Negotiating change in today's schools*, edited by Jane Hannaway and Andrew Rotherham, 203–28. Cambridge, MA: Harvard Education Press.

Lawn, Martin. 1996. *Modern times? Work, professionalism and citizenship in teaching*. London: Falmer Press.

Sachs, Judyth. 2003. *The activist teaching profession*. Maidstone, UK: Open University Press.

Sahlberg, Pasi. 2010. *Finnish lessons: What can the world learn from educational change in Finland?* New York: Teachers College Press.

Seifert, Roger. 1984. "Some aspects of factional opposition: Rank and file and the National Union of Teachers 1967–82." *British Journal of Industrial Relations* 22 (3): 372–90.

Stevenson, Howard. 2003. "On the shopfloor: Exploring the impact of teacher trade unions on school-based industrial relations." *School Leadership and Management* 23 (3): 341–56.

Stevenson, Howard. 2011. "Coalition education policy: Thatcherism's long shadow." *FORUM* 53 (2): 179–94.

Stevenson, Howard. 2012. "New unionism? Teacher unions and school governance in England and Wales." *Local Government Studies* 40 (6): 954–71.

Stevenson, Howard, and Allison Gilliland. 2014. "Natural allies? Understanding teacher-parent alliances as resistance to neoliberal school reform" Paper presented at the AERA annual meeting, Philadelphia, PA, April 2.

Stevenson, Howard, and Justine Mercer. 2012. "School sector industrial relations in transition: Assessing the impact of academies." Last modified December 2012. https://www.belmas.org.uk/write/MediaUploads/Stevenson_Mercer_Final_Report.pdf.

Stevenson, Howard, and Nina Bascia. 2013. "Teacher unions and multi-unionism: Identifying issues of gender and militancy in Ontario and England." Paper presented at the AERA annual meeting, San Francisco, CA, April 27–May 1.

Stevenson, Howard, and Phil Wood. 2013. "Markets, managerialism and teachers' work: The invisible hand of high stakes testing in England." *International Education Journal: Comparative Perspectives* 12 (2): 42–61.

Tattersall, Amanda. 2013. *Power in coalition: Strategies for strong unions and social change*. Ithaca, NY: ILR Press.

Tomlinson, Sally. 2006. *Education in a post-welfarist society*. Buckingham, UK: Open University Press.

Unterrainer, Tom. 2014. "Standing up for education: Organising at the local level." *FORUM* 56 (2): 293–98.

Vasager, Jeevan, and Allegra Stratton. 2010. "Geoffrey Canada warns Michael Gove teacher unions 'kill' innovation." *Guardian*, October 5.

Waterman, Peter. 1993. "Social movement unionism: A new union model for a new world order." *Review* 16 (3): 245–78.

Weiner, Lois. 2012. *The future of our schools: Teachers unions and social justice*. Chicago: Haymarket Books.

Wheatley, Sheena, Susi Artis, and Tom Unterrainer. 2013. "Organising to win: How Nottingham teachers defeated the 'five term year' and organised to win." Accessed March 1, 2014. https://vote4sheena.files.wordpress.com/2014/03/organisingtowin.pdf.

Yarker, Patrick. 2009. "'This is determination': Grassroots opposition to academies." *FORUM* 51 (3): 319–22.

CHAPTER 12

The Teachers' Trifecta: Democracy, Social Justice, Mobilization

Lois Weiner

Across the United States, we are in the midst of a great struggle over the nation's education system. On one side is a bipartisan effort to privatize schools and undermine the promise of public education. Opposing that effort are large numbers of parents and teachers.

However, working-class parents of color see the current battle over public education quite differently than do those from the white middle class. For this reason, when I talk to teachers about what is driving the changes that they see destroying their careers and schools, I always start by sharing the story of my own education. In 1954, I was in the first grade in the David W. Harlan elementary school in Wilmington, Delaware. I could buy a hot lunch prepared by cafeteria workers who were employed by the Wilmington Public Schools (WPS). I took music lessons—violin—for free, using a violin the city schools lent to me. We had a school library, chorus, and band. We had art classes three times a week. However, schools on Wilmington's east side got the leftover musical instruments and much less money for books, supplies, and maintaining school facilities like the playground. Harlan was all white, intentionally segregated. Real estate developers and brokers in its attendance zone had homeowners sign racial covenants that prohibited the sale of homes to blacks. This information was subsequently used by the NAACP in its successful suit to desegregate the WPS (Raffel 1980).

To be credible to the parents and community members who should be our strongest allies—the poor and working parents of color who are targeted by neoliberal propaganda—we must acknowledge the complicity of the education establishment, labor, and teacher unions in allowing this gross inequality to persist. Labor did not create residential and school segregation, but accepting it was an unarticulated assumption in its post–World War II pact with capital. Those practices and assumptions must no longer be accepted by parents, teachers, and our unions.

The rich and powerful, who control the media and educational policy of both political parties, use lofty-sounding slogans about "putting students first" and "making schools work" that obscure their aims. The linchpin of educational policy of both Democrats and Republicans is that schooling is, to quote Arne Duncan, "the one true path out of poverty" (US Department of Education 2010). This assumption obviates the need for the state to fight poverty through economic policy by creating well-paying jobs that support a sustainable economy and by requiring a minimum wage that does not leave people in poverty. Schooling is not and cannot be the "one true path out of poverty" for the vast majority of children because our economy consigns millions to unemployment or work that pays poverty wages. Yet we are told students must be made "college and career ready" to have well-paying jobs, or as the US Department of Education phrased its goal in the reauthorization of the Elementary and Secondary Education Act, "The goal for America's educational system is clear . . . Every student should have meaningful opportunities to choose from upon graduation from high school" (US Department of Education 2011). The Common Core, the new national curriculum funded in good part by Bill Gates, is explicitly defended by its proponents, including teacher unions, to make individuals and the country economically competitive (Schneider 2013).

Schools in the United States have been affected by inequality outside their walls while also functioning in ways that both challenge and reproduce it (Bastian et al. 1986). We have a remarkable body of high-quality empirical scholarship describing "schools as places where social reproduction occurs but also where human agency matters and makes a difference in students' lives" (Wells et al. 2004). Social movements effectively challenged the inequality of outcomes in education but, in the end, were unable to disrupt social processes in schools as fully as was needed. In good part, this occurred because schooling was made to carry a weight that it cannot by itself bear and because education is enmeshed in social, political, and economic conditions that support or undercut what can occur in classrooms.

Probably the most important liberal defender of public education today is Diane Ravitch. In battling her former cothinkers with the personal resources and connections she acquired in supporting neoconservative policies, Ravitch has contributed mightily to public awareness of the threat to democracy and to children in the current drive to create a privatized school system funded by public money but without collective, public oversight. *Reign of Error: The Hoax of the Privatization Movement and the Danger to America's Public Schools*

(Ravitch 2013), her newest book, is an authoritative compendium of why these reforms are so dangerous. Ravitch has almost single-handedly developed and publicized a liberal rebuttal to neoliberal "reforms," in effect substituting not only for the teacher union establishment but for labor as well.

Still, while she has repudiated the policies she helped craft and promote under the George H. W. Bush administration, she has not yet distanced herself from assumptions that led to her support for the initial iteration of the current reforms. The central political flaw in her analysis is seen when she argues about education's purposes, past and present. Public education was established in the nineteenth century, she explains, to educate future citizens and to sustain our democracy. The essential purpose of the public schools, the reason they receive public funding, is to teach young people the rights and responsibilities of citizens. A secondary purpose was to strengthen our economy and our culture by raising the intelligence of our people and preparing them to lead independent lives as managers, workers, producers, consumers, and creators of ideas, products, and services. She then adds a third purpose: "to endow every individual with the intellectual and ethical power to pursue his or her own interests and to develop the judgment and character to survive life's vicissitudes" (p. 237).

Ravitch explains that education's purpose was—and is—to strengthen the economy and prepare people for work. Yet the book does not acknowledge that schools have educated most working-class students for working-class jobs, and most children of professionals for similar careers and the social status of their parents. She challenges the claim that education is the "one true path" out of poverty by making poverty exclusively to blame for inequality in education. Previously, Ravitch contended that her own education was ideal, and it is to her credit that in *Reign of Error* she steps back from that assertion and argues that residential and school segregation cause harm. Her shift in thinking shows a new willingness to address racial segregation, an unpopular but necessary step in equalizing school outcomes (Raffel 2013). However, the overarching argument that US public education was doing as well as could be expected given the effects of poverty is a serious flaw in her analysis and opens her—and the movement—to the charge that we want to defend an unequal status quo.

Ravitch does not address the contradiction between schooling's noneconomic purposes, its role in educating the next generation of citizens and nurturing each individual's potential, and its use as a sorting mechanism to allocate a diminishing number of well-paying jobs. Unfortunately, neoliberal reforms resonate with poor, minority parents precisely because they want the same opportunity for their children to compete for good jobs as children of middle-class parents have. Calls for schools that make children happy and develop creativity will not assuage parents' fears that their children will not be strong competitors in an increasingly punishing labor market. Arne Duncan's contemptuous dismissal of opponents of high-stakes testing and the new Common Core curriculum as "suburban moms" who can't face their children's limitations demonstrates that our opponents will fully exploit the utterly hypocritical and inaccurate claim that they protect poor, minority children against white liberals who want to maintain the status quo, to advantage their own children.

Ravitch marshals evidence that bipartisan reforms aim to destroy the template for mass public education in the United States that was created in the nineteenth century. Unfortunately, the artificial national border she draws in telling the story of US educational reform obscures the global dimension of the project and the relationship of the changes being made to US schools to demands of capitalism globally and its transformation of schooling throughout the world. In effect, she proposes a return to the post–World War II social democratic compact, inflected by commitment to the civil rights movement's campaign for school integration. One insurmountable problem with this strategy is that capitalism rejects the compact. But even if we could win back the compact, it was a Faustian deal. Teacher unions, like the rest of labor, were bureaucratized and greatly weakened by the quid pro quo that gave them collective bargaining but took away the capacity to intervene directly in issues that go to the heart of teachers' work, especially school organization and curriculum. This is not a past to which we should want to return, even if we could.

Her electoral strategy also reflects a desire to return to the (idealized) past. Ravitch recognizes that big money and corporations control the Democratic Party, and her solution is to push Democrats to be the defenders of public education that she says they once were. She therefore encourages opponents of corporate school reform to embrace Democrats willing to criticize (however vaguely) privatization, testing, and charter schools and defend (however meekly) teacher unions. However, she (and those who agree with this political strategy) does not explain how we will hold candidates responsible to the activists who have worked on their behalf and avoid betrayals. Yet this issue is more pressing with each election cycle and each desertion of Democrats whom progressives have supported. Al Franken, liberal sweetheart, has endorsed Teach for America and charter schools, as has Howard Dean. Ras Baraka, campaigning for mayor of Newark, easily won support of activists, including Ravitch, based on his harsh criticisms of Newark's school closings and creation of charter schools. Yet Baraka has allied himself with the mayor of Jersey City, who was elected on a program to bring to the Jersey City schools precisely the reforms that Baraka criticizes in Newark, reforms that Democrats for Education Reform (DFER) and New Jersey's newest Democratic senator and Newark's former mayor, Cory Booker, embrace wholeheartedly.

Although pressed by activists to criticize teacher union leaders, in particular her longtime friend, Randi Weingarten, president of the American Federation of Teachers (AFT), for endorsing the Common Core and commending legislation that links teacher evaluation to students' standardized test scores, Ravitch declines, arguing that this creates divisions. But the divisions already exist, because union reformers are challenging the local and national leadership in both the AFT and the NEA. The question is, will we encourage activists to democratize their unions, to make them social movements, or will we decide that the model of "service" or "business unionism" should remain the norm?

The "Trifecta": Mobilization, Social Justice, Democracy

A new generation of teachers is being politicized and radicalized very rapidly. While there is still much fear, nodes of resistance are emerging. In some cases, organizations of parents and teachers opposed to testing are supporting creation of reform caucuses in unions. Teachers have been both energized and inspired by the Chicago Teachers Union (CTU), and are terrified at the enormity of the task they face. Many are asking how they can apply lessons from those who formed the Caucus of Rank and File Educators (CORE) and then transformed the CTU.

In spring of 2014, activists in Massachusetts, Colorado, and North Carolina formed statewide caucuses in their NEA affiliates. After losing a contract fight, the AFT union reformers of Newark, New Jersey, won a majority in their union's executive committee; they lost the union presidency by only a few votes. Seattle, an NEA affiliate, and Philadelphia's AFT local now have reform caucuses, as does Minneapolis. In school districts large and small, grassroots groups of teachers and parents that oppose testing or charter school colocations are spawning change in the local teacher unions.

In the Los Angeles union, the second largest in the country, reformers elected to office years earlier failed to build a union presence at the school site and captured the union apparatus without developing a base of support. Activists learned from their mistakes and reorganized as Union Power; they nurtured a new culture and program of building a "member-driven union." While Union Power worked diligently to build the chapters, developing a program modeled on CTU's, out of 31,505 members only 7,158 returned ballots. The turnout was disappointing but was still a higher percentage of voters than in the 2011 citywide union elections. Alex Caputo-Pearl, who headed the slate, narrowly missed winning the 50 percent plus 1 he needed to be elected president, but his opponent essentially ceded the runoff to him.

Union activists seem in agreement about three issues: (1) mobilizing union members during contract disputes, (2) working with parent allies, and (3) developing contract demands that embed economic issues in a program for quality schools that names social inequality, corporate domination of the government, and racism as impediments to schools students deserve. While these are essential elements themselves, they are insufficient. Too often overlooked is the centrality of organizing a union presence "on the shop floor," that is, at the school site, developing new leaders and activists, and fighting for democratic norms and procedures.

Unfortunately, marginalized in discussion of union reform is strengthening union democracy. This was apparent in the left media's coverage of the near strike of the Portland Association of Teachers (PAT), an NEA affiliate. PAT's leadership used the contract to defend aspects of teachers' work that directly affect learning rather than focusing on salary. They reached out to parents and mobilized members, involving them in the contract fight. But key questions about the process were ignored. How were bargaining demands developed? Was the team elected directly by the membership? The contract campaign is the opportunity to involve more members as leaders, deepening the membership's participation in decision making.

Chicago had an elected bargaining team of dozens of people and spent months gathering, refining, and voting on contract demands. Did the PAT? Another question we should ask is how discussion and ratification of a proposed settlement occurs. Is the discussion organized so that union officers "sell" the proposed settlement to members—or does the process encourage members to raise questions, concerns, and problems? Contract ratification directly influences how strong the union will be in the school site after the heat of the contract fight subsides. Members have to defend the contract, so it is essential that they understand the specifics of the final agreement. In Chicago, in the midst of a strike, CTU's negotiating team brought the proposed agreement to the union's representative assembly, which refused to endorse it before taking it back to members for a closer look. CTU's process has to be the standard to which we hold unions.

The history of the Service Employees International Union, including its lawsuit against individual dissidents who formed an independent union, the National Union of Healthcare Workers, illustrates why we need union democracy as well as social justice commitments (Benson 2013). Not just member voice is needed but also power that emerges from the ranks in the shops and that challenges and informs the leadership's actions. A social justice program combined with member mobilization is a volatile and unsustainable mixture. The combination can fuel militant struggles, but it cannot translate those victories into the deep alteration in power relations on the shop floor that teacher unions need today to counter the vastly unequal power of teachers and administration.

Herman Benson, the unofficial dean of union democracy studies, has pushed left reformers to consider the relationship between union democracy and the other elements of their agendas, arguing that bureaucratization in unions is not neatly linked to union reformers' (left-wing) politics. Benson's challenge to understand how the struggle for democratic unions relates to our program for social justice is a matter of the utmost importance for teacher unionism today, and yet it has been ignored.

I suggest that trade unionism's two essential principles, solidarity and democracy, challenge notions of individual competition and hierarchical relations embedded in capitalism and expressed in power relations in the workplace. These twin ideals, solidarity and democracy, are essential in creating societies that support the full flowering of human potential. Unions, owing to their unique situation in the workplace, provide the filament that sustains democracy. When unions are not democratic, even if they fight for social justice, they perpetuate hierarchical relations that disempower working people, allowing bigotry and oppression to remain embedded in social relations. Undemocratic unions cannot educate workers to create a democratic society because the substance of union life reinforces workers' subordination to others that (purportedly) know what is best for them. And most often those others come from groups in society that have more power and privilege.

However, democracy is very fragile, and vigilant enforcement of regulations that give members the right to decide policy and elect officers is a necessary but insufficient condition. Deep, thorough union democracy depends on the union having a presence in the workplace, such that members understand that *they* are the union. This process is in turn nurtured by the union defining its members' self-interest very broadly so that members bring their concerns into the union.

Nelson Lichtenstein notes that "rights are universal and individual, which means employers and individual members of management enjoy them just as much as workers" (Lichenstein 2013), but what makes unions unique is that unions represent members' individual interests through expression and struggle for their collective interests. The accuracy of Lichtenstein's observation is seen in the way neoliberalism has exploited the rights discourse against teachers and teacher unions, in lawsuits arguing that tenure and seniority protections conflict with the rights of children to equal educational opportunity. At the same time, a rights discourse also fueled social movements that created opportunities for millions of students who previously were excluded from education—those with special needs and native speakers of languages other than English. Neither the NEA nor the AFT helped these movements for increased educational opportunity, using their political clout only after legislation was introduced. The laws creating special education and bilingual education programs were flawed in taking "disputes out of the hands of those directly involved," as Lichtenstein (2013) argues. Yet, millions of children once refused an education today receive services. Children in these groups are better off because they claimed their (human) rights—without support from the unions.

Teacher unions plant the seed of democracy in schools by giving teachers collective voice about the conditions of their labor. Even when collective bargaining restricts the union's legal authority, a teacher union with a highly conscious, active membership that has assimilated the lesson that members are the union, not staff or elected officials, can exert pressure over many informal work arrangements. However, while the union's presence provides opportunity for teacher voice, it does not automatically do the same for parents, students, or the community. To the extent that the teacher union does not consciously push to extend democracy in the school to include those affected by union agreements, it undermines its legitimacy and contradicts labor's claim of speaking for working people. So while Benson is correct that as a rule when unions "raise the standards of those who are victorious, they tend to lift the standards of the class, even those not organized," it is also the case that support for unions, including teacher unions, eroded precisely because of the attenuated impact of union victories on those who were not union members (Panitch and Gindin 2012).

Bringing the Trifecta to Politics

Teacher union activists generally understand that the destruction of public education and the profession is a bipartisan project, even as they see individual candidates as more sympathetic to the perspective of teachers. The question I think we need to consider is not whether we need a new electoral vehicle that will project the vision of a transformed teacher union movement, but how to achieve it.

In embarking on this discussion, it's important to acknowledge that electoral activity is not a substitute for the trifecta I have previously described. Nor can we ignore the success of neoliberalism's "scorched earth" war against unions. When teacher union reformers succeed in becoming leaders of newly mobilized unions, as they have in Chicago, they are often isolated in a fairly bleak labor landscape. Education is often the sector of the economy with the highest union density, but public employee unions have been greatly weakened and private sector unionism is marginal. This puts newly elected teacher union reformers in a very precarious situation. On the one hand, they see that they have few dependable allies in the Democratic Party, which is controlled by capital. On the other hand, they bargain with the people who are elected. It is very, very difficult for union leaders to argue that we need to create an independent political vehicle, because in the process of creating that vehicle we may lose elections that seem to jeopardize the union's ability to maintain the status quo, including members' jobs and benefits.

However, just as defending teachers and public education means doing battle with economic attacks while recognizing the dangers of doing so, advancing that struggle into the electoral sphere means facing dangers inherent in developing an independent electoral vehicle. The elite that controls the state, exercising their control through both the Democratic and Republican parties, directs the global capitalistic project that aims to destroy us. We contradict and undercut our efforts to contest that project when we support either party. Candidates cannot serve two masters—on the one hand, the Democratic Party of Arne Duncan, DFER, and Rahm Emanuel, and on the other, the movement opposing them.

Electoral activity is an extension into the public realm of the trifecta of principles and politics we use in building the union: democracy, social justice, mobilization. Candidates for office (and officeholders) should have the same relationship with a union and the social movement of which it is a key element as we want union officers to have with the membership. We elect candidates to carry out our program, but we in turn are responsible for helping them push electoral initiatives by mobilizing. Elected officials are supported by and responsible to the people who elect them. On the local level, teacher unions may be able to initiate the trifecta through an ad hoc political coalition, but such a formation is unstable. In the longer run, locally and nationally, we need a new political party.

Many problems complicate the proposition of forming a new electoral vehicle, I acknowledge. Clearly, though, the Democratic Party is owned by forces that aim to destroy everything that teacher unions must defend. We cannot give money and votes to a party that aids and abets our destruction. And if not now, when? When we are weaker as a result of unrelenting political attacks and the continued absence of political voice?

What will this new electoral movement and vehicle look like? We know it must be democratic with mechanisms that make leaders and candidates responsible to the activists and constituencies who have put them into office. Here again we can look to what occurred in Chicago: CORE activists did not delay their challenge to the old CTU leadership while developing a blueprint of what a transformed Chicago teacher union would look like. They brought principles and a vision, developed in struggle. They honed their strategy further in carrying out that vision as union officers and staff. The same process can occur in developing a new electoral vehicle, in Chicago and elsewhere. Union Power's victory in Los Angeles opens the door to teacher unions having an independent electoral vehicle in two of the three largest US cities.

A vibrant new movement is emerging, though it is under the radar of the mass media. Teachers and parents who were previously not political and not engaged are seeing that children and the profession of teaching are being harmed by policies in which ordinary people have no voice or influence. New national and international networks are emerging among teacher union activists. Much hinges on radical activists in the United States understanding that we cannot repeat the mistakes teacher unionism made in its birth in the 1960s. Fifty years ago, teacher unions could trade power in the workplace, articulate how schools are organized, and what and how we teach for improvements in members' wages and benefits. However, those days are gone. To protect teaching as a profession and public education we need to win the trifecta of democracy, mobilization, and social justice, in union life and politics.

References

Bastian, Ann, Norm Fruchter, Marilyn Gittell, Colin Greer, and Kenneth Haskins. 1986. *Choosing equality: The case for democratic schooling*. Philadelphia, PA: Temple University Press.

Benson, Herman. 2013. "Sober thoughts after inspiring years of union organizing." *Union Democracy Review* April/May: 3–5.

Lichtenstein, Nelson. 2013. *A contest of ideas: Capital, politics, and labor*. Urbana: University of Illinois Press.

Panitch, Leo, and Sam Gindin. 2012. *The making of global capitalism: The political economy of American empire*. New York: Verso Books.

Raffel, Jeffery. 1980. *The politics of school desegregation: The metropolitan remedy in Delaware*. Philadelphia, PA: Temple University Press.

Raffel, Jeffery. 2013. "The changing challenges of school segregation and desegregation." *Education Review* 16 (5): 1–15.

Ravitch, Diane. *The death and life of the great American school system: How testing and choice are undermining education*. Basic Books, 2011.

Schaffer, Connie. 2013. "Unmasking the reformers: An essay review of Ravitch's *Reign of Error*." *Education Review/Reseñas Educativas* 17 (3): 1–9.

Schneider, Mercedes. 2013. "A brief audit of Bill Gates' Common Core spending." Huffington Post. Last modified August 8. http://www.huffingtonpost.com/mercedes-schneider/a-brief-audit-of-bill-gat_b_3837421.html.

US Department of Education. 2010. "US Department of Education awards promise neighborhoods planning grants." Last modified September 21. http://www.ed.gov/

news/press-releases/us-department-education-awards-promise-neighborhoods-planning-grants.

US Department of Education. 2011. *A blueprint for reform: The reauthorization of the Elementary and Secondary Education Act*. Washington, DC: US Department of Education.

Wells, Amy, Jennifer Holme, Anita Revilla, and Awo Korantemaa. 2004. "How society failed school desegregation policy: Looking past the schools to understand them." *Review of Research in Education* 28: 47–99.

CHAPTER 13

Conclusion

Nina Bascia

The 11 chapters contained in this book consider the past, present, and future prospects of teacher unions in the United States, Canada, and England. The case studies manage the balance between specificity and universality in different ways. Some provide only limited treatments of how local context shapes union agendas, instead of emphasizing the lessons that may be learned across contexts. Other chapters foreground context, underscoring how individual and collective social commitments, histories, relationships, and political dynamics form the basis for particular organizational directions. Some make no claim of universality in their depictions of specific circumstances, while others situate the particular in more general contemporary trends.

Over the last 50 years, the research on teacher unions has grown in both quantity and variety. Following the establishment of collective bargaining, treatments of teacher unions by researchers could be said to have fallen largely into several camps. One camp was intent on capturing the dynamics of the sea change in the 1960s and 1970s, when teacher unions first began to flex their muscles in earnest as they campaigned for the right to collective bargaining (e.g., Berube 1965; Seldon 1964). In another camp was research fueled by the concerns of educational decision makers that newly strengthened teacher unions would introduce a host of new ills, such as the promotion of a conception of teaching as labor, the formalization of administrator-teacher relations, the standardization of teaching tasks, and policy making driven by teachers' "special interests" (Carlson 1992; Englert 1979; Kerchner and Mitchell 1986; Loveless 2000; McDonnell and Pascal 1988; for critiques, see Johnson 1984; Mitchell and Kerchner 1983; Price 2009; Williams 1979). In yet another camp were researchers urging teachers' organizations to present themselves more like professional organizations, in order to improve public confidence in teachers (Darling-Hammond and Berry 1988; Haberman 1986; Kerchner and Koppich 1993; see Ozga and Lawn 1988 for a critique). Starting in the 1980s, some researchers began urging and documenting collaborative working relations between unions and decision makers in order to create local opportunities for innovation and teacher professionalism (Johnson 1988; Kerchner and Koppich 1988; Rosow and Zager 1989). A number of good historical treatments of the origins of teacher unions were published throughout the time period between the 1980s and the present (see, for example, Murphy 1990; Rousmaniere 2004; Urban 1981).

In recent decades, criticism of teacher unions has increased—not only in the press (Cooper and Sureau 2008; Goldstein 2011) but also by governments intent on sidelining them or outlawing them outright. In the United States, collective bargaining has been directly challenged by recent reform initiatives such as Race to the Top, which provides incentives to state and district policy makers to establish greater freedom from "restrictive" policies traditionally found in teacher union contracts (Strunk and Grissom 2010). In Canada and England, governments have deliberately limited the purview of teacher unions through legislation, deciding many of the issues, including salary and working conditions, that previously had been subject to negotiation. Even in the Scandinavian countries, which have had a practice of, and a legal basis for, close working relationships between government and teacher unions, fiscal austerity and neoliberal reforms have led to open hostility. Recent research on teacher unions is necessarily preoccupied with the rise of neoliberal reform. Several recent volumes have addressed the negative impact of neoliberalism on teaching and unionism around the world (Bascia and Osmond 2013; Compton and Weiner 2008; Robertson and Smaller 1996).

The chapters in this book represent many of the current developments in teacher union research. They provide the basis for inquiry and action that can fruitfully be further explored in the next generation of teacher union research. What follows are a few examples of research that can be extrapolated from work in this volume.

One development showcased in this volume is the treatment of teacher union actions over time rather than in shorter, episodic snapshots. Whereas teacher union research has tended to focus on contemporary events, many of the chapters in this book reveal longer-term patterns of conflict and strife, and the ebb and flow of relations between teacher unions and other entities.

Few studies exist that depict the lives and career histories of union-active teachers. Such histories would enable us to see how union activities allow teachers to expand the scope and impact of their work beyond their classrooms, through informal and nonformal professional learning, curriculum development, political organizing, and other pursuits. Such career histories as are portrayed in this book, would enable us to develop a broader understanding of teachers' work and their contributions to educational policy and practice.

Teacher unions are multifaceted organizations populated by groups of educators with diverse priorities and agendas. Collective bargaining and professional development units are two common examples of the different activities undertaken by teacher unions simultaneously. Teacher unions increasingly provide services to compensate for the loss or lack of infrastructure in the greater educational system. Moving beyond established units to examine initiatives proposed by teachers under union auspices (e.g., curriculum development) would allow us to more clearly discern the contributions of union organizations to educational systems.

In many jurisdictions in this time of profound crisis, old and familiar relationships between teachers and their unions cannot be taken for granted. Many long-standing structures and arrangements have been lost or transformed, and teacher unions must adopt new ways of organizing teachers in order to remain viable. Several chapters in this book address this phenomenon directly, and there is room for further work.

While there are a number of single-case teacher union investigations, there are few studies that make multiple-union, cross-case comparisons. Those that do exist tend to emphasize commonalities across the cases rather than differences between them. There is room for more research that compares and, perhaps more importantly, contrasts two or more divergent unions—their contexts, their strategies, their structures, the personalities within them—so that we can develop more robust understandings of how union organizations function more broadly.

As the educational environment continues to change, teacher unions will be required to evolve. Teacher union research, always rich and varied, will evolve with it, topically, methodologically, and conceptually. Because teacher unions are involved in, and relevant to, so many aspects of educational policy and practice, studies of teacher unions will continue to provide unique vantage points from which to observe the workings of the educational realm.

References

Bascia, Nina, and Pamela Osmond. 2012. *Teacher unions and educational reform*. Washington, DC: National Education Association.

Bascia, Nina, and Pamela Osmond. 2013. *Teacher unions' role in educational reform*. Brussels, Belgium: Education International.

Berube, Maurice, and Marilyn Gittell. 1969. *Confrontation at Ocean Hill-Brownsville: The New York school strikes of 1968*. New York: Praeger.

Carlson, Dennis. 1987. "Teachers as political actors: From reproductive theory to the crisis of schooling." *Harvard Educational Review* 57 (3): 283–308.

Compton, Mary, and Lois Weiner. 2008. *The global assault on teachers, teaching and their unions*. London: Palgrave.

Cooper, Bruce, and John Sureau. 2008. "Teacher unions and the politics of fear in labor relations." *Educational Policy* 22 (1): 86–105.

Corwin, Ronald. 1970. *Militant professionalism: A study of organizational conflict in high schools*. New York: Appleton-Century-Crofts.

Darling-Hammond, Linda, and Barnett Berry. 1988. *The evolution of teacher policy*. Washington, DC: RAND Corporation.

Englert, Richard. 1979. "Collective bargaining in public education: Conflict and its context." *Education and Urban Society* 11 (2): 255–69.

Goldstein, Rebeca. 2011. "Imaging the frame: Media representations of teachers, their unions, NCLB, and education reform." *Educational Policy* 25 (4): 543–76.

Haberman, Martin. 1986. "Licensing teachers: Lessons from other professions." *Phi Delta Kappan* 67 (10): 719–22.

Johnson, Susan. 1984. *Teacher unions in schools*. Philadelphia, PA: Temple University Press.

Johnson, Susan. 1988. "Pursuing professional reform in Cincinnati." *Phi Delta Kappan* 69 (10): 746–51.

Kerchner, Charles, and Douglas Mitchell. 1988. *The changing idea of a teachers' unions*. Philadelphia, PA: Falmer Press.

Kerchner, Charles, and Julie Koppich. 1993. *A union of professionals: Labor relations and educational reform*. New York: Teachers College Press.

Loveless, Tom. 2000. *Conflicting missions? Teachers unions and educational reform*. Washington, DC: Brookings Institution Press.

McDonnell, Lorraine, and Anthony Pascal. 1988. *Teacher unions and educational reform*. Washington, DC: RAND Corporation.

Mitchell, Douglas, and Charles Kerchner. 1983. "Labor relations and teacher policy." In *Handbook of teaching and policy*, edited by Lee Shulman and Gary Sykes, 214–38. New York: Longman.

Murphy, Marjorie. 1990. *Blackboard unions: The AFT and the NEA, 1900–1980*. Ithaca, NY: Cornell University Press.

Ozga, Jennifer, and Martin Lawn. 1981. *Teachers, professionalism and class: A study of organized teachers*. London: Falmer Press.

Price, Mitchell. 2009. *Teacher union contracts and high school reform*. Bothell: Center on Reinventing Public Education, University of Washington.

Robertson, Susan, and Harry Smaller. 1996. *Teacher activism in the 1990s*. Toronto: James Lorimer and Company Ltd.

Rosow, Jerome, and Robert Zager. 1989. *Allies in educational reform*. San Francisco, CA: Jossey-Bass.

Selden, David. 1964. "A report from the UFT: Class size and the New York contract." *Phi Delta Kappan* 45 (6): 283–87.

Strunk, Katherine, and Jason Grissom. 2010. "Do strong unions shape district policies? Collective bargaining, teacher contract restrictiveness, and the political power of teachers' unions." *Educational Evaluation and Policy Analysis* 32 (3): 389–406.

Urban, Wayne. 1982. *Why teachers organized.* Detroit, MI: Wayne State University Press.

Williams, Richard. 1979. "The impact of collective bargaining on the principal: What do we know?" *Education and Urban Society* 11 (2): 168–80.

List of Contributors

Nina Bascia is a professor in the Department of Leadership, Higher, and Adult Education and founding director of the Collaborative Educational Policy Program at the Ontario Institute for Studies in Education at the University of Toronto. She has conducted research about and for teacher unions for the past 25 years in the United States and Canada and is one of the best-known teacher union researchers internationally.

James Chamberlain has been a social justice activist and educator for the past 22 years. He is currently a vice principal with the Vancouver School Board. Previously, he coordinated the social justice program at the BCTF. He has been an activist on LGBTQ issues in school for two decades.

J.-C. Couture is associate coordinator, research, with the Alberta Teachers' Association. His research interests include strategic planning and cultural psychoanalytic theory applied to organizational change. His most recent publications focus on teachers' work life and school improvement.

Larry Kuehn is director of Research and Technology at the BC Teachers' Federation. He is a former president of the BCTF and holds an EdD from the University of British Columbia.

Justine Mercer is associate professor of Educational Leadership at the University of Warwick, England. In an international career spanning nearly 20 years, she has lived and worked in countries as diverse as China, Hungary, Oman, Thailand, Turkey, and the United Arab Emirates. She has conducted research funded by the Russian National Training Federation; the United Kingdom's Department of Innovation, Universities, and Skills; the National College for School Leadership; the British Educational Leadership, Management, and Administration Society; the Society for Research into Higher Education; and the Leadership Foundation for Higher Education. These studies have focused on cross-cultural understandings of educational leadership; senior leadership teams in high schools; the academic leadership provided by full professors; and employee relations within both K–12 schooling and the higher education sector. Her work has been published in international peer-reviewed journals, including *Oxford Review of Education*, *International Journal of Educational Development*, *Compare*, and *Women's Studies International Forum*. Her most recent coauthored book is entitled *Human Resource Management in Education: Contexts, Themes and Impact*.

Charlie Naylor is the senior researcher at the British Columbia Teachers' Federation in Vancouver, where he supports the union's teacher inquiry projects across BC while also conducting a range of research in areas such as teachers' work lives, teacher inquiry, teacher leadership, inclusion, teachers' professional development, and twenty-first-century learning. He taught in a secondary comprehensive school in Sheffield, England, while completing his undergraduate degree and postgraduate teacher education. He also taught in programs for unemployed youth in Melbourne, Australia, participating in Action Research networks across the state of Victoria. Since coming to Canada in 1988, he has completed an MA degree at Simon Fraser University, with a research focus on high school dropouts in a large urban school district. Charlie's PhD research at the University of British Columbia explored teacher inquiry as professional development in a multiliteracies research project.

Pamela Osmond-Johnson is a PhD candidate in the Educational Administration and Collaborative Educational Policy programs with the Department of Leadership, Higher, and Adult Education at the Ontario Institute for Studies in Education at the University of Toronto. She is a former teacher and vice principal in the K–12 context, and her interest in researching teacher unions stems from her experiences as an active member of the Newfoundland and Labrador Teachers' Association and has been influenced by her work as a research assistant on various union-related projects with Dr. Nina Bascia. Currently in progress, her doctoral dissertation explores how active involvement in teachers' organizations influences the ways teachers define and enact teacher professionalism in their day-to-day work.

Ben Pogodzinski is an assistant professor in the College of Education at Wayne State University. His research focuses on how state and district policies, school organizational context, and labor relations influence teachers' instructional practices, effectiveness, and labor market decisions.

Wendy Poole is an associate professor in the Department of Educational Studies at the University of British Columbia. Her research focuses on teacher unionism, the impacts of neoliberal education policy, and organizational studies in education.

Kara Popiel is staff director and secretary of the Yonkers Federation of Teachers (YFT). Over the course of her 25-year teaching career, she has taught English as a foreign language (EFL) to adults in Morocco and Hungary with the United States Peace Corps, high school ESOL in Brooklyn, New York, and elementary ESOL in Yonkers, New York. She first became active in the YFT in 2001. Kara earned her EdD at Teachers College, Columbia University, in 2010 in Organization and Leadership, with a specialization in Leadership, Policy, and Politics, and she is currently conducting research on teacher union activism and union-management collaboration.

Cindy Rottmann is a research associate with the Institute for Leadership Education in Engineering (ILead) at the University of Toronto and adjunct professor in the Faculty of Education at the University of Manitoba. She has spent the past eight years researching teacher activism, teacher leadership, and teacher unionism in a Canadian context and recently served two terms as program chair of the American Educational Research Association's Special Interest Group on Teachers' Work and Teacher Unions.

Harry Smaller's research interests include teachers' work and teacher unions, in both historical and contemporary contexts.

Howard Stevenson is professor of Educational Policy and Leadership Studies at the University of Nottingham. He has considerable experience in researching the interface between education reform, the impact on teachers' work, and the implications for teacher trade unionism. Work undertaken has been commissioned by both teacher unions and academic bodies. He was coinvestigator, with Bob Carter (University of Leicester), of the ESRC-funded project Workforce Remodeling, Teacher Unions, and School-Based Industrial Relations (RES). He has published many articles related to teacher unionism, including in the *American Educational Research Journal*, and is a coauthor (with Bob Carter and Rowena Passy) of *Transforming the School Workforce: Industrial Relations in Education* (Routledge, 2010).

Christine Stewart/Galksi-Gibaykwhl Sook' is a teacher with the Vancouver School Board, currently in the role of counselor at Britannia Secondary

School. She is a member of the Nisga'a Nation. Previously, Ms. Stewart was an assistant director on the staff of the BC Teachers' Federation, with responsibility for overseeing aboriginal programs. Active in her community, Ms. Stewart has been a member-at-large on the BCTF executive committee, as well as on her Vancouver Secondary Teachers' Association local executive. She currently serves as a board member with the Tsamiks Society.

Katy Swalwell is an assistant professor in Teaching and Learning, Policy and Leadership at the University of Maryland, College Park. Living in Madison, Wisconsin, during the protests sparked her interest in researching the relationship among teachers' political activism, their pedagogical decisions, and the contexts in which they work.

Jane Turner is a retired secondary Social Studies teacher and a committed activist in the BCTF. She was a member of the BCTF Status of Women Committee and then a BCTF staff member for several years in the Professional and Social Issues Division. She also worked in the Faculty of Education at Simon Fraser University.

Lois Weiner is a member of the New Politics editorial board and is professor of Education at New Jersey City University, where she coordinates a graduate program for experienced teachers. Her newest book, *The Future of Our Schools: Teachers Unions and Social Justice*, explains why and how teachers need to transform their unions to save public education.

Index

B

C

U